The Mercenaries

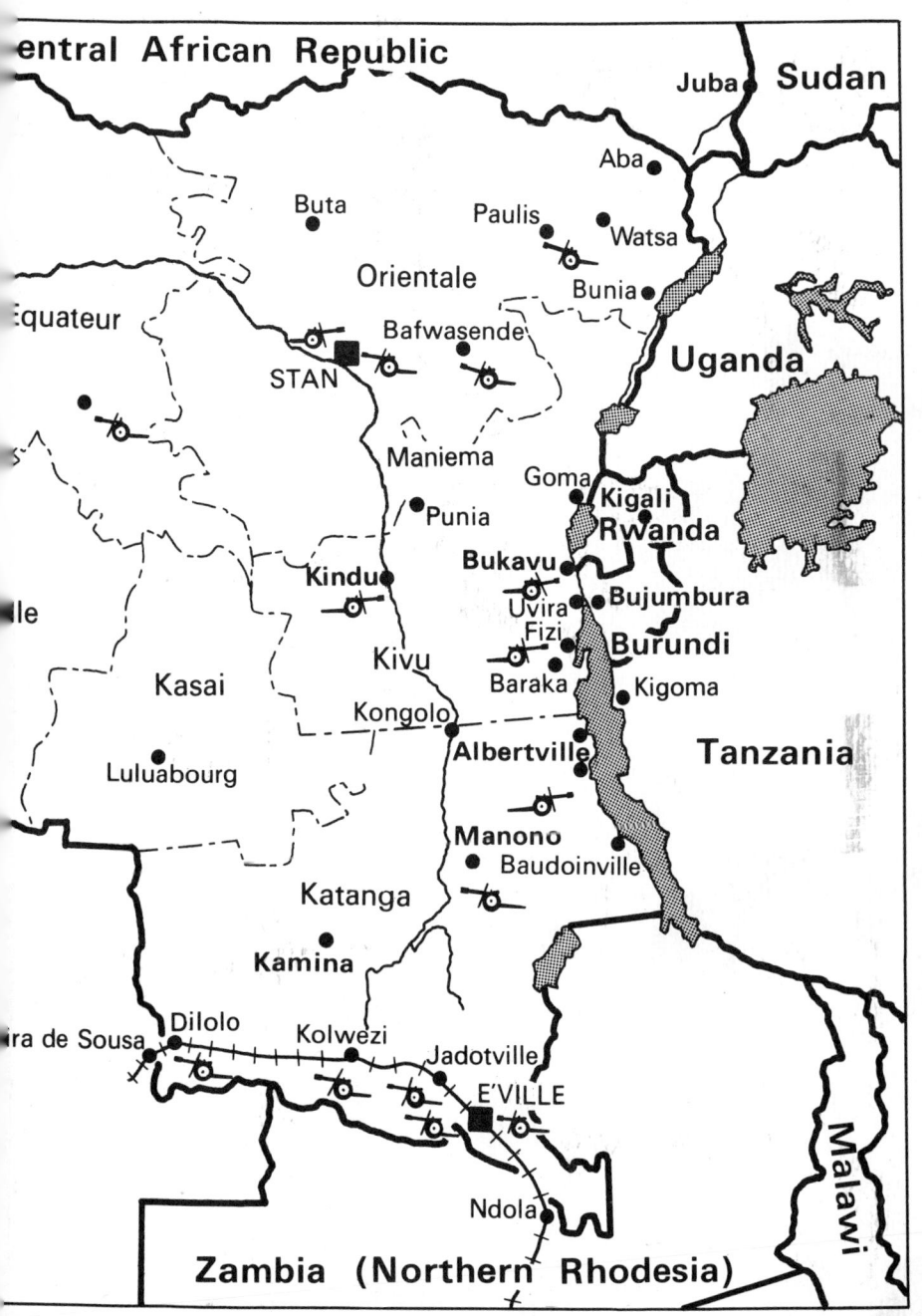

986614

**Lamar State College of Technology
Beaumont, Texas**

PRINTED IN U.S.A.

The Mercenaries

by Anthony Mockler

The Macmillan Company

Copyright © 1969 by Anthony Mockler
All rights reserved. No part of this book may be reproduced or transmitted in any form or by any means, electronic or mechanical, including photocopying, recording or by any information storage and retrieval system, without permission in writing from the Publisher.

The Macmillan Company
866 Third Avenue, New York, N. Y. 10022

First published in France in 1969 by Éditions Stock

First published in English in 1970 by Macdonald and Company, Ltd., London

First American Edition 1970

Library of Congress Catalog Card Number: 73-88837

Printed in the United States of America

Permission to quote from "Epitaph of an Army of Mercenaries" from *The Collected Poems of A. E. Housman* granted by Holt, Rinehart and Winston, Inc. Copyright 1922 by Holt, Rinehart and Winston, Inc; copyright 1950 by Harclays Bank Ltd.

For Leone

Acknowledgments

The author and publishers would like to thank the following:

For permission to quote:
John Murray, Publishers   P. C. Wren: *Beau Geste*
Penguin Books Limited   Froissart: *The Chronicles*, translated by
   G. Brereton. Machiavelli: *The Prince*, translated by G. Bull.
   Castiglione: *The Book of the Courtier*
Society of Authors   A. E. Housman: *Epitaph on an Army of Mercenaries*

For the maps: Oxford Illustrators Limited

For the pictures between pages 160 and 161:
Berne Historical Museum   the 'thousand flowers' tapestry showing the Golden Fleece and the arms of the Duke of Burgundy
Mansell Collection   Colleoni: equestrian statue by Verrochio. Portrait and arms of Bartolomeo Prignano, Pope Urban VI. Ludovico il Moro, from the 'Pala Sforzescha', Milan. Gattamelata: statue by Donatello. Federigo da Montefeltro, reading in his library at Urbino. Sir John Hawkwood (Giovanni Acuto): fresco by Paolo Uccello. Battle of Marignan: bas-relief on the tomb of King Francis I
John Murray, Publishers   Jacket of *Beau Geste* by P. C. Wren
Radio Times Hulton Picture Library   Battle of Crécy. Landsknecht, by Holbein. French legionnaire
Roger Viollet   Foreign Legion *cuisine*
Associated Press   Mueller.
   Puren. Schramme
Camera Press   von Rosen. Lumumba memorial. Mercenary by Congo River. Hoare (Donald McCullin)
Dalmas   Simba war. 'Jungle bunny'
Jean Guyaux   Tshombe. Defence of Bukavu.
John Hillelson Agency   Death of Goosens (Gilles Caron-Gamma). Steiner (Gilles Caron-Gamma)

Keystone Seige of Bukavu. Mercenaries interned at Rwanda
Magnum Capture of Bukavu (Donald McCullin)
Anthony Mockler Guard of honour. Mercenary in 'liberated' villa. Unit diary of 56 Commando. Battle honours of 53 Commando
Reporters Associés Denard
Paul Ribeaud Denard's 'invasion'

Contents

Author's foreword 11
1 What Is a Mercenary? 13
2 The Decline of Feudalism and the Free Companies 25
3 The Condottieri and the Renaissance 42
4 A Nation of Mercenaries 74
5 Mercenaries in the Age of Reason 105
6 The Myth of the Legion 130
7 World Opinion and Twentieth Century Mercenaries 143
8 What the Mercenaries Did in the Congo 155
9 Strength and Weaknesses of the Mercenaries 194
10 The Mercenary Life 220
11 The Yemen and Biafra 254
12 The Future of Mercenary Soldiers 276

APPENDIX I 282
APPENDIX II 292
INDEX 297

Illustrations

PHOTOGRAPHS

Between pages 160 *and* 161
Devotion to war: the mark of a mercenary
Battles and booty
Marignan
The age of the condottieri
Federigo da Montefeltro
The Legion
Death in the Congo
Life in the Congo: 5 Commando at Stan
The mercenaries' revolt
Employers and employed
Death in Biafra

MAPS

France   29

Italy   46

The Thirteen Cantons   77

The mercenaries' revolt: Denard's 'invasion' of Katanga in support of Schramme   197

The mercenaries' revolt: in practice, in theory   212, 213

Biafra   263

Author's Foreword

AUTHORS, LIKE MERCENARIES, live on a plethora of hopes and a penury of means; without hope they would hardly have the will to survive, without practical help hardly the strength. For their practical help and kindness over the two years or so that this book has taken to write, my thanks are especially due to: Dr and Mrs Carey, Donna Anna Velardi, Mr and Mrs Salmon, M. and Mme de Cock, Sarah Georges-Picot, Kasia Crouzat and Hope Leresche.

I would also like to thank Geoffrey Taylor, Alastair Hetherington and Brian Beedham, without whose indirect assistance it would have been impossible to assemble the material for the second half of this book; and for their direct assistance or advice: Robin Mannock, John Ridley, Mert Gusweiler, John Worrall, Lideke Hoffscholte, Judy Cottam, Peter Kemmis Betty, Lord Gifford, Fomdac, and others who may prefer to remain anonymous.

Anthony Mockler
Paris, February 1970

1 What Is a Mercenary?

'AN ARMY OF MERCENARIES,' the Kaiser, jibing, called his British enemies. 'Epitaph on an Army of Mercenaries' A. E. Housman, ironizing, entitled his poetic retort:

> Their shoulders held the sky suspended;
> They stood and earth's foundations stay;
> What God abandoned, these defended,
> And saved the sum of things for pay.

But Housman was defending on grounds of motive what the Kaiser was attacking on grounds of status. Others both before and after them have continually fallen into the same verbal trap, and all discussions on mercenaries are befuddled by this same confusion, which arises from the difficulty of defining precisely what a mercenary is. In the case in point, Housman was throwing scorn on the idea that the soldiers in the British army were mercenaries in the sense that money was their main reason for fighting. The Kaiser, on the other hand, was basically doing no more than to point out that many soldiers who were not British—the Indians, for example—were fighting under the British flag. Both, as was natural, exaggerated: the one the moral high-mindedness of his side's motives and the other the preponderance of the foreign-born element in his opponent's army.

Both assumed also that the term mercenary was necessarily insulting. So it was at the time. Yet it was hardly for the Kaiser to criticize. His ancestor Frederick William I of Prussia had raided all Europe for the seven-foot giants who were the pride and joy of his heart and the *corps d'élite* of the Prussian army. Even under Frederick the Great and his successors only one-third of the army had to be Prussian citizens. There was nothing extraordinary in such proportions at the period. The continual wars that followed the end of the Thirty Years' War were quarrels fought out among monarchs who used small professional field armies that were almost entirely mercenary in character. That is to say that although, for example, the army of the United Provinces might well consist at any given moment largely of Dutchmen, it was not considered either unusual or discreditable for the United Provinces to employ troops and officers born elsewhere and serving primarily for money rather than for motives of loyalty or idealism. Moreover, though particularly noticeable at this period, the use of mercenary soldiers in wars fought between European powers has generally been common and often predominant.

This may appear at first to be a rash and indefensible statement. It certainly needs to be qualified. The qualification I propose is this: that it is only with the growth of the nation-state in Europe that mercenary soldiering has become disreputable and that it is only with the introduction of universal conscription that it has fallen out of use.

At least a negative definition is possible. A mercenary is neither a tribesman fighting for his tribe nor a conscript fighting for his country. This juxtaposition is not frivolous: the nation state is a revival of the tribal state in the sense that it is a geographical and (usually) cultural and linguistic bloc where devotion to the tribal gods is expected and glorified by the name of patriotism and where each male member of the tribe is expected to be trained and ready to take up arms.

Until the French Revolution it had seemed both logical and acceptable that the professional soldier should fight while the ordinary citizen stayed at home. But the massacre of the Swiss

Guard at the Tuileries by a Parisian mob was a sign marking the end of the days of the professional mercenary who sold his loyalties and his service to the traditional employers. The French hordes rose and the armies of the Revolution invaded all Europe; over a million Frenchmen took up arms in four months—a figure that staggered the kings and had been unseen in Europe since the days of the Germanic tribal invasions. After the French Revolution it was considered correct that every man should fight for his own country and dishonourable that a man should serve under another flag. This principle was applied in practice in 1798. General Jourdan's law introduced universal conscription, unknown in Europe since the decline of feudalism and in England since the end of the fyrd. The idea, now so widely spread, that a man can be obliged to fight for his country could only be accepted when a man had a country that was more than a geographical expression to fight for. The Franco-German War of 1870-71 marked the real triumph of the nation state and, in the military field, of the nation-in-arms; in it a short-service German army of conscripts beat a professional long-service French army, and Germany's success was so thorough and so outstanding that all the nations imitated her methods. Bismarck had changed the rules by making conscription in practice as well as in theory universal and by allowing no foreigners at all to serve in the army. His system is still generally observed throughout Europe, where every young man is liable to military service and where every army is based on national loyalties. In an army of conscripts the mercenary soldier can have no place. He is a fish out of water, for since men must have a moral basis to make unpleasant duties tolerable, the cry of patriotism excuses the burden of military service, and for the mercenary soldier the cry of patriotism is the knell of doom.

In these last hundred years, from the Franco-German War to the present day, the unwritten rule that forbids the use of mercenaries in a European war has come to be thought of without any real justification as almost a moral law. In their colonial wars the European powers used mercenary troops—I am thinking in particular of the Gurkhas employed by the British and the Foreign Legionaries employed by the French—but when the battleground was in Europe itself, the use of African or Asian troops invariably caused ill-defined but enormous resentment, as the Kaiser's remark shows. Other examples of this are the use of Moroccan troops by the Free French in the Second World War, of Moroccans by General Franco in the Spanish Civil War, and of their Asiatic levies by the Russians. For even longer the use of European mercenary troops in a European war has been considered outrageous, precisely because it outrages the basic myth of the nation state that patriotism is the only justification for taking up arms. The outrage has always been avenged on the actual foreign-born troops; in the post-Napoleonic civil wars in Spain, Don Carlos ordered that any British or French fighting against him should if taken prisoner be shot out of hand. In the more recent civil war the followers of Franco specially detested the foreigners of the International Brigade; so strong is this almost instinctive feeling that to be a mercenary is in itself immoral that it is generally forgotten how recent and how illogical this sentiment is.

Throughout most of European history any such moralizing attitude would have seemed ridiculous—which is not to say that it was never adopted. Logically, however, the further states progressed from tribalism and the more civilized they became, the more they tended to use mercenary troops. The logic was simple and unanswerable: war being a barbaric pursuit, the citizens of a rich and flourishing state preferred to hire needy foreigners to fight for them rather than themselves to interrupt their profitable and enjoyable lives. This was particularly the case with the great commercial powers and, though it occasionally led to disaster, it often led to triumph. The Carthaginian armies were entirely mercenary, and Hannibal's invasion of Italy which so nearly destroyed Rome was an invasion by a great mercenary army that defeated in three pitched battles the patriotic citizen army opposed to it. Venice by law forbade her citizens to serve in the land forces not merely as soldiers but even as officers;

Venetian generals were always hired mercenaries. England, in her similar period as a rich commercial sea power, fought her wars in Europe on semi-mercenary principles by subsidizing—in effect by hiring—the armies of such leaders as Frederick the Great. Indeed there is only a very fine distinction to be drawn between a foreigner subsidized to fight and a foreigner directly hired to fight. As for the Middle Ages, its whole military system in practice as opposed to theory was semi-mercenary, of which more will be said later. The imperial armies of Rome and of Byzantium, the dynastic armies of Charles V or of Napoleon—all such armies fall rather into the category of mercenary than of national. By modern standards their loyalty was bought rather than owed; their service paid for rather than given; their unity temporary and circumstantial rather than permanent and natural.

In these last paragraphs, however, the word mercenary has been used in a loose though acceptable way, almost as the equivalent of 'professional soldier'. But though a mercenary is a professional soldier, a professional soldier is not necessarily a mercenary: the difference may lie only in a nuance, but the nuance is important in that it implies a moral judgment. That mercenaries are un-principled and unpardonable is a generally accepted proposition, but a proposition that helps very little in deciding who or what a mercenary soldier is. By the principles of justice no man should be condemned without a hearing; by the principles of logic no man should be condemned without a definition.

'*Soldat qui sert à prix d'argent un gouvernement étranger*' is the definition given by Larousse. It covers extremely well the French Foreign Legion; it would equally cover the Swiss regiments for long in French service, the irregular Swiss bands that preceded them, the Gurkhas in the British army, also the Gurkhas in the Indian army, the International Brigade in Spain, the British officers—whether seconded or hired—of the Arab Legion in Jordan, and the mercenaries in the Congo. It would not cover such mercenary leaders as Wallenstein or Tilly in the Thirty Years' War since they were hired not by a foreign government but by their own Holy Roman Emperor. It would not cover any of the condottieri employed by the Pope, since the Pope was ruler of Christendom. It would not cover the Sikhs or the Rajputs enlisted by the British at the time of the British Raj since the Sikhs and the Rajputs were subjects of the Crown, whereas the Gurkhas were technically independent. In other words, Larousse's definition is in one sense too loose and in another sense not broad enough. Any definition that couples both the Foreign Legion and the International Brigade must be inadequate. Yet members of both were certainly paid, and paid by a foreign government.

The idealistic young men who went off to Spain to join the International Brigade, though they were paid, did not join for money. Possibly 'soldier who fights with money as his main objective' would be a better definition, thus defining the mercenary by motive rather than by status.

This, however, is an oversimplification, comforting only to those who prefer to base their definitions on prejudice rather than on analysis, for the mercenaries in the Congo were certainly mercenaries in the fullest sense though not all of them were fighting primarily for money. Money, as Hoare in his book *Congo Mercenary* makes clear, was the main motive for almost all of them, but is one therefore to say that the minority who fought for other reasons were not mercenaries? This would be an absurdity. Besides, from another point of view the definition would stretch too far—to include, for example, most of the conquistadors, whose disappointment after the sack of Mexico at finding hardly any loot is vividly described by Bernal Diaz, the companion of Cortes. The professional, too—the ordinary regular army officer or NCO in any army in the world—fights for money and, as a comparison between recruiting figures and wage increases shows, often mainly for money.

Even a combination of the two points—that the mercenary must be fighting first for money and secondly for a foreign government—is not really satisfactory. It would not cover the Provençal who voluntarily went to fight for Charles of Anjou in the Neapolitan Wars or the Hessian conscript who involuntarily was sent to fight for George III in the American War. It would hardly cover the semi-feudal soldiery of France, of whom de Vigny wrote: 'The regiment used to belong to the Colonel, the Company to the Captain, and both of them knew very well how to lead their men when their conscience as citizens rejected the orders which they received in their capacity as soldiers. This independence of the Army lasted in France until the time of M. de Louvois who was the first to bring the army under the control of the civil servants and to place it, bound hand and foot, in the hands of the Sovereign Power.'

It is not enough, then, to base a definition either on status or on motive or even on a combination of the two. The conclusion imposes itself: it is useless to attempt to give a formal and final answer to the question 'What is a mercenary?' because the meaning of the word has varied throughout history and has depended at any moment on the force of the spirit of nationalism at that particular epoch. At times of great empires and almost universal citizenship, the term mercenary is applicable or not, at choice. At periods of close national unity and limited citizenship when the nation state or the city state is the form of government dominant, it can be defined precisely. In the feudal era when loyalties were confused and multitudinous, the term is almost meaningless and yet in a sense more meaningful than ever, for this was the one period in European history when men served as soldiers entirely without pay—the feudal levy is the least mercenary too (in the strictly verbal sense) of any army ever raised, for the feudal levy had a duty to serve but the lord had no duty to pay.

When a rich state goes to war, its poorer allies are mercenaries, and when a poor tribe enters *en masse* the service of a more powerful neighbour, a group or even a society becomes mercenary. At periods when the bonds of loyalty and patriotism grow tighter, the word mercenary acquires an evil, in addition to a merely descriptive, meaning, and varies greatly at different epochs during which personal loyalty may be due to either an impersonal government, a personal chief, or an imperial or supranational ideal. The mercenaries who fought in Katanga in the early 1960's called the troops of the United Nations '*les super-mercenaires*'; and indeed there is little difference in principle between the troops contributed by the modern law-abiding nation states to the organization that has the task of enforcing peace in the world but lacks the physical power to do so, and the soldiers occasionally offered by the secular rulers of Christendom to popes whose purpose was considered in much the same terms and whose prestige was considerably greater.

But it is not so much by principles as by practice that mercenaries are judged and recognized. So great has been the fascination of both moralists and novelists with the mercenary soldier that the image of the typical mercenary is clearly established in the general mind. Why this fascination should exist, de Vigny perhaps explained when he wrote, 'Military servitude is heavy and inflexible like the iron mask of the nameless prisoner and gives to every fighting man a cold and standardized aspect.' In this passage he was writing of the modern armies of the nation state. When there is uniformity in the most individualistic of professions, that of the soldier, there is a perennial fascination with the semi-independent leader, whether guerrilla or mercenary, who is above the laws and above the specious appeals to loyalty and to the common good with which politicians and commanders-in-chief normally attempt to keep their colonels under control. For one mark by which the mercenary can be recognized is his lack of loyalty or, to be precise, his lack of more than a temporary loyalty. By this criterion the colonels and captains whom de Vigny described in the first passage quoted were mercenaries; by the same criterion the Gurkhas and the International Brigade were not mercenaries, for their loyalty to a cause was permanent, however temporary their actual service paid to that cause may have been. By it, the truest mercenaries of all were the condottieri whose loyalties were literally governed only by the length of their contracts and who fought now for one side, now for the other, with an ease that not even the Swiss, far less the Congolese mercenaries, ever managed to rival.

The second mark of the mercenary comes out in Xenophon's character sketch of the Greek mercenary leader, Clearchus. It is a portrait of an individual, but also of a type that is recognizable throughout history.

'He could have lived in peace without incurring any reproaches or any harm but he chose to make war. He could have lived a life of ease but he preferred a hard life with warfare. He could have had money and security but he chose to make the money he had less by engaging in a war. Indeed he liked spending money on war just as one might spend it on love affairs or on any other pleasure. All this shows how devoted he was to war.'

Here is the real mark of the mercenary—a devotion to war for its own sake. By this the mercenary can be distinguished from the professional soldier whose mark is generally a devotion to the external trappings of the military profession rather than to the actual fighting. The Greeks, lacking the Christian ethos, saw nothing outrageous in this love of war. They were aware of its miseries too; they did not view the utter devotion to war of an Achilles or a Clearchus with the admiration which it would have received in traditionally warlike societies such as those of ancient Scandinavia or feudal Japan. They considered such devotion exceptional but not morally wrong. Christian society, however, demanded that pleasure in war should be masked, often hypocritically, under the pretence of devotion to duty. This attitude still exists, and it is, I believe, the unspoken reason behind the general distaste that has always been shown towards self-confessed mercenaries. The regular army officer of modern times would say he was serving his country, the conscript that he was defending his family and home; but an open devotion to war as an art and a way of life is the mark of the mercenary, and the mercenary's casting aside of a moral attitude to war that is often hypocritical, at best uneasy, both fascinates and repels.

A history of mercenaries would be very little less than a history of warfare throughout the ages, and even a mere list of mercenaries with dates, achievements, and the minimum of historical background would fill a potted volume or two. In a work of this sort, which makes no claim to be definitive and aims rather at entertainment than at instruction (though would-be mercenaries or employers of mercenaries should certainly read it with close attention), the problem is not one of too few facts but of an *embarras de richesse*. It will already be clear that I do not intend to deal with mercenaries outside the European context, although the military history of Japan, India, and China is studded with their influence. But even within the context of European history certain categories of mercenaries will be eliminated and certain periods of history too.

Among categories of mercenaries a common-sense division is easily made. There are three main groups: first the individual soldiers of fortune who flourished particularly in the seventeenth and eighteenth centuries, driven often by persecution to seek service abroad. The 'Wild Geese' are the typical example of these—the Irish Catholic gentry who, after the Battle of the Boyne, refused to take the oath to King William and joined armies all over Europe; to them, as to the Scotsmen who also served in such numbers, the title of mercenary seems far less suitable than that of soldier of fortune.

A second category consists of the various guards with which by tradition, or by their own initiative, heads of state surrounded themselves. Till recently, General Franco had a Moorish guard; the emperors of Byzantium hired Norsemen for their Varangian guard; and there was at one period hardly an enlightened despot in Europe who did not consider it *de rigueur* to have a body of Swiss Guards, of which the most famous example still serves the Vatican. The phenomenon is as widespread as its origin is invariable—the fear of an absolute ruler who, mistrusting his relatives or his fellow countrymen, surrounds himself with a group of foreigners who owe everything to him, who are isolated by their language, by their customs, and particularly by the loathing of the ruler's subjects, in such a way that their loyalty goes to him alone. Dionysius of Syracuse, that most successful of all dictators, rose to power with the help of such a band of Greek mercenaries. The Praetorian Guard of the Roman emperors was a variation of the same system.

Of the third category of mercenaries, almost certainly the most fascinating and in any case the category that alone will be the subject of this book, the free companies of the Middle Ages form the type. Bands of professional soldiers, often dispersing but often temporarily united, under leaders of strong personality, fighting for pay and loot but not entirely indifferent to the claims of honour and legality or to the interests of their country of origin, above all militarily effective—these are the type of mercenaries with which this book will deal. These bands reappear in one form or another throughout European history; their power and influence is always opposed to the power and influence of the formal authorities of the time. Usually the formal authorities succeed in suppressing them either by direct action or more often by absorbing them indirectly into the organization of the state. Occasionally they succeed in overturning the whole structure of society and politics, as happened in Italy just before the Renaissance. When the feeling of patriotic nationalism is strong, they fade; where it is weak, they flourish. On one occasion, in Switzerland, the two elements combined and produced the most formidable soldiers to appear in Europe since the Roman legions. Therefore my aim in this book is twofold: to choose first of all those periods of history when these bands of mercenaries had most influence, direct or indirect, not only on warfare but also on politics and society, and secondly to show how continuous mercenary history has been.

For, though history in the general sense may not, mercenary history certainly repeats itself. If Hoare and Schramme of the Congo had read their Xenophon, they could have foreseen many of the mistakes that they committed. Xenophon's *Anabasis* should be the bedside reading of every mercenary leader and of every employer of mercenaries too. It is the only memoir of more than a mere passing value ever written by a mercenary leader; in it the complex relationships between mercenary leaders, the princes who employ them, the troops who follow them, the native allies who mistrust them, and their countries of origin which attempt to use them are described and illustrated with that lucidity and lack of rhetoric which were the mark of Athenian writers. Throughout mercenary history the balance among these groups has always been delicate, and the vicissitudes tend to follow the same pattern. To take the most striking example, the treacherous killing of Clearchus and the Greek generals is the end that more often awaits mercenary leaders than death in battle or a rich old age; it illustrates the rule of which many instances will occur in the chapters to follow—that no mercenary leader should separate himself even momentarily from his troops, particularly when the most difficult of all problems, that of disbanding a mercenary force, is being negotiated.

The Ten Thousand most certainly fall within the third category defined above—that of roving mercenary bands. Any attempt, however, to deal with them in this book would be a mere paraphrase of Xenophon's full and unique account, which can easily be had either in the original Greek or in translation. I intend therefore to pass directly on to the more obscure, more complex, and more fascinating era of mercenary history which begins in France as the feudal system declines. All mercenary history thereafter up to and including that of the twentieth century can be traced (somewhat in the fashion of a shaky genealogical table) back to the free companies.

2 The Decline of Feudalism and the Free Companies

MILITARILY the feudal system never functioned perfectly. In theory, when war threatened, the king called out the feudal levy, and an array of dukes, counts, and barons, each with their own vassal knights, assembled and, as was their duty in return for the privilege of landholding, fought for their king, receiving no pay. In practice things were very different.

The rights and duties of every landholder were fixed by a charter; legally the whole medieval system depended on an enormous complexity of charters which defined sometimes in incredible detail the contract that existed between vassal and lord. There was no such thing as a standard charter; each knight's obligations to his lord varied to some extent. The only common point was that a knight's fief was held against an obligation for military service, and this military service was commonly forty days a year. This period was certainly the standard in twelfth-century Normandy; there is not enough evidence to prove it was so in England or France. What was also standard was a further clause in the charter which exempted knights and magnates from serving outside their king's realm for these forty days. In Hungary the Golden Bull of 1222 confirmed this privilege—except for those counts and knights who were serving for pay. In León a statute of 1188, in Aragon a statute of 1283, and in Provence a statute of 1212 laid down the same principle.

Strictly speaking, therefore, the feudal host was of very little use to a warlike king. An army composed of knights, each of whose charters must be examined to define their precise duties, which moreover can be held together for only forty days and can refuse to serve abroad, is not the ideal instrument for a king bent on military glory and conquest.

Furthermore, by no means was all the land held by knights in the form of fiefs. In England, to take one example, this was only one of the four basic forms of feudal land tenure.

There are many learned arguments about how many knights' fiefs existed in England—in other words, how many knights the feudal host could muster at best. None are conclusive; what is sure is that the number of knights owed steadily declined. Around 1100 in England the great ecclesiastics, abbots and bishops, owed the King for their lands a total of 784 knights; but when Edward I called out the feudal host in 1277, he could get the great ecclesiastics to send him only 13 knights in all and 35 sergeants (a sergeant was considered equivalent to two knights). And at the same time Humphrey de Bohun who held the earldom of Essex offered the King the service of a mere three knights, a miserable total for an earl's vast fief.

Basically what happened was that the feudal military system gradually broke down and made way for a semi-mercenary system. From approximately 1066–1166 the feudal host was the great military force of England; and as a system, this functioned. But its disadvantages were so great both for knight and King that in 1159, Henry II introduced scutage. Scutage in effect was a tax: a knight by paying scutage, that is, by paying an agreed sum of money, could escape his feudal obligation of so many days military service per annum, and with the money thus brought in the King hired an army. The effect, of course, was that the King had a permanent or semi-permanent army composed of his most warlike knights and vassals, who would normally but not necessarily be his subjects.

It was the great ecclesiastical fiefs which, as much as the innate defects of the system, caused feudal military service to collapse;[1] they were often unable to force their knights to give the due service and almost as a measure of self-defence tended to sub-divide knight's fiefs into small holdings held by squires and small yeomen. This sub-infeudation undermined the whole basis of the feudal idea by splitting a now theoretical knight into four or more small holders, none of whom were capable of giving the King the service that a fully trained knight would have done.

The tenants-in-chief, however, the barons and the great earls, were bound to serve in person or, if not, to send not merely a substitute but also a valid excuse. Barons who refused to obey the summons to a feudal levy had to pay not only scutage but also a heavy fine.

Therefore at the period of the Hundred Years' War a royal army would tend to consist of the King and his barons and earls, plus their personal retainers, the strictly feudal nucleus, and a swarm of knights who served not basically for reasons of feudal duty or loyalty but for pay. In 1337 when Edward III decided to revoke his homage paid as Duke of Aquitaine to the King of France, and thereby started off the Hundred Years' War, the greatest attempt the English ever made to conquer France, a parliament held at Westminster imposed a double tax on wool to last for as long a period as the war should last and decreed that every knight and soldier in the royal army should 'draw the King's pay,' though paying for their living expenses out of their own personal funds and being allowed to keep for their own personal profit any war gains, either in the way of property or prisoners. This army was a very far cry indeed from the simple feudal host; by this time it was considered normal that knights

---

[1] In 1237 the Abbot of St. Albans, who held his land from the King in the form of six knights' fiefs, managed to field two knights and eight esquires, but the expense of equipping a knight was getting heavier and heavier—it cost him 100 marks, and in addition he had to pay each knight two shillings a day for living expenses.

should draw pay and that their motive for fighting should be gain. There are those who hold that the Hundred Years' War was a vast plundering expedition in which the needy English gorged themselves on the riches of a peaceful France. It is not a point of view which it is easy to dismiss.

Nor was the French army in different case. Landholding by socage—in effect by paying rent—was by then the normal system of tenure throughout France, and knight's service had fallen into disuse. The King could only assemble an army by promising high pays and greater rewards; Genoese[1] and German mercenaries flocked to his standards.

The opening decades of the Hundred Years' War made the the English almost masters of a ruined France. The first Valois, Philip VI, was defeated at Crécy (26 August 1346) and ten years later his successor, John the Good, was captured by the Black Prince at Poitiers. John was still in captivity in 1361 when the Treaty of Bretigny was concluded, marking the end of the first period of the conflict. It also marked the rise of the free companies, which owed their origin to the decline of feudalism and very nearly succeeded in overthrowing the whole feudal structure.

Treaties of peace were all very well for kings and barons and the common people, but they offered no means of livelihood to the knight who held little or no land and lived by war. When peace was concluded—indeed even before, while anarchy reigned throughout France after the capture of King John—groups of knights and professional soldiers joined together as 'free companions'. Their very title was a challenge; feudalism held no place at all for 'companions'; every man was fastened for life in his place on the hierarchical ladder. But for those who were not of noble and perhaps not even of good birth, but who had proved themselves excellent soldiers, the system offered no status.

---

[1] The rout of the Genoese crossbowmen by the English archers turned the scale at Crécy. As they fled in panic, the Genoese suffered the usual fate of unsuccessful mercenaries: the King in disgust called out, 'Quick now, kill all that rabble. They are only getting in our way!' and those who survived English arrows were finished off by French swords.

THE DECLINE OF FEUDALISM AND THE FREE COMPANIES | 29

France.

It was impossible that they should ever win a respectable place in society, but at least in war they won honour—honour, and riches too, in the form of plunder but more particularly of ransoms. Peace for them was intolerable.

After the Peace of Bretigny the free companions spread all over France like the plague that had preceded them only a few years earlier. Here are the names of some of the more famous of their leaders: Regnault de Cervoles, known as the Archpriest, Sir Robert Knollys, Perrot le Bearnais, Geoffrey Tête-Noire, Sir John Aimery, Sir John Hawkwood, Bertrand de la Salle, Aymerigot Marcel, the Bascot de Mauleon, Sir Bertrand du Guesclin, Sir Hugh Calveley, the Bourc de Capenne, the Bourc Anglais, the Bourc of Lesparre, Carsuelle, Larnit, the Captal de Buch, Eustace d'Auberchicourt, Sir James Piper, Bernard d'Albret. These captains were not generally noblemen; the very ring of their names is vulgar and plebeian; yet some of the most famous military leaders of the time are here. Bertrand du Guesclin, the Breton, went on to become Constable of France, and Sir Robert Knollys protected young King Richard at the time of the Peasants' Revolt. But most of them died violent deaths before attaining a respectable old age. As the Bascot de Mauleon told Froissart, 'I know of very few except myself, who were not killed somewhere in battle.' And if the battles of Crécy and Poitiers were won by English bowmen against the cavalry of France, all the succeeding battles of importance for many years were decided by the free companies. They fought for the King of Navarre against the King of France and were beaten at Cocherel. They decided the succession to the duchy of Brittany at the battle of Auray where the Comte de Blois was killed; they fought on both sides in the Castilian civil war between Pedro the Cruel and his brother, Henry the Bastard of Trastamare—a war that was finally won by Bertrand du Guesclin. In all these battles they were hired and led by feudal lords or princes. But at the battle of Brignais, their greatest achievement, the free companies united to oppose a feudal army sent by the King of France to wipe them out. And although the Archpriest was at the time fighting, none too enthusiastically, for the King, the companions won a fantastic victory and killed the Constable of France, Jacques Comte de la Marche, defeating an army of over two thousand lances and gaining enormous wealth through ransoms and enormous power through their subsequent capture of castles up and down the Rhone.

Froissart, a great supporter of the medieval system, recounts their exploits with a mixture of horror and admiration. He continually refers to the companions as 'wicked,' but in the end his love of a good story overcomes his disgust at their disrespect for feudal obligations. Some of the most vivid and detailed accounts in his chronicles deal with the free companions. The wrong side may have won at the battle of Brignais but no one, least of all Froissart, could help admiring the companions for their military ability and describing it in detail. He reports the reminiscences of the Bascot de Mauleon and how only the summons to dinner prevented him from hearing of all the adventures of his friend the Bourc de Capenne. He describes in detail the death of Geoffrey Tête-Noire and how his castle of Ventadour was recaptured by the officers of the French King. There is the story of Perrot le Bearnais and that of Ambrogiot Marcel and the incredible story of how the Archpriest[1] collected a band (probably the first) soon after the battle of Poitiers in 1358, invaded Provence, and so terrified Pope Innocent VI and the cardinals that he was invited to dinner at the palace in Avignon several times, 'as if he had been the King of France's son,' and not only had his sins forgiven him but received forty thousand crowns to distribute among his companions. The Pope previously excommunicated all the companies when Geguin de Badefol, who styled himself 'king of the companions,' seized Pont-Saint-Esprit near Avignon on December 28, 1360 and, in the words of the Bascot de Mauleon, had 'made war on the Pope and cardinals

---

[1] 'Archpriest' was an honorific title of precedence given to a senior parish priest at a large church. The other famous archpriest of history was the Archpriest of Hita who was a canon of Seville and wrote bawdy medieval ballads. The title does not appear to have been conducive to holiness.

and really made them squeal'. How preoccupied the popes were with the companies and the curious relationship that developed between them, the next chapter will show.

'What then,' wrote a medieval jurist, Bartholomew of Saliceto, 'shall I say of those companies of men-at-arms who overrun the territories of our cities? I reply that there is no doubt about their position, for they are robbers . . . and therefore as robbers they should be punished for all the crimes they have committed.'

The companions ran great risks; as long as they were fighting for their feudal overlord or indeed for any feudal magnate who had the right to levy war, they were considered to be justified in their style of life. But when peace came, this style of life all of a sudden became that of a bandit: not only was their pay cut short but they had no legal right to pillage, to burn, or to take prisoners. Therefore they were continually looking for legal excuses to continue their way of life; and it was not enough for them to find a new war—they had to find a war that was legal.

The pitfalls were many. First of all, the war that they were to fight in had to be, as the great Doctor of the Church Aquinas had laid down, 'in a just cause'—that is to say, in practice it had to have a legal pretext. In 1370, Sir Robert Knollys met another leader of companions, Perduccas d'Albret, and talked him into deserting the French cause to join the Black Prince, 'who had advanced him to so much honour'. Knollys was a fine example of villain turned preacher: in 1358 he had headed the Great Company in the Loire Valley and had intercepted vast sums being sent in to Paris for the ransom of King John after Poitiers; he is said to have made over 100,000 crowns in booty and rashly declared that he fought neither for the King of England nor the King of Navarre but for himself alone. His banner displayed the device:

> *Qui Robert Canolle prendera*
> *Cent mille moutons[1] gagnera.*

---

[1] Mouton: probably a pun. A florin, was so called because of the sheep's head on it.

Next year he led the Great Company down from Brittany and threatened (following the Archpriest's example) to plunder the Pope. His ravages in May 1359 were so terrible that the charred gables that marked his route were known as 'Knollys' mitres.' *'Robert Canolle,'* wrote the chronicler, *'qui moult greva Françoiz tous les jours de sa vie.'* But on his return from his raid down into Provence he proclaimed that all the towns and castles captured by him were at the King's disposal. And Edward III pardoned him for his previous insolent and dangerous presumption.[1]

Knollys had very nearly fallen into the second pitfall: he had waged war without lawful authority. As, however, he retracted and as the Peace of Bretigny had not yet been signed, his were little more than windy boasts; whatever he might proclaim, he was a vassal of the King of England fighting at a time of war against the enemies of the King of England. But at the battle of Brignais (April 6, 1362) none of the companions were fighting on lawful authority: they were guilty of illicit war, a crime for which the feudal authorities punished with death those who fell into their hands.

In medieval theory wars that were not declared by a prince were not properly wars. But who was a prince? Strict legalists said that only with the permission of the Pope or Emperor could any feudal lord declare war; at the other end of the scale Beaumanoir held that 'every baron is sovereign in his own barony.' In practice kings and the major magnates were held to be so entitled. But in any case no one inferior to a baron had the right to wage war, either public war or private war. (Private war was an old feudal privilege of the nobles; in private war the antagonists had the right to wound or kill but not to spoil or burn or ransom. It was therefore of virtually no interest to the companies and in any case was dying out at this period.)

Finally the companion had to make sure that he was fighting in a war that he had the right to take part in personally. This could be a very knotty problem. In May 1364 the Archpriest,

---

[1] In 1376 the Commons petitioned that Sir John Hawkwood might receive a similar pardon. This was at the time of Hawkwood's unexpected burst of piety—see page 59.

who was in the employ of the King of France, refused to fight at Cocherel because he held lands from the Captal de Buch who commanded for the King of Navarre. In this case his oath of fealty stood in the way. Later the Black Prince made the Captal de Buch return some gifts sent to him by the King of France, for, had the Captal accepted the gifts, he could not honourably have taken up arms against the King of France. It needed very little to create a personal relationship in which the honour even of a companion was involved. In 1369 the Captal de Buch was captured by King Charles, who to his disgust refused to ransom him; the Captal considered that he was bound by gratitude to arm when the King of England asked him to, but King Charles did not. Perrot le Bearnais, unlike other companions, felt himself obliged to refuse service with the Count of Armagnac, a great Gascon noble, because the Count was the sworn enemy of his own lord, Gaston Phoebus Count of Foix.

Of course, not all the companions cared to be or could afford to be as scrupulous as they should have been. The rules were not clear-cut and anyway were too complex in many cases for a companion to be sure how he should act. But any companion who waged illicit war risked his life. He was guilty of *lèse-majesté* in usurping public authority. One of the terms of the Peace of Bretigny was that the kings should agree to disperse the free companies, and in an Order of November 18, 1361, Edward III commissioned two knights to go to France, seek out those who were his subjects and were continuing to loot, rob, and ransom 'as if it were still time of war,' and to set them a time limit to leave France; if they did not observe this, to arrest them and, if it was impossible to arrest them, to report their names to the Council.

Such commissions were often, though not always, ineffective; the companions had recourse to two methods to avoid punishment. Either they would attempt to obtain a pardon as Knollys did (usually paying for it—a fine or a bribe, both terms are applicable) or, if they were in a position of strength, they would themselves attempt to get a payment from the royal lieutenants, a formal bribe in return for which they would agree to leave the territory. There are endless examples in Chancery records in both kingdoms of pardons being given, leaving a companion secure in his profits but with no right to insist on, for example, unpaid ransoms, since no legal claim could arise out of an originally illegal act. As for payments by royal lieutenants, it took Jean de Blasey twenty years of effort to clear Auvergne, Rouergue, Gevaudan, and Velay by this method: some companies he had to buy off half a dozen times, for they insisted on full payment of the ransoms owed them. There was even a system set up for trials of cases arising from these difficulties: one judge appointed by the royal lieutenant and one by the companies. It was in these wild and mountainous areas between the borders of Aquitaine and Provence that the companies were particularly well established. Among the many that infested France were: the White Company, the Compagnie de la Margot, the Compagnie des Tards-Venus, the Compagnie des Bâtards, and any number of 'Grandes Compagnies'.

But many were executed after trial, and Pierre de Saquainville, 'who was in his time a good esquire,' was beheaded at Evreux after being captured on the wrong side at Cocherel. Enguerrand de Bournonville, idol of the French companies in Lombardy, was condemned for defending Soissons against Charles VI, and Sir Henry Boynton, who had taken service under the King of the Scots, was judged guilty by the Constable of England for defending Berwick against Henry IV.

One fully documented trial is that of Merigot Marches who was tried in Paris in July, 1391; he had fought on different occasions for the kings of France and England and the counts of Armagnac and Foix. He had broken the truce which all the companies had agreed with Jean de Blasey in 1390 by seizing a castle and waging apparently illicit war; his venture had terminated by his surrender. The trial turned on what 'a soldier can or ought to do in a just war.' Merigot tried to establish first that he owed basic allegiance to the King of England as a Gascon and secondly that his war was just, for he was acting on secret orders from the Duke of Lancaster (at the time governor of Aquitaine). Alternatively he pleaded that he had seized the castle as surety for a debt, because the castle belonged to the Count of Armagnac, who owed him unpaid wages. The judges, however, rejected his defence and condemned him for treason, murder, robbery, and arson. He was beheaded in Les Halles.[1]

On the other hand, war waged by a feudal lord on the companies was not considered to be war but the execution of justice. Many an accusation of 'illicit war' was met by the defence that the other feudal lord, the enemy, had been employing companies. And the companies, when they were unemployed, suffered from the further disadvantage that they were at the ban of the kingdom. According to the law of arms, knights who were captured by them and released on promise of ransom were justified in not paying, and no loyal subject of the King could trade or communicate with them in any way (French Chancery records show many examples of pardons for dealings with Navarrese, Gascon, and English companies).

In practice, however, the companies could almost always be sure of finding a licit war to take part in. The Breton Company of St Denis had two banners ready under which to fight: the white cross of Armagnac and the Burgundian cross of St Andrew. The raising of a banner and the shouting of a war cry indicated, formally, for which king or lord one was fighting; there was no legal distinction between an English army raised in England and led by English lords and a band of adventurers who used the same cry and the same colours. Thus when the Navarrese war broke out again in central France shortly after the Peace of Bretigny, the companies there changed their cry from 'St George!' to 'Navarre!'

This could lead to difficulties when it came to the division of spoils. For instance, in 1358 a band of English companions

---

[1] An ominous quarter of Paris for free companions. Alleyne and Peter Roux, the nephews and successors of Geoffrey Tête-Noir, were hanged, drawn and quartered there after the surrender of Ventadour; and Aymerigot Marcel lost first his castle of La Roche de Vandais in Auvergne and then his head in the same market-place at Paris.

captured the castle of Poix under the cry of 'Navarre!' not that of 'St George!' But King Edward still considered that they were his vassals fighting in his war and claimed the ransom money due to be paid by the lord of the castle, Jean Tyrel. Robin Walton, the English captain, claimed it for himself; Jean Tyrel who had paid it into the hands of a neutral guarantor named Rayneval reclaimed it, and the Count of St Pol (possibly for the Navarrese?) also put in a claim. The situation was complicated by the local truce that existed between France and England at the time of the capture of the castle.

But this is just a particularly confusing example of a confusing situation. The companions naturally enough wanted all the spoils of war for themselves, but the English rules with regard to plunder were that the King took one-third, the captain one-third, and the remaining third was divided among the soldiery. (In Spain the royal portion was only a fifth and the captain's share a quarter or a tenth according to his standing.) Whenever a town was plundered, therefore, the King was extremely interested to know whether it had been done under the war cry of 'St George!'

In any case, looting and plunder were comparatively minor sources of wealth. Most of the companies derived a permanent income by 'appatising' local villages and towns—a form of blackmail or protection money by which these villages and towns bought immunity from being attacked or plundered. Many of the companies had a formally appointed official to deal with these extortions, the *clerc de patis*. But by far and away the greatest source of sudden wealth was ransoms: a companion who captured a noble lord was set up for life, and the relationship between prisoner and captor was considered to be an entirely honourable and personal one. Throughout this whole period there were any number, naturally enough, of disputes about the payment of ransoms, and if a Frenchman who had captured and then released an Englishman against promise of payment was not in the end paid, he had to have recourse to the English courts. The extraordinary thing is that even at a time when the kings of

France and England might be bitterly at war, the Frenchman could still expect justice in the English courts, and vice versa.

It was, of course, more difficult for a free companion who was fighting an illicit war to be sure that his released prisoner would pay ransom. But it seems that after the battle of Brignais the noble French captives, even though they had every excuse not to pay their ransoms, did so, for the companions, who had been very poor, grew rich after the battle. Presumably honour triumphed over legality. No doubt fear, too, entered into it, for at the time the companies must have appeared invincible—and it would have been a hard death for any feudal lord who had evaded paying his ransom and who fell a second time into the hands of his erstwhile captors.

A few years later, however, many free companions who were assembling for the Castile expedition were loud in their complaints against French prisoners taken at Montauban who refused to pay their ransoms on the grounds that the companions had been excommunicated. Excommunication was far from being a merely spiritual weapon at this time; it entailed precise legal consequences of which this is a fine example. The companions took their case to Sir John Chandos, Constable of Aquitaine, who set up courts to settle the dispute.

Were the companions guilty of atrocities? Froissart says that the Navarrese companies would never entirely respect the safe-conducts which they themselves issued; as soon as they saw a beaver hat or ostrich feathers, they would plunder it, safe-conduct or no. The truth of the matter seems to be that they were no less cruel than the feudal lords and kings. Henry V and Perrot le Bearnais both had excellent reputations for respecting the laws of war and the immunity of the three major categories of people who should not be attacked—churchmen, pilgrims, and peasants. On the other hand, most of the companions seem to have massacred the peasants without compunction—possibly because they were themselves of humble origin. In the suppression of the Jacquerie they were even more ferocious than the nobles. The Bascot de Mauleon helped to kill more than six thousand 'Jacks' at Meaux in 1359, and boasted of it. At the occasion of Wat Tyler's death at Smithfield, it was Sir Robert Knollys who advised the young King to kill all the assembled peasants and was 'more than angry' when his advice was rejected.

Toward the Church the companions naturally behaved with less respect than the feudal nobles, though they generally avoided the sacrilege of killing ecclesiastics. Sir John Hawkwood, before he went to Italy and entered papal service, was one of the leaders of the White Company which in the anarchy after Poitiers in 1359 raided down into Gascony; they took Pau by storm, robbing the clergy and letting the laity go free. Froissart describes him as 'a fine English knight'; he was certainly original. Next year he was at the taking of Pont-Saint-Esprit and received a sixth of the sum with which Pope Innocent VI bought off the threatening companies. And two years later when the White Company was crossing the Alps with the Pope's blessing, Hawkwood stayed behind to take part in the battle of Brignais, the result of which was a challenge to the whole feudal structure, both lay and ecclesiastical.

But in the end the feudal structure proved too strong for the companies. Their rise was caused by the weaknesses of the feudal military system, and they in their turn eventually brought about the complete collapse of the military system and, with it, indirectly, the end of the majestic feudal idea.[1] Meanwhile they shook the whole bastion of feudalism, the whole kingdom of France, and by their successes undermined eventually the ideas of noble birth as the *sine qua non* of prowess, of land as the basis of a chain of authority, of the Church as an unassailable structure, and of loyalty and personal honour as the motives for fighting. But at the time feudal prejudices were too strong for them; despite their title they were never really free and never really companions. The captains had much the same relationship to the ordinary 'companions' as the feudal baron had to his retainers; he took (if it were an English or Gascon company) the captain's third; he armed and trained his men, admitted responsibility for their

---
[1] See p. 69.

unauthorized pillaging, and he might even go so far as to replace their horses and pay their ransoms if they were captured in battle—though Perrot le Bearnais would only ransom those of his men who were captured when fighting at his side. Nor were they really 'free'; they were still bound not only by the law of arms, as has clearly enough been shown, but also by their residual feudal allegiance. When Edward III was about to renew the war after the interval of the Peace of Bretigny, he sent word to the free companies ranging around France to pass from the defensive to the attack, and they were overjoyed to have orders to obey.

It was not till the companies came into contact with a non-feudal society in Italy that they really became great powers in their own right, semi-permanent moving states capable, occasionally, of following a political policy with at least as much consistency and success as the average Italian city.

In the years following Poitiers and the Peace of Bretigny when the companies were at the height of their power and threatened kings and popes alike, all the feudal authorities banded together to take steps to get rid of this new, embarrassing, and dangerous threat that the kings had with so little foresight created. There was a move, backed by the Pope with pardons and privileges galore, to send them off on a crusade against the Turks. Many companies started off for the wilds of Prussia; they got as far as Alsace and then turned back. Eventually it was to be the Spanish expeditions which decimated the companies and exhausted their strength to a point where they remained a nuisance certainly but no longer (for the time) a serious threat.

But earlier the Pope and the cardinals had been driven to desperation by the capture of Pont-Saint-Esprit. As the Bascot de Mauleon explained to Froissart, they could not get rid of the companies 'and never would have done until everything had been destroyed if they had not thought of a way out. They sent to Lombardy to invite the Marquis of Montferrat, who was at war with the Lord of Milan. When he reached Avignon the Pope and cardinals made an agreement with him and he talked to the

English, Gascon and German companies.' And as a result, a large number of captains and companies went off across the Alps, taking, according to Froissart, three-fifths of all the men with them. This was in the year of grace 1361. It is doubtful whether Pope Innocent VI would have taken this action had he been granted the divine gift of foresight and shown what troubles he was storing up for his successors to the Holy See.

3 The Condottieri and the Renaissance

OF ALL THE EQUESTRIAN STATUES in Italy, perhaps indeed of all the myriad equestrian statues in Europe, none has quite such an air of dominance as that of the condottiere Colleoni. Horse and rider seem to bestride not merely a piazza but a civilization, and the bland portraits of popes and princes are obliterated by this terrible face, this harsh energy, this monotonous and potent mass of stone. Here, feels the uneasy spectator, is the brute force that lay behind the colour and refinement of the Renaissance: a barbarian, devoid of pity or scruples, incapable of that finesse that was the mark of the civilization around him. Surely Colleoni must have been a power in the land; surely men like these must have been masters of the times.

Werner of Urslingen wore on his breastplate the device: 'Lord of the Great Company, enemy of God, of pity and of mercy.'[1] Sir John Hawkwood—Giovanni Acuto—in the massacre at Faenza found two of his constables quarrelling over a young nun; with Solomon-like judgment he decreed, 'Half each!' and cut the unfortunate woman in two. Braccio Fortebraccio is described by his biographer as 'a fine figure of a man except that he was scarred all over.' Yet the fresco of Sir John Hawkwood in the

---

[1] *'Signore della Gran Compagnia, nimico di Dio, di pieta e di misericordia.'*

Duomo at Florence shows a man of a very different stamp from Colleoni—almost melancholy, a man with a sense of responsibility and care, a citizen without ambition or fire—and Federigo da Montefeltro reading in his library at Urbino is clearly a man of good humour, urbanity, competence, and culture. No less an authority than *the* authority on behaviour, Baldassare Castiglione, noted in *The Courtier* that Iacopo Piccinino was renowned even in the Italy of that elegant period for his wit. Yet all these men were mercenary captains; they form a historical class in the same way that the popes of the Renaissance form a historical class— which is to say that if individuals must be compressed into a category, then a category can be found to compress even such individuals as these into. Werner of Urslingen was known, unjustifiably, as '*il duca Guarnieri*'; Federigo da Montefeltro, justifiably, as Duke of Urbino; between these two dukes there is a gap of almost a century and an even greater gap in character. They have nothing in common but the name of condottiere. Both dominated in a sense certain years of Italian history, and all the other condottieri of the intervening decades had in them that life force of which Verrocchio's statue is the indecent and brutal but symbolic expression.

The history of France can—just—be imagined without the free companies, but the history of Italy is unimaginable without the condottieri. They fascinated the minds of their contemporaries, who followed their achievements with a mixture of repugnance and admiration but evolved no consistent mental standards by which to analyze them or moral standards by which to judge them.[1] They still fascinate to a certain extent all who admire or are interested in the Italian Renaissance, with the fascination aroused by an obscure but obviously important phenomenon. Historians of the Renaissance and writers about Italy of that epoch tend to refer to the condottieri *en passant*, in the tones commonly used when referring to the picturesque but disreputable. It is, however, only too clear that the condottieri were more

---
[1] Machiavelli's standards of judgment and analysis were horribly inconsistent—see below, pp. 47, 50 ff.

than picturesque; they were an essential part of that most complex civilization. And the purpose of this chapter is to attempt to place them historically as more than merely decorative extras.

The title of condottiere is functional in origin. A condottiere was a mercenary captain who signed a '*condotta*,' or written contract, with a prince or a city for the hiring of mercenary troops.[1] The *condotta* specified length and terms of service, number of men, pay, and so on; it was a document drawn up with great care by lawyers on both sides, and though there was no standardized form, there were several main varieties. The following were the most common forms of *condotta* used by the Florentine Republic:

Condotta a soldo disteso—for a condottiere employed under a native-born (e.g., Florentine) captain-general, with a fixed number of soldiers, for active service.

Condotta a mezzo soldo—a looser form, in which the condottiere was not controlled by any captain-general but was free to raid the lands of the enemy more or less as and when he wished.

Condotta in aspetto—basically a retainer paid to condottieri in time of peace in order to keep their loyalty.

Throughout Italy the *condottas* of this period tended to have various common features; however limited the time for which the *condotta* was to run, the condottiere would normally bind himself for a further and longer period to take no part in hostilities against his late employer. Thus Werner of Urslingen when he left the service of Louis of Hungary had agreed neither to enter the service of any of Louis of Hungary's enemies—to wit, the rulers of Naples, the Pope, and the ruler of Milan—nor to attack cities friendly to his late employer—Florence, Perugia, and Siena, among others. How effective these guarantees were can be judged by Louis of Hungary's action in writing an open letter of recommendation for Werner to the Florentines but secretly

---

[1] It was my intention to include among the appendices an example of a *condotta* between Fortebraccio and the Apostolic Chamber (the papal mercenary-hiring office), but space precluded this—the *condotta* in 27 clauses is approximately as long as this chapter.

sending a message to warn them that 'there is no faith or pity in those who follow battles; and the said duke Werner has been accustomed to doing on other occasions very dangerous things under the protection of his company. So be on your guard. . . . We will if necessary come to your help.'

When Braccio in 1420 made peace with his great enemy Pope Martin V (Colonna), he received as part of the peace treaty a papal *condotta;* its terms were that he was to maintain 300 lances in the March[1] and, if so required, 800 lances for active service in the Kingdom[2] or wherever else they might be required. This *condotta* was to last for three years during which he would continue to hold the cities he had seized illegitimately in central Italy (Perugia and others) as papal vicar; for the first eighteen months he was to be paid 52,000 florins and for the second eighteen months 60,000 florins, plus another 54,000 florins for keeping an extra 600 lances in papal service in lands directly controlled by the Pope. His excommunication and interdiction were lifted; his dispute over the possession of Assisi with Guid'Antonio da Montefeltro was to be settled by arbitration.

Two points will immediately be noticed. The first is that the relationship between condottiere and employer was purely a matter of business; there was no pretence on either side of any claim to loyalty or allegiance outside the terms of the *condotta*, in contrast with the rules governing the behaviour of the free companions in France. The second is equally clear: that as the *condottas* became more formalized and more varied, the condottiere's position shifted from that of military captain in temporary service to that of independent power in temporary alliance. Braccio's *condotta* was basically nothing more or less than a formal alliance for three years. Giovanni Bentivoglio of Bologna was given *condottas* by various states and princes continually over a

---
[1] The March—the March of Ancona, part of the Papal States.
[2] The Kingdom—the title by which Italian writers of the period refer to the Kingdom of Naples (known confusingly as the Kingdom of the Two Sicilies). In order to avoid this confusion, I will imitate them by using the short title.

Italy.

period of thirty years. He was rarely seen in the field. The purpose of *condottas* like these was to prevent the resources of a minor but important state from going to the enemy and to obtain free passage for friendly troops; if long-term, they were a means of extending a sphere of influence. They were in fact treaties of alliance between a major and a minor power, for historical reasons termed *condottas*. Thus many of the lords and *signori* who took *condottas* can only be called condottieri in a purely technical sense. And it is worth noting that the title of condottiere was in any case only rarely used by contemporary chroniclers and historians, though in a later period it became a convenient and accepted way of distinguishing the Italian-born mercenary captains from the foreigners who had preceded them.

No one has contributed more to the evil reputation of the condottieri than Machiavelli, and it is a matter of amazement that the liberal historians with whom Machiavelli enjoys the most evil of all reputations should in this instance accept uncritically from the lips of the devil a judgment that, if it were on any other subject, they would sceptically submit to searching and rigorous tests. 'I want to show more clearly,' writes Machiavelli in *The Prince*, 'what unhappy results follow the use of mercenaries. Mercenary commanders are either skilled in warfare or they are not; if they are, you cannot trust them because they are anxious to advance their own greatness by coercing you, their employer, or by coercing your enemies more than you intended. If, however, the commander is lacking in prowess, as often as not he brings about your ruin. . . . Experience has shown that only princes and armed republics achieve solid success, and that mercenaries bring nothing but loss.'

This argument has a superficial logical appeal but not very much historical backing when tested against the actual events of the period. Machiavelli himself in an earlier chapter contradicts his conclusion by citing the 'solid success' achieved by Francesco Sforza and about to be achieved, had not fate struck an unexpected blow, by Cesare Borgia. Admittedly he was then considering

Sforza and Borgia in their role as princes, forgetting their past as mercenaries; his analysis does not go very deep. And when he writes that 'mercenaries are disunited, thirsty for power, undisciplined and disloyal; they are brave among their friends and cowards before the enemy, they have no fear of God, they do not keep faith with their fellow men,' he might with far more accuracy have substituted 'princes and republics' for 'mercenaries' and the epithets would have applied with even more truth.

For if mercenaries were faithless, it is at least arguable that they were mere amateurs in treachery when compared with their employers. Carmagnola, returning in triumph after a series of victories won for Venice, was escorted with pomp and ceremony to the Doge's palace, placed in the chair of honour and warmly applauded while he spoke. As evening drew on, the *sbirri*, the military police, suddenly arrested him and for twenty days he was 'examined by torture before the Secret Council.' What he was accused of only the Secret Council knew and they kept their secret. Finally he was led into the Piazza di San Marco, gagged to stop his protests of innocence, placed between the twin columns, 'and there beheaded amidst a trembling people.' Albert Sterz, captain of the White Company, was beheaded by his employers the Perugians. Fra Moriale was suddenly arrested at Rome by Cola di Rienzo, to whom he had been unwise enough to lend money, thrown into a dungeon, tortured, and beheaded.[1] Gianpaolo Baglione was executed on the orders of Pope Leo X (Medici), and his brother-in-law, Bartolomeo Alviano, was probably poisoned by the Venetians. The savage Ottobuono Terzo was trapped and killed treacherously by Muzio Attendolo Sforza. Iacopo Piccinino eventually married Francesco Sforza's daughter, Drusiana. Despite this blood alliance, Francesco arranged for Iacopo to be killed; he advised him to go to Naples where he was feasted by the King, Don Ferrante, for seven days; at the farewell banquet he was arrested and strangled in Castel-

---

[1] The story of his death, one of the most colourfully written descriptions in Italian literature of the period, is told in the *Vita Anonima di Cola di Rienzo*.

nuovo by Don Ferrante's men. Muzio Attendolo Sforza when he was Grand Constable of the Kingdom was twice within one year arrested by Queen Joanna and thrown into prison, escaping death only by a combination of luck and support from his numerous family. He was eventually drowned trying to lead his cowardly troops across a raging stream. His great enemy Braccio was taken prisoner in battle and then struck down by an exile from Perugia. Rare was the condottiere who like Sir John Hawkwood died honoured and respected in old age. In danger of betrayal at the hands of their employers, in danger of defeat and death in battle at the hands of their employers' external foes and of sudden assassination at the hands of their employers' internal enemies, it seems extraordinary that any condottieri of the time should have survived at all.

Boldrino da Panigale, a minor condottiere, was poisoned at a feast in Macerata given by the Pope's brother. His band of four hundred swore a vendetta and two years later descended on Macerata and demanded the person of the killer of 'their beloved condottiere.' The Florentines arranged a truce by which the bones of Boldrino were handed over instead, and the company received the bones with great honour as they were borne out of the city by a procession of weeping ladies and priests, and put them in a casket that served as their standard for long after.

Cesare Borgia surpassed all his predecessors by arranging a veritable razzia of mercenary leaders formerly employed by him. At the castle of Sinigaglia he called his condottieri together and had Paolo Orsini, Vitelozzo Vitelli, and Oliverotto da Fermo strangled. Gianpaolo Baglione only escaped thanks to that well-justified wariness which later deserted him. Machiavelli, needless to say, considered this one of Cesare's master strokes and thoroughly approved. If mercenaries were expected by him to keep faith with their fellow men, princes were not.

Machiavelli's was not a voice crying entirely in the wilderness. 'Locusts who leap here and there,' St Bernard of Siena, the great anathematizer of all vices and weaknesses, called the mercenaries, and he complained that he had himself 'been in a city wherein these executioners of God entered, and in the houses where there was some wine do you know what they did with it? They let it flow and washed their horses' hoofs in it.' But even St Bernard did not consider them evil, merely barbaric. Sometimes when he met them on the highway they would call out, 'Fra Bernardino, remember the poor free-lancers!' and he would stop and tell them that they had more excuse than merchants who traded with the enemy since they depended on their profession for their daily bread. Once two friars greeted Hawkwood with the customary phrase, 'God give you peace!' to which he retorted, with that light and airy wit of which we have already noted a practical example, 'God take from you your alms!' The friars said they meant no offence. 'How,' said Hawkwood, 'when you pass by me and pray that God would make me die of hunger? Do you not know that I live by war and that peace would ruin me?'

Machiavelli complained that mercenaries in Italy 'directed all their efforts to ridding themselves and their soldiers of any cause for fear or need for exertion; instead of fighting to the death in their scrimmages they took prisoners without demanding ransom. They never attacked garrison towns by night; and if they were besieged, they never made a sortie; they did not bother to fortify their camps with stockades or ditches; they never campaigned in winter. All these things were permissible under their military code and this policy was followed by them so that, as I said, they might escape both exertion and danger.' Machiavelli would presumably have approved of, though not believed, Hawkwood's retort. With a total disregard for consistency, Machiavelli accused mercenaries, as many have done since him, of being both too warlike and not warlike enough; of fighting wars at all and, almost in the same breath, of fighting them without enthusiasm; of being incapable cowards and of being only too ferociously efficient. The friars, no doubt, were shocked at Hawkwood's rough attempt at humour and went away shaking their heads and telling each other that these mercenaries were the cause of all the troubles and wars in Italy. In fact, however, the mercenaries were not the cause of wars, they were rather the instrument by which wars were fought. And once they reached a position where they had the power to cause wars, they were only in a very limited sense mercenaries at all.

Machiavelli was a jaundiced observer who tended to blame the mercenaries for their faults and their virtues alike. He finished the diatribe above with the phrase 'and as a result they have captained Italy into slavery and ignominy.'

Admittedly he was writing at a time when the French, the Swiss, and the Spanish (largely mercenary troops themselves) were totally outclassing the Italians in the field, but his direct criticisms which have had so much influence on the generally accepted picture of the condottieri are founded on prejudice rather than on study. He was attempting to revive the Florentine militia (he did so, and it was soundly beaten in 1506) and any stick was good enough with which to belabour the condottieri. Night attacks—the White Company and Fra Moriale were famous for them. Fighting to the death—Braccio and Sforza had never shown any fear of that. It was the princes and the signori who so rarely died in battle, loath to risk their lives on the battlefield. As for the desire to escape exertion and danger, the history of the condottieri is, if nothing else, a history of constant exertion attended by continual danger.

And yet a man of Machiavelli's acute intelligence is unlikely to have given way to entirely unfounded propaganda. At the period at which he was writing, the wars in Italy, minor wars conducted by the condottieri, had tended to become more and more stylized. His error lay in attributing to all the condottieri those military failings that had only appeared in the forty-year period of comparative calm in the history of Italy that lasted from the Peace of Lodi in 1454 (by which the five great states of Italy accepted the balance of power as a system) until the first of the great French royal invasions in 1494. These forty years were mething of a golden age, and its military faults were but the marks of a civilization—the only one in European history—which had refined the barbarity out of war, a point that will come up again later in this chapter. That this civilization crumbled militarily when faced with the organized brutality of the French, the Swiss, the Spanish, and the German invaders was not surprising; it is rather a matter of amazement that it managed to resist so long. But in any case the criticisms which Machiavelli formulated could certainly not be directed against the earlier condottieri and mercenary captains who dominated the century of confused, turbulent, and bloodthirsty warfare which preceded the Peace of Lodi.

As always, mercenary bands originated in the difficulties that legitimate feudal princes found in dispersing their troops when a war was over. Toward the end of the Middle Ages, Italy was the richest and most populous, the most commercial, the most fertile, and the most prosperous part of Europe, and as bees to flower buds, so mercenary bands gravitate toward riches. Rough figures will serve as a rough guide. Milan had a population of about four hundred thousand; Venice and Naples about three hundred thousand; Florence and Paris about two hundred thousand; Rome and London were comparatively small, with about fifty thousand inhabitants each. The state of largest extent and of the greatest riches was the Kingdom (which at times included Sicily and at times did not); the territories of the Kingdom stretched up almost to the gates of Rome and swept round on the east to include the mountainous region of the Abruzzi. The Kingdom was bounded on the north by the Papal States, a belt of semi-independent territories and city-states over which the popes held feudal sovereignty and upon which they were always trying to impose their authority. In the north of Italy, Milan under the Visconti was the papacy's main enemy; Venice was largely occupied with her colonial empire in Greece and the Mediterranean. Florence, normally a papal ally, barred Milan's expansion south. And around these five great states a swarm of smaller cities buzzed and hummed, all with a life and policy of their own.

Between 1300 and 1375, four great waves of mercenary companies, all foreign, swept into Italy. As the century began, Charles of Anjou, brother of St Louis King of France, was struggling against Don Peter III of Aragon for the possession of the Kingdom. Twenty years of war were ended by the Treaty of Caltabellota by which Sicily was detached from the Kingdom and transferred to Aragon while the House of Anjou was installed at Naples. The comparative and unexpected success of Aragon was due partly to popular support, partly to sea power, and partly to the Almogavares.

The Almogavares were a type of professional mercenary infantry, recruited mainly in the territories of Aragon and Navarre. In an age when armour was almost indispensable, they wore no armour at all but were clothed in skins and shod in brogues. Their weapons were javelins and a short sword, their defence a shield. Their name was derived from the Arabic *Al-Mughúwir* ('Raiders'). And half a century before the Peace of Bretigny they achieved success in an enterprise which was never equalled either by the free companies in France or by the condottieri in Italy.

The peace between Anjou and Aragon left them unemployed, unwanted, and unoccupied—but not unorganized. The conditions were precisely those which led to the rise of the free companies in France; and in the exploits of all the future 'Great Companies' can almost certainly be traced a desire to imitate the success of these bands, who formed themselves into a company entitled the Grand Catalan Company under a leader named Roger di Flor.[1] This first wave menaced Italy briefly but the menace passed on and away, merely hinting at what was to follow. The Grand Catalan Company crossed from Sicily over to Constantinople and took service, 6,500 strong, under the Byzantine Emperor, Andronicus II (Palaeologus), against the Turks. Roger, who had

---
[1] His real name was Roger von Blum; but in that cosmopolitan society nationalities of origin mattered very little and the Italians invariably altered foreign names to a more mellifluous form.

a very murky past as a blackmailer, spoke excellent Greek. He was given the title of grand duke and later that of caesar, as well as the hand of a Byzantine princess in marriage. But such favour had its dangers; he was assassinated by the Emperor's son, Michael, at Adrianople.

The Grand Catalan Company took a bloody revenge on the Byzantines, then entered the service of the Frankish Duke of Athens, Walter of Brienne. Finally they turned against their employer, and at the battle of Cephissus, in March, 1311, killed Duke Walter and set up their own Catalan duchy in Athens. This duchy of mercenaries lasted for the almost unbelievably long period of sixty-three years until the Catalans were finally ousted by a Navarrese company who in their turn held Athens for nine years until they, too, were ousted by the Italian Lord of Corinth, Nerio Accaiouli. No company or band of mercenaries before or after ever achieved such political power and held it for so long a period—though many tried to—as the Grand Catalan Company. Their exploit was an inspiration to many would-be imitators and is a passage of mercenary history that deserves to be studied in far more depth and detail than is here possible.

Half a century later an internecine war between two branches of the Anjous tore the Kingdom and began the century of civil wars, foreign invasion, looting, plundering, and atrocities which complicated its history and ruined its prosperity. Louis King of Hungary, head of the senior branch of the Anjou line, set out from Budapest in the autumn of 1347 with a thousand knights in order to avenge the death of his brother Andrew, murdered by Queen Joanna I of Naples, Andrew's wife and cousin. The war that followed in the Kingdom lasted for just over three years until peace was finally signed in January, 1351, before Pope Clement VI at Avignon. In the words of a chronicler of the time, 'This was the beginning of the desire among Germans and Hungarians to prey on the Kingdom—delights which attracted soldiers from everywhere like birds to a carcass, to the great harm of all the country, as our story will show.'

In itself the war was indecisive and benefited none of the House of Anjou; its importance lies not in its direct but in its indirect results. Indirectly those three years changed the whole character of warfare in Italy, destroyed the feudal system in the Kingdom, introduced bands of foreigners to a looting ground of incomparable richness, and involved the papacy in its first timid attempts to manoeuvre mercenary bands for its own ends. It was therefore one of the most extraordinary and significant wars ever to take place in Italy.

Louis of Hungary spent merely four months in the Kingdom before returning to central Europe. He left the conduct of the war to his vicars, Hungarian and German captains such as Conrad Wolf, Sprecch, and Count Landau, and to a Provençal, a knight of St John,[1] Fra Moriale. Werner of Urslingen, whom Louis of Hungary had dismissed before he left, was hired by Queen Joanna before passing, semi-treacherously, back to the invaders' side. These Germans and Hungarians rode light but wiry horses; they were known as '*barbute*,' from the conical form of their helmets. They proved their military superiority decisively in a battle at Meleto, only four miles outside the walls of Naples, where after less than an hour's fighting they defeated the feudal barons of the Kingdom. 'This cannot properly be called a battle,' comments the disgusted chronicler 'but a trap set to catch barons.' No hour's work in the whole of Italian mercenary history was ever as richly rewarded. The spoils of harness, horses, and arms alone must have been worth a fortune—but the ransoms were prodigious. Five major barons paid 100,000 florins among them, and the other barons a total of 50,000 florins. The knights added another 50,000, and as a *douceur* on the side the Neapolitans paid 20,000 more for the privilege of being allowed to collect their harvest. Queen Joanna was offered—and had to accept—the opportunity of buying back two of her cities for another 120,000 florins.

After this battle there could be no question of the superiority of the foreign invaders to any local forces, feudal or other, that

---
[1] Knight of Malta

could be raised against them, whether in the Kingdom or in the considerably less powerful states to its north. Italy was at their mercy if they could make use of their strength. Also the invaders had had a taste of the immense riches which their military superiority could earn them. Many of the Germans returned home after dividing the booty (which in the end included crucifixes, vestments, women's clothes, and the women inside the clothes) but many others, particularly the Hungarians, felt no desire to leave so rich a country.

The invaders were not at this stage mercenaries in the full sense; they were still fighting, as they always had been, for Louis of Hungary in a legitimate war and with complete legal justification. It was not till the peace was signed at Avignon that they were faced with difficulties of status and the need to decide whether they would stay in Italy and, if so, on what terms. Their position then became peculiarly awkward—powerful, but deprived of that force which the possession of a legitimate status, however absurd, gives to soldiers who have never been without it. These were not the condottieri of a later age but soldiers tied by the same feudal rules of war which bound the free companies who at just this period were spreading over France. Conrad Wolf, 'with typical German astuteness' and remembering the rules of licit and illicit war, put up an Imperial banner. But he was bought off with a bribe of 35,000 florins and left the Kingdom with his followers, having signed a pact not to return for two years, after which he would be entitled to come back as a baron, paying homage. The other leaders faded away. Werner of Urslingen returned to his native Swabia and Count Landau raided desultorily in the Campagna. Fra Moriale attempted to hold on to a city in the Kingdom but was driven out by Sigismondo Malatesta of Rimini whom Queen Joanna employed as her vicar.

Technically demobilization appeared to have been accomplished. But at this stage 'the Friar of St John, Fra Moriale, seeing that the Prefect di Vico with whom he had been at the siege of Lodi could not keep up his pay, and being very desirous of booty, got the idea of collecting armed men from every part of Italy and of forming a company of foot soldiers with whom he could march or raid against any place or any man he wanted.' From all over Italy foreign soldiers came in to join the first 'Great Company' that really deserved its title. Fra Moriale was a military leader of talent, and an organizer of genius, the first true condottiere untrammelled by any respect at all for established authority and the feudal system of precedence. The Great Company became a moving city-state, carefully administered internally and exchanging ambassadors on equal terms with the republics of central Italy. It owed loyalty to no man except Fra Moriale, and it was not so much employed as bought off by any city whose territory it approached. For two years its movements, actual or feared, dominated the politics and diplomacy of central Italy, and his contemporaries believed that Fra Moriale aimed at establishing his power over the whole peninsula. He might have done so, had he not made the mistake that has so often been fatal to the mercenary leader—that of separating himself physically from his troops. After his death, the Great Company's importance faded. Count Landau led it in the service of the Visconti, Lords of Milan, and there he died, stoned to death by English soldiers when the relics of the Great Company were overwhelmed by the third wave of mercenaries to invade Italy, the free companies from France whom the Pope had urged across the Alps into the service of the Marquis of Montferrat.

The most important of these free companies was the White Company, led at the time by Albert Sterz, but later to be taken over by Sir John Hawkwood. Each knight, heavily armed, had one or two pages, and 'the pages' job was to keep their armour polished so that when they appeared in battle array, their arms and armour gleamed like mirrors and so were all the more frightening.' The Italians were amazed at their warlikeness, at the archers in the company, at their fashion of fighting on foot, leaving their horses to be held by the pages, and at their penchant for night attacks. The White Company evidently based its tactics and organization on the English armies of the time. Militarily the light-armed Hungarian-German cavalry bands that had preceded them were completely outclassed.

It was at this time that the term lance began to be used in Italy. A lance consisted of a knight and a squire both mounted on chargers and a page on a palfrey. Five lances formed a company commanded by a corporal, and five companies a troop commanded by a constable; a company therefore consisted of seventy-five mounted men and almost always a certain number of foot followers too. An army of 1,000 lances would be basically a mounted army 3,000 strong.

Very soon all central and northern Italy was pullulating with new companies. Among the rivals of the White Company were the Compagnia del Capellotto or the Black Company led by Hartmann von Wartenstein, the Compagnia del Fiore of Hugo von Melchingen, the Compagnia della Stella of Hans von Bongard, and the first of a series of companies called the Compagnia di San Giorgio. Pisa, Florence, Siena, Perugia, and Lucca employed them all, with varying fortune but no long-lasting results, against each other. The Pope, who had hoped only that the companies and the Visconti would exterminate each other, found his projects to regain control of the Papal States ruined by their activities. In 1365, the new Emperor, Charles of Bohemia, visited Avignon and concerted plans with Urban V for dispatching the companies on a crusade against the Turks. St Catherine of Siena wrote to her 'dearest and beloved brother in Jesus Christ, Messer Giovanni'—none other than Sir John Hawkwood—urging him and his followers to 'become a company of Christ and go forth against the dogs of infidels who possess our holy places.' Like similar schemes before, this came to nothing. On April 13 the next year Pope Urban excommunicated all the companies and had a papal bull of anathema read from every pulpit in Italy. The captains laughed. It was his successor, Gregory XI, who a decade later reversed this policy and decided to employ the companies as an instrument of papal authority; this decision, perhaps inevitable, was later to lead to fearful complications in the period of the Great Schism when three rival popes employed bands of mercenaries against each other. At the time, however, it succeeded in its immediate arm—the crushing of the Great Rebellion against papal authority of 1375.

This rebellion was led by the usually loyal papal ally, Florence. In order to crush it, the Pope decided to return himself to Rome, finally abandoning Avignon, and to send ahead Cardinal Robert of Geneva leading 6,000 knights and 400 infantry. These were free companions, the fourth and final wave of foreign mercenaries to sweep down into Italy. These companies were the last remaining in France, the relics of the Spanish expeditions that had decimated their ranks in the years following the Peace of Bretigny. That same year they had been hired by King James of Majorca (third husband of Queen Joanna of Naples) for yet another attack on his brother, Don Pedro the Ceremonious of Aragon. But at Val di Soria, King James fell sick and died. The companies dispersed and made their way back to Provence, where they were hired by the Pope and handed over to Cardinal Robert.

It is noticeable that each wave of foreign mercenaries brought in its wake a new nationality into Italy. The nucleus of this army was a Breton company commanded by Sir Silvester Bude—'a very gallant knight,' according to Froissart—Jean Malestroit, and Bertrand de la Salle. The Great Rebellion was soon over, ended by their military ability, by Cardinal Robert's threats (he had warned the Bolognese that he would wash his hands and feet in their blood), and by two massacres that served as a warning to the rest of Italy. Both of these massacres were perpetrated by Sir John Hawkwood; he had, probably with tongue in cheek, changed the name of his company to the Compagnia Santa, the 'Holy Company,' and entered papal service. The sack of Faenza was a comparatively humane affair, as such affairs went, but the massacre of all the inhabitants of Cesena, apparently carried out by Hawkwood under protest and on the direct orders of Cardinal Robert, horrified all Italy and remains the greatest atrocity ever committed in this period.

* * *

The year 1379 marks the turning point of mercenary history in Italy. The Great Schism began with the election of two rival popes—a native Italian, Urban VI, and the bloodthirsty Cardinal Robert as Clement VII. Faced with the Bretons of Cardinal Robert, Urban VI appealed for help to a native Italian of the Romagna, a pupil of Sir John Hawkwood's who had served in the White Company, by name Alberigo da Barbiano. Alberigo had formed a company of his own on a national basis: *Societas Italicorum Sancti Giorgii*, the 'Italian Company of St George', which up to this time had always fought under the tutelage and at the side of Hawkwood, though nominally independent. In answer to Pope Urban's appeal Alberigo took the completely revolutionary decision to risk his Italian Company, all on its own, against the ferocious and war-hardened Bretons.

St Catherine, supporter of the Italian pope, promised these 'new martyrs'—she cannot have been optimistic—eternal life. The decisive battle of Marino took place on April 30, twelve miles outside Rome. It lasted for five hours and to the general amazement resulted in a complete victory for Alberigo. This was the end of the Bretons. The survivors dispersed. Malestroit died obscurely of illness three years later in Naples; Sir Silvester Bude was killed at Avignon in a quarrel; and Bernard de la Salle died in France in the civil wars of the Armagnacs. As for Alberigo, Urban VI, barefoot, welcomed him back to Rome, created him a knight of Christ, and gave him a white banner with a red cross inscribed '*Italia liberata dai Barbari.*' This battle marks, neatly enough, the beginning of the period when Italian condottieri took over military power from foreign captains. Only twelve years later Pier Paolo Vergerio, the flowery neo-classical letter-writer, was talking of Germans 'who come to Italy to learn military discipline, it being the best possible school of warfare' and declaring that 'he who hasn't fought in Italy is of no military use anywhere.'

In that year Iacopo del Verme, a Milanese condottiere, had beaten a French company led by Duke Jean III of Armagnac whom Vergerio accuses—so quickly had national reputations changed—of 'gallic frivolousness, impetuous charges but no discipline or staying power.' Ten years later Alberigo da Barbiano and other Milanese condottieri were to beat Rupert, the Emperor-elect, at Brescia, and in the middle of the next century the Venetian condottiere Colleoni defeated the French under Renaud Dresnay and the Duke of Savoy in three successive battles.

The next generation of military leaders had nearly all served under Alberigo da Barbiano, just as he in his turn had served under Hawkwood. Among them were Iacopo del Verme, the savage Facino Cane, and as young men the two rivals who were to become the greatest condottieri of the age—Muzio Attendolo Sforza, the peasant from Cotignola, and Braccio Fortebraccio, the minor noble from the hill fortress of Montone outside Perugia.[1]

It was about the turn of the century that the actual title of 'companies' appears to have died out. The idea of a company with its underlying anti-feudal prejudice and its appeal to the north European love of equality and camaraderie around the campfire was out of place among the Italians, who admired above all individual ability and who, never having been as tightly bound by feudal chains as the French, Germans, and English, felt no compulsion to react so strongly against them. Italian mercenary soldiers followed individual leaders and laid no claims to being treated as equals by their masters.

Even great potentates at this period quailed before the Italian condottieri. On April 5, 1390, the impoverished Duke of Bavaria, Stefan III, signed a *condotta* at Munich with the Florentines for a six months' campaign against the Visconti to begin in early June. He agreed to supply 2,000 lances for 21,000 florins a month and borrowed 10,500 florins as well to set up his army. He came down into Italy in July but only went out on rare occasions for military ceremonies. The Florentines accused him of being bribed by the Visconti, which was not unlikely as he was the father of the Queen

---

[1] Sforza and Fortebraccio were both nicknames. Sforza was given by Alberigo to his young but impudent follower who tried to '*sforzare*'—impose his will upon—his captain. Fortebraccio—'strongarm'—is an obvious pun.

of France and the French were allies of the Visconti at the time. The Germans said he '*ass und trunk und hub sich an ein Huren an Ihm.*' In any case his stay was ignominious. He departed 'happy not to have left his bones on Italian soil, the tomb of so many barbarians,' and the Florentines decided for the future to employ Italian mercenaries.

In the symphony, or cacophony, of Italian political history, mercenaries began timidly enough, a minor chord struck here, a major chord sounding there, but gradually the tone rises and the volume swells till they dominate the whole orchestra. Roger di Flor and Conrad Wolf began as typical feudal soldiers following a feudal lord; only when the lord made peace with his enemies, did they, like the leaders of the free companies, set up semi-independent bands, though *au fond* they never succeeded in breaking their feudal or national ties. At one stage Hawkwood acted as legate for the King of England at the Vatican, and as the story of his final burial shows,[1] the King always considered Hawkwood his subject and would no doubt, if the occasion had arisen, have used Hawkwood directly to further his policy in Italy.

The ambition of these early mercenaries was limited, in Italy as in France and Spain, to making money, holding a castle or two, and becoming great in the service of one or several legitimate lords. They did not seriously aspire to carve out fiefs, still less independent principalities for themselves. Fra Moriale, if the chroniclers are to be believed, did have such an ambition and he had the example of another self-made man, Cola di Rienzo, before his eyes to encourage him—but also to deter him, for Fra Moriale no doubt knew the history of Cola's few months of real power in Rome several years before they met and had seen how Cola had been unable to hold onto power when the Pope and the

---

[1] Hawkwood died in 1394 and the Florentines gave him a magnificent funeral in the Duomo. Next year at the special request of King Richard II, Florence granted Lady Hawkwood the right of transferring her husband's remains to England. He is buried in the parish church of Sible Hedingham in Essex, in a tomb decorated with hawks.

feudal barons, the Colonna, combined against him. Whatever projects Fra Moriale may have had in mind, certain of his actions show him to have been a man who was restrained and still mentally held fast by the basic feudal code of behaviour: his fear, for instance, on the day of his execution that he might be hanged rather than beheaded places him irretrievably in the feudal, knightly context.

Hawkwood for his part never seemed to have aimed at power; Machiavelli argues that this was merely because he was unsuccessful as a general, 'but everyone will admit that if he had been successful in battle, the Florentines would have been in his power.' This seems a total misconception of Hawkwood's ambitions and character; he was generally a loyal soldier during the periods in which he was directly employed by a state, pope, or prince. At one stage he arranged a *coup d'état* in Pisa, but this was in favour of a Pisan noble and there is no evidence at all to show that he ever thought of winning a state and direct political power for himself. He was less of an adventurer, less of an innovator, than Fra Moriale, and it is difficult to resist the conclusion that he was a typical Englishman with the English soldier's respect for civil power.

But by the end of the fifteenth century all had changed. Condottieri had become dukes, and dukes had become condottieri. The last Visconti, Duke Filippo Maria, of a family often allied with the royal houses of France and England, married the widow of Facino Cane, his father's low-born condottiere. Francesco Sforza, son of the peasant Muzio Attendolo, in his turn became Duke of Milan and founder of the dynasty of the Sforza there. Federigo da Montefeltro, Duke of Urbino in his own right, became a most famous and successful condottiere. The Pope's own son, Cesare Borgia, was in his time cardinal, duke, condottiere, and employer of other condottieri. The lines had become crossed and tangled: mercenaries had become rulers and rulers had become mercenaries. The most successful and most famous condottieri sprung no longer from peasant origin or from the minor nobility but from the great Houses of Baglione,

Caldora, Orsini, Medici, Bentivoglio, and Colonna. Definitions had gone all awry.

The easy and superficial explanation for the vast importance of mercenaries in Italy and their comparatively minor role in other European countries is that Italy was divided into a number of warring and independent states, small and large, which offered the ideal conditions for the formation of mercenary bands, their growth, and finally their seizure of power. This explanation, though traditional, is not very satisfactory; it is based on the presumption that 'Italy' existed. The Italian peninsula existed but an Italian state did not exist, and the so-called minor powers of Italy were at the time, many of them, very major powers indeed by European standards, both in wealth and population. The duchy of Milan was far more important than even the county of Flanders; the kingdom of Naples was as rich and as populous as the kingdom of England; Venice had a colonial empire greater than that of the kingdom of Aragon; and the smaller Italian states under the nominal control of the Pope were as important as the smaller Germanic states under the nominal control of the Emperor. Yet it was only in Italy, not in Germany or in France, that mercenary leaders came to dominate first military, then political, and finally social life.

The reasons for this lay not in the continual wars in Italy, which were no more and no less continual than the wars in the rest of Europe, but in the lack of two elements present in all other European countries; a native militia of one sort or another and, more important still, the feudal spirit.

Both these elements were closely connected, and both depended on and in a sense were caused by the basic fact that made Italy so different from the rest of Europe—its wealth. In the poorer countries such as Spain and Germany and to a lesser extent France and England, land was wealth; to possess land was all important, and landowners were involved in and bound by the feudal loyalties and the concepts of feudal authority and duty. But in Italy trade had brought wealth, and wealth was reckoned in florins not in castles. City dwellers and traders are never great warriors; rich states normally in history prefer to hire poor states or at least men coming from poor states to fight their wars for them.

Wealth was important but not in itself decisive; the peculiar political circumstances of Italy and in particular the predominance of the cities over the countryside, absolutely exceptional in the Europe of this period, played its part too. By about 1350, all over the Romagna and Lombardy the *Capitano del Popolo*, the commander of the city militia, the semi-feudal host, was becoming *il Signore*, the tyrant, whose first preoccupation was to disarm his former fellow citizens and equals, now his new subjects and potential enemies. In Bologna the militia were sent out to drill with blocks of wood, and this city which had been able to raise a force of 2,200 horses and 20,000 infantry among its own citizens hardly ever sent its men into the field again. The populace of Milan were formally absolved by the first Visconti from their obligation to do military service, though the countrymen in the surrounding territories continued to serve where necessary.[1]

Even the free communes gave up their militia. In Florence, out of every census group of a hundred, five infantrymen had had to serve for ninety days a year. But in 1351 the Florentines commuted this service for cash (in the same way as feudal kings accepted scutage in lieu of knight service) and thus raised 52,000 florins a year. It must have seemed to the commune only sensible to spare their own citizens, who would remain more gainfully employed at their crafts, trades, and commerce, this annoying and tiresome obligation, and possibly cheaper as well as more convenient in the long run to hire professional soldiers whenever needed, whatever their origin might be.

The merely business relationship that developed between the condottiere with absolute control over his own troops and his paymaster grew up noticeably and quite rapidly once the foreigners had disappeared or been eliminated. This could only have happened in a basically non-feudal society. Here there is a

---

[1] For three florins a month per fully armed soldier. This figure gives some idea of the value of the florin.

temptation to exaggerate: feudal ideas remained very important in Italy, as the investitures, the oaths, the acts of homage, and the challenges to single combat show. But the whole basis of feudal society, the idea that each man has from birth to death a fixed position that gives him unalterable rights and duties, had never been very strong in Italy, became even less strong as wealth increased and as tyrants set themselves up illegitimately, and eventually vanished entirely. 'Man,' wrote Jakob Burckhardt, the great Renaissance historian, 'was conscious of himself only as a member of a race, people, party, family or corporation—only through some general category.... The liberality of the northern princes of the thirteenth century was confined to the knights; to the nobility which served and sang. It was otherwise with the Italian despot. With his thirst for fame and his passion for monumental works, it was talent not birth which he needed. In the company of poet and scholar' and, one might add, of mercenary, 'he felt himself in a new position—almost indeed in possession of a new legitimacy.'

Only the early foreign condottieri felt any need to maintain a pretence of loyalty and feudal devotion to their employers; the charade by which Werner of Urslingen, in order to have a pretext for changing sides, arranged for himself and his men to be captured asleep by the 'enemy' was the performance of a man with a feudal conscience. Though in fact holding no land in the Kingdom, he felt the need to act as if he were still a vassal tied to a liege lord. But Alberigo da Barbiano, though he had been solemnly consecrated a knight of Christ and been given a special papal banner after the battle of Marino, did not scruple in his later life to fight for Ladislas, King of Naples, against the Church. Braccio's *condotta* from Pope Martin, referred to earlier in this chapter, implied no loyalty on either side, and the clause limiting his vicariate to three years gave an obvious *casus belli* when that period should expire.

Unhampered therefore by the codes of personal and political honour which still prevailed in the other lands of Europe, the most able of the condottieri seized amid the general admiration those opportunities of attaining power which circumstances or the weakness of their enemies offered to them. That some of them founded states and dynasties is less a matter of amazement than that so many of them failed to do so. Braccio's powerful state in Umbria fell apart immediately after his death; Muzio Attendolo Sforza failed despite many years of striving to seize power in Naples in the place of Queen Joanna II. Francesco Sforza himself failed at Pesaro before he succeeded, though only after immense effort and intrigue, in winning the duchy of Milan. Iacopo Piccinino, whose father Niccolo had been Braccio's right-hand man, did not succeed, despite opinion generally in his favour throughout Italy, in founding a princely house. The established authorities fought back with the weapons at their disposal and, in an age when career was open to the talents, employed the talented, often successfully, in mutual destruction. They also attempted to absorb the condottieri by more subtle means, noticeably by marriage. Bernabò Visconti married off his illegitimate daughter Donnina to Sir John Hawkwood amid splendid pomp and feasting and jousting at Milan; it was a means of attaching his condottieri which he in particular was well equipped to apply—he had seventeen legitimate and twenty illegitimate children. Marriage as a means of taming the condottieri, however, was a two-edged weapon and was more often turned against the established dynasties by condottieri thus given a pretext to the succession (as in the case of Francesco Sforza) than accepted as an obligation to remain loyally subservient. Muzio Attendolo Sforza was imprisoned by Queen Joanna II's lover, the Grand Seneschal Pandolfello Piscopo. In order to meet a threat from the barons, Pandolfello, who had planned to have Sforza executed, released him and reinstated him as Grand Constable provided that Sforza should marry Pandolfello's sister. Yet a few months later Pandolfello himself was beheaded without Sforza making any attempt to save him. In that age and that period family ties had no power to restrain the inordinate ambition of talented military leaders.

*   *   *

Thus conditions in the Italian peninsula peculiarly favoured the rise to influence and to power of the mercenary captains. Yet the same phenomenon might have occurred in France, and it will be instructive to see how the threat posed by the free companions was finally removed. Two waves were siphoned off into Italy and many other companies were eliminated by the various Spanish expeditions, but when the Hundred Years' War blazed up again after the long lull following the Peace of Bretigny, inevitably new bands were formed, which posed a perpetual threat to legitimate feudal authority. By this time, as in Italy, their leadership was passing from the hands of base-born professional soldiers, true 'companions,' into the far more dangerous hands of minor but legitimate feudal nobles. In 1375, Enguerrand de Coucy, a cousin of the dukes of Austria, invaded Alsace at the head of no less than 40,000 mercenaries, known as Juglers from the curious shape of their helmets. But he was defeated thrice in the territories of the Empire across the Jura, and came back ignominiously into France. Sixteen years later the Duke of Armagnac, that too powerful Gascon noble, was encouraged by the King's uncles, the dukes of Burgundy and Berry, who wished to be rid of him, to try the Italian venture that ended in his death.[1] Successive defeats such as these naturally helped to damp down mercenary ardour in France. The Treaty of Arras in 1435 marked the end of the war and the final explusion of the English; but then, as had happened after Bretigny, the peace left France full of disoccupied and potentially dangerous professional soldiers whose only trade and experience were war. Once again the King of France, now Charles VII, tried to siphon them off into foreign adventures. The Emperor Frederick III, Duke of Austria and head of the House of Hapsburg, hired vast bands of these adventurers (now known as Écorcheurs—'Scorchers'—rather than free companions) in order to enforce his ducal rights over some rebel peasants on the imperial side of the Jura. This army, well over 40,000 strong this time, were called 'the Armagnacs'; they were mostly Gascons

---

[1] See page 60.

but were led not by the Duke of Armagnac but by the Dauphin in person. To the general amazement they were beaten and twelve hundred of them killed by a couple of thousand rebellious peasants at the battle of St Jacob-on-the-Birs (St Jacques-sur-Birse), and poured back in confusion over the Jura.[1] Aeneas Sylvius Piccolomini, the future Pope Pius II, compared their defeat to that of the Persians by the Spartans, and the peasants scornfully nicknamed them not Armagnacs, but Arme-Jacken ('Poor Jackets') and Arme-Gecken ('Poor Fools').

Poor fools they may have been but they were still tens of thousands strong and bootyless, an even greater threat than before to feudal authority in France. Charles VII solved his dilemma in an entirely new and revolutionary way: he took the bands permanently into his pay and formed the first regular standing army in Europe. The great, glorious, and renowned French army thus had its origin in the formal union of bands of French and Gascon mercenaries, and the cause of its creation was the desire of the King of France to free himself once and for all from the threat that these mercenaries presented. The indirect result was the end of the feudal era in France, for a regular standing army could not be fitted at all into the feudal scheme of society, and its formation inevitably though not immediately ruined the power of the great feudal lords. By the famous Royal Ordinances of 1445 fifteen companies were set up as a start, each company to consist of 100 lances[2] paid not by their captains but directly by royal officers, subject to strict rules, and living normally a garrison life. Furthermore, each captain was limited to the command of a single company. The wheel had turned full circle: the bands that had originally sprung up as free companies ended as tightly controlled royal companies, and feudal society in overcoming the direct threat posed by their existence indirectly undermined itself.

In Italy a similar solution, which might have succeeded, was

---

[1] The battle was fought in the year 1444. See page 78.
[2] The French lance unlike the English lance comprised six men: knight, squire, page, two archers, and a valet.

never attempted. Possibly the condottieri's professional pride would have resisted any attempt made to form them into a regular and subservient army. Militarily, as this pride grew each condottiere developed and refined his own tactics. Alberigo da Barbiano was the first to protect his horses with long tanned leather coverings, painted and decorated. His two pupils, Sforza and Braccio, formed their own schools of war; the *'bracceschi'* of the *'scuola braccesca'* were renowned for the impetus of their assault, and the *'sforzeschi'* for their tactical cunning and skill in manoeuvring. The later condottieri were all formed in one or the other of these schools, though each developed his own military style. Indeed warfare in Italy, fought between condottieri who knew and to a certain extent respected each other, became more and more stylized. Carmagnola in his later days fought a great battle against Piccinino and captured 5,000 horsemen and 5,000 footmen: no one was killed, 'though the slaughter of horses was incredible.' Military theorists like Clausewitz for whom the aim of war was to seek out and destroy the opposing army would never have agreed with this. Nor would those critics of the condottieri who basically accept the Prussian view, incapable of recognizing the good sense of men who reduce the most bloodthirsty and senseless of human activities to a skilled but almost bloodless rite of manoeuvre. How many lives throughout human history would have been saved if every general had surrendered when he saw himself outmanoeuvred and almost inevitably defeated, if war was carried on right up to the moment of impact but then stopped by the rational assessment of the chances of victory by both sides? These later condottieri were the most civilized and humane of all war-makers, but the modern nation states, accustomed like tribal barbarians to reckon the seriousness of a war by the slaughter it involves, would sneer foolishly at such proofs of civilization. Imagine how Carmagnola and Piccinino would be struck by such evidence of progress in military science and general humanity as is afforded by the First World War and all the subsequent history of our century.

If the condottieri civilized warfare, they also embellished

civilization. Great fortunes were made by the successful, even though the pay steadily fell.[1] The great days of 'traps for barons' and vast ransoms in the Kingdom were soon over, and after the Peace of Lodi in 1454 wars became fewer and the profession overcrowded. Condottieri at that time had to go far afield in search of fame and fortune: the Conte di Campobasso took service under Charles le Téméraire, Duke of Burgundy, and Giuliano Giustiani masterminded the defence of Constantinople before it finally fell to the Turks, to the horror and amazement of the whole Christian world, in 1453.

Even so, the widow of Facino Cane brought Duke Filippo Maria a dowry of no less than half a million florins. The fortunes of the leading condottieri were used with a taste rarely characteristic of successful military men. Sir John Hawkwood, though reduced at the end of his life to financial difficulties, had endowed the English Hospital at Rome, together with Sir Robert Knollys and Sir Hugh Calveley, as fine a trio of mercenary captains as ever endowed any hospital. Francesco Sforza built palaces and set up monasteries all over the Milanese. And among the most glorious of the later condottieri was Federigo da Montefeltro; 'on the slopes of the Appenines, almost in the centre of Italy towards the Adriatic is situated as everyone knows the little city of Urbino.' The court of Urbino became so renowned that Baldassare Castiglione chose it as the setting for his classic book, *The Courtier*.[2] Duke Federigo was the most cultured prince of his age; his library, later to form the nucleus of the Vatican library, was the richest and most famous in Europe. And yet Urbino was just one small hill town in poor country. Duke

---

[1] In 1371 the Apostolic Chamber paid eighteen florins a month per lance. This had fallen to nine florins by 1430.

[2] 'Among the blessings and advantages that can be claimed for it [Urbino],' he wrote, 'I believe the greatest is that for a long time now it has been governed by outstanding rulers.... Without looking any further, we can find a splendid example in Duke Federigo of glorious memory who in his day was the light of Italy. Nor are there lacking today any number of reliable witnesses to his prudence, humanity, justice, generosity, and unconquerable spirit, and to his military skill, which was brilliantly attested by his many victories, his ability to capture impregnable places, his swift and decisive expeditions, his

[Footnote continued overleaf

Federigo had made his fortune entirely as a condottiere, serving first with the *sforzeschi*, then under Florence, then for Pope Pius II against Piccinino, then against Malatesta and Carmagnola's pupil, the Venetian condottiere Colleoni, and finally as captain-general of a Florentine league against the Pope and Venice. The money he made in mercenary service he lavished as if he were by birth what he became by talent, a great prince, and founded the most refined and polished court in Italy.

When men like these were condottieri, it becomes hard to argue that mercenaries were the ruin and the curse of Italy. It might be argued with just as much reason that the condottieri were the glory and the light of Italy and that the Italian Renaissance needed the initiative that only self-made men, successful adventurers, could supply.

This would perhaps be to claim too much and to go too far. Generalizations are difficult; the distance is too great, as I pointed out at the beginning of this chapter, between the different individuals who formed that one class, the condottieri. Yet a final theory can tentatively be ventured: that the victory of Alberigo da Barbiano over the Bretons in 1379 was not only of great importance in the military and mercenary history of Italy but also set off a sudden explosion of Italian self-confidence and national pride. This new-found confidence, this new-found sense of Italian unity (symbolized by the papal banner inscribed 'Italy Liberated from the Barbarians') was a *sine qua non* of the Renaissance. As long as the Italians felt themselves to be militarily inferior to other nations or peoples, the Renaissance could not

having routed many times with few troops great and formidable armies, and his never having lost a single battle.... Among his other commendable enterprises, Duke Federigo built on the rugged site of Urbino a palace which many believe to be the most beautiful in all Italy, and he furnished it so well and appropriately that it seemed more like a city than a mere palace. For he adorned it not only with the usual objects such as silver vases, wall-hangings of the richest cloth of gold ... but also with countless antique statues of marble and bronze, with rare pictures and with every kind of musical instrument. Then at great cost he collected a large number of the rarest and finest books, in Greek, Latin, and Hebrew, all of which he adorned with gold and silver, believing they were the crowning glory of his great palace.'

properly get under way, for it appears to be an inevitable rule of history that a great new culture starts to flourish only among states or peoples that are militarily superior to their neighbours. Why this should be so is another question—perhaps a matter of personal psychology, perhaps one of cultural roots. Here I merely state a rule that appears to be historically accurate, and draw the conclusion that without a victory such as that of the Italian Company of St George at the battle of Marino the Italian Renaissance as we know it would not have taken place. Alberigo da Barbiano, obscure condottiere, deserves his niche in the hall of fame and the gratitude of all post-medieval Europeans.

4 A Nation of Mercenaries

'Point d'argent, point de Suisse.'

URI, UNTERWALDEN, AND SCHWYZ—these three little mountain villages against every expectation were to make all Europe tremble. No story is more fascinating than that of the slow formation of the Swiss Confederation, its sudden rise to fame and glory, the vast efflux of mercenary masses which followed, and that brief period when Machiavelli forecast that the Swiss would be 'the new Romans.' The Swiss never produced a great general or even a great political leader; a few names here and there flit across the stark canvas of their early history but they are no more than brush strokes. In Italy and France and Germany an extraordinary variety of characters and individuals, colour running riot, delight the eye, while in the mountains between them sombre and anonymous masses group and regroup and incidentally wipe out their chevalieresque opponents, like destroying lions.

On the river Aar, in what is now northern Switzerland, Guntram the Rich built, shortly before the year 1000, the castle of Habitsburg, the Hawk's Castle. The power of his descendants gradually spread south, north, and east; they became counts of Zurich, landgraves of Upper Alsace, counts of Kyburg, dukes of Austria, and eventually, in 1273, Rudolph I of Hapsburg was elected German King and Rex Romanorum. Among his many personal feudal possessions were the mountain villages, in the centre of what is now Switzerland—Uri, Unterwalden, and

Schwyz. To Uri, Rudolph sent a governor named Gessler so cruel and oppressive that eleven men from each village (or canton) met in the plain of Rütli and swore to throw out the oppressor; among them was William Tell. A document was drawn up, a treaty of perpetual alliance among the three peasant cantons, and with it the history of the Confederation properly begins, in 1291.

The fourteenth century saw a long and bloody struggle between the peasants, trying to preserve their rights while acknowledging their feudal lords, and the same feudal lords, the Hapsburgs, trying to impose a tighter control on these unimportant but annoying territories. Duke Leopold of Austria and a small band of knights descended on them, but at a mountain pass at Morgarten the peasants bombarded the noblemen with rocks and stones and then descended to finish off the wounded: 'Their murderous hallebards chopped into pieces as if they were birds even the most heavily armoured of their enemies. This was not a battle but a butchery. Duke Leopold's knights had been led to the slaughterhouse and the Duke himself, half-dead with shame and sorrow, having lost the flower of his band, fled.'

This was in fact a minor skirmish, but against all the rules peasants had beaten armed knights and for the first time the murderous weapon, the hallebard, part grappling hook and part dagger, had been successfully used by footmen against horsemen.

Lucerne, impressed, allied with the three cantons (known collectively as the Waldstätte), becoming the first town to join the Confederacy.

Duke Leopold the Valiant[1] descended with a larger army. But at the battle of Sempach (July 9, 1386) the *Montani Bestiales*—'Bestial Mountaineers'—proved that Morgarten had not just been a lucky accident. Two hundred knights were left dead in the field, including Duke Leopold himself. This was a disaster for the Hapsburgs and for knightly chivalry. The news of it went out beyond the borders of the Empire and was noted momentarily even in Italy and France amid the distraction of their own great

---

[1] Nephew of the previous Duke Leopold.

wars. In the immediate region it had more lasting effect: the town of Zurich allied itself with the Waldstätte and, more important still, the free imperial city of Berne, high bourgeois in tendency and militarily renowned, also joined the alliance. Two more mountain villages, Glarus and Zug, followed their example shortly afterward. But this was a league rather than a state; these cities and villages were all allied with the Waldstätte but not directly with each other; they all kept their own autonomy, and Berne and Zurich, for example, were quite free if they wanted to war on each other. The league was defensive rather than offensive, and directed against the dominating power of the dukes of Austria in defence of local feudal liberties and charters. Many other leagues like it, greater and smaller, were in existence all over the Empire.

Politics and rivalries were none the less bitter for being on so small a scale. In 1394 Glarus beat off on its own a small punitive expedition and fiercely reproached its allies for not coming to its aid. The Confederates called a Diet (assembly) to which each ally sent ambassadors and agreed on the first Swiss military code, the Covenant of Sempach. The points were:

1. Every ally, every canton, should see to strict military training of its men.
2. Pillage was not permitted unless the captains expressly allowed it, and in that case it was up to the captains to share out the booty.
3. Holy places and clerics, women and children were to be spared.
4. Deserters were to be punished.

By the end of the century the eight Confederates were a force to be reckoned with within the Empire, and the dukes of Austria made a peace treaty with them, recognizing their rights and exacting a symbolic annual tribute as a sign of their feudal allegiance. But this was still a loose alliance of towns and villages whose territories were surrounded by powerful and aristocratic neighbours, the counts of Neuchâtel and Romont, the Bishop of

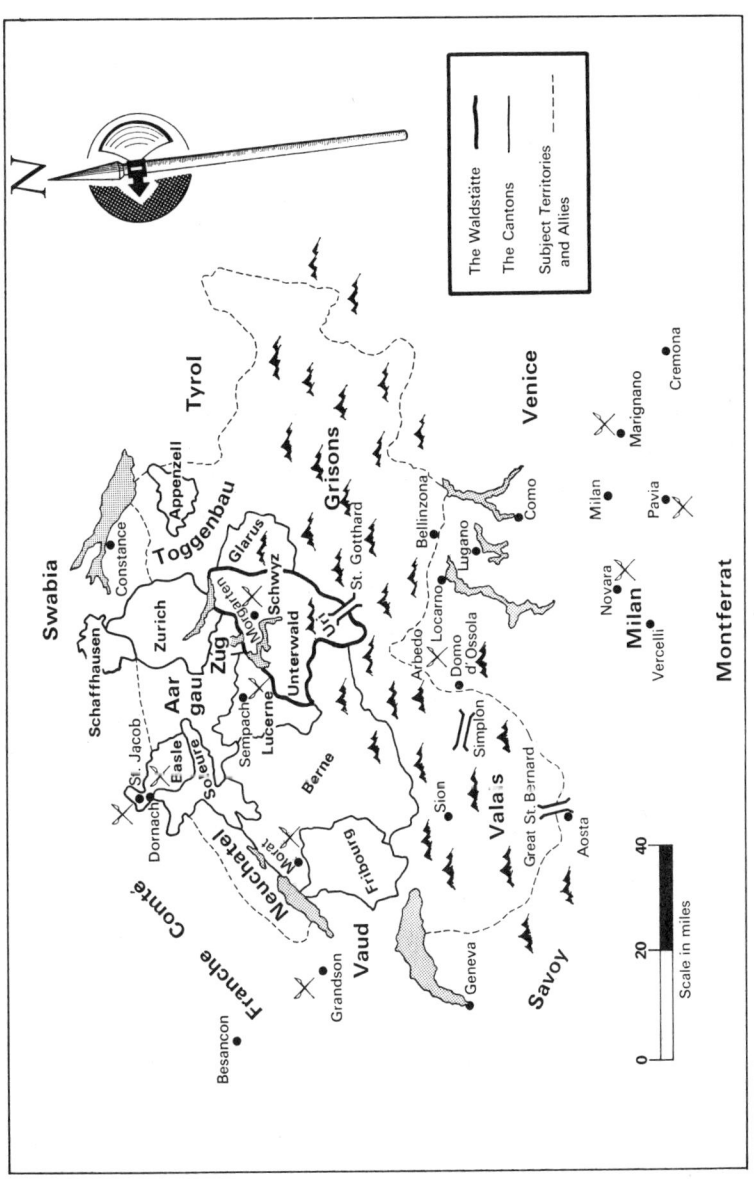

The Thirteen Cantons.

Sion, and the Count of Savoy. They were united only in their hostility to the dukes of Austria as such.

During the first decades of the next century the Confederacy grew shakily in strength. A new canton joined, Appenzell, but although seven of the Confederates allied with it, Berne, jealous of Schwyz's influence, refused. To the south Uri and Unterwalden tried to expand, taking advantage of the confusion in the Milanese territories after the death of Gian Galeazzo Visconti. Together they took the town of Faldo, and Uri bought the town and castle of Bellinzona from a needy Milanese vassal. But Duke Filippo Maria pulled his territories together and sent the condottiere Carmagnola against the peasants. Uri and Unterwalden raised their troops and appealed to the Confederates: Zurich hesitated, the Bernese stayed at home, and Schwyz tried on its own to invade the valley of Ossola. Eventually most of the contingents appeared and a battle was fought at Arbedo. The result was not decisive: Carmagnola's cavalry lost a lot of men in their first charge but his army was 16,000 strong, and since the Confederates had managed to raise a mere 2,000 men, they retreated.

About this time the Emperor Sigismond placed Duke Frederick of Austria under the ban of the Empire and ordered the Confederates to overrun the Hapsburg lands. They hesitated and then complied, conquering small territories in the Aargau around the original Hapsburg castle. For the first time they were faced with the question of governing territories held in common by all the nine Confederates; this common interest reinforced their very fragile unity, but only very temporarily. Schwyz and Zurich quarrelled over the lands of the dead Count of Toggenbau and war broke out. Zurich was isolated but appealed to the Emperor. The Emperor was now once again a Hapsburg—Frederick III—and being only too keen to settle accounts with these troublesome vassals, he hired vast mercenary bands, the Armagnacs, from the King of France. At the battle of St Jacob-on-Birs the Confederates utterly beat their formidable opponents, though outnumbered twenty to one.[1] Their military fame spread throughout Europe,

---
[1] See page 69.

though their lack of discipline except on the actual battlefields was noted too.

This battle had twin political results: on the one hand, the Confederates turned against the Empire and from this time on aimed at independence; on the other, the King of France was so impressed by their military ability that he made the first of a long series of alliances that were to follow between the Confederacy and France. This was the first alliance the Confederates had ever made outside the Empire and the first step taken toward independence and a sense of nationality. Hundreds of Swiss began to go off and take service under the new King of France, Louis XI, and fought as a minor element in the royal army in the Picardy wars.

But the Confederacy was still a poor, loose, small, and basically unimportant league. It was not till twenty years later that its great period of glory suddenly came.

Louis XI of France well deserved his sobriquet, *l'universelle araignée*, 'the universal spider'; for the feudal virtues of chivalry and arms he had neither taste nor aptitude. The two aims of his policy were to keep France internally peaceful by giving the ever aggressive English no excuse for another invasion and to centralize royal power by eliminating the great vassals. Of these the greatest was Charles le Téméraire, Duke of Burgundy.

Charles le Téméraire was the fourth, the most appealing, and the last of the dukes of Burgundy. His predecessors had built up a vast state in Europe of which the title Burgundy gives only the faintest indication. Originally the power of Burgundy was founded on the union by marriage between the duchy of Burgundy (capital: Dijon) and the county of Flanders (capitals: Bruges and Ghent). Marriage, inheritance, annexation, conquest, and treaties had gradually built up around these two powerful fiefs a whole chain of states in each one of which the Duke of Burgundy was feudal lord, though each state retained its local institutions—a sort of monarchical union entirely different in structure from the feudal kingdoms of the time. Although all the territories were held formally either from the King of France or the Emperor, the feudal system of allegiance was crumbling and the power of Burgundy was virtually independent. Charles le Téméraire's father, Philip the Good, had been known as the Grand Duke of the Occident and had exchanged ambassadors with the Turks. Three generations of wise rulers and peace throughout most of the Burgundian lands had made its states incredibly rich and prosperous. Charles le Téméraire dreamed of reviving the ancient ideal of a middle European state, Lotharingia, balancing Germany and France. It is an ideal which, had it succeeded, might have prevented the antagonism between France and Germany that has been the cause of so many wars. But it was ruined by the Swiss Confederates.

A minor incident, the confiscation by the Count of Romont of a wagonload of Swiss sheepskins, led to the fall of Burgundy. By 1470, Charles le Téméraire ruled by inheritance or conquest over the states of Flanders, Brabant, Hainaut, Friesland, Zeeland, Limburg, Zutphen, and Guelders in the north; over ducal Burgundy, the Nivernais, the Charollais, the Auxerrois, Picardy, Lille, Artois, the Vermandois, and Rethel inside France; and in the centre, over Namur, Liége, Luxembourg, Upper Alsace, and the Franche-Comté. The Duke of Savoy was his subservient ally; all he needed to join his two vast dominions together was the little duchy of Lorraine (capital: Nancy), most of which indeed he controlled by right of conquest.

The dispute started by the confiscation of the sheepskins led to a quarrel between the city of Berne, always eager to expand westward, and the Count of Romont, a vassal of the Duke of Burgundy. Louis XI from France did all he could to inflame the quarrel. Charles le Téméraire decided to crush the intimidated Confederacy, which sent ambassador after ambassador to placate the Grand Duke.

'If God had not abandoned the said Duke,' writes Comines, 'there was no reason why he should have been in danger over such a little matter, seeing the offers that were made to him by the Swiss—and in a conflict against people like them where he could acquire no material gain nor glory. For at that time they were in no way esteemed as they are now and there was nothing as poor as them. And I heard one of their people tell how he had been one of the first ambassadors sent to the said Duke, and he had told the Duke, trying to dissuade him from making war, that he would gain nothing, for their country was very sterile and poor and could pay no good ransoms; and that he believed that the spurs and the horses' bits of the Duke's host were worth more money than all his own countrymen could raise altogether.'

But Charles le Téméraire would never take advice. The Confederates called up their pitiful host as the Burgundian chivalry advanced into the territory of Berne. But at Grandson a sudden panic overtook the Burgundians and a flight by one section led to a flight by all. Only seven knights were killed but the Confederates held the field.

They not only held the field, they captured the abandoned Burgundian camp, with 420 cannons, 300 tons of powder, 10,000 horses, 1,500 wagons, and tents, chapels, tapestries, seals in gold, dinner plates in silver, oriental slaves,[1] a box full of ropes to hang prisoners, and a million florins of gold. Comines recounts the surprise and ignorance of the Confederates when confronted with such unheard-of wealth. One of the largest diamonds in Christendom was picked up by a peasant, sold for a florin, and resold for three florins. There is still a room in the museum at Berne devoted to *die Burgunderbeute*—'the booty of Burgundy.' For the first time the peasants saw the possible profits of war, 'which,' writes Comines a little acidly, 'thereafter taught them very well to recognize what money was worth.' From this battle stemmed the desire for loot, plunder, and sudden riches which was to make the Swiss the most formidable mercenaries ever known.

Their ambassadors came to the court of France and were sent back with full purses, silk garments, and the promise of annual retainers—both to cantons and to individuals

---

[1] The unusual beauty of Swiss women in one canton traditionally lucky stroke.

'*Sa Grandeur le Duc*' swore revenge. He promised to inspire the Swiss with 'a holy terror' and that 'as many as he will take, so many will he hang.' He now led the army of Burgundy in person against the Confederates and the minor Duke of Lorraine. On June 22, 1476 they met at Morat: the Burgundian army was 23,000 strong and by the end of the day 18,000 Burgundians and 500 Swiss lay dead on the field. Never had such a slaughter occurred in any battle of the epoch. The modern era of infantry warfare began as the death knell sounded for chivalry and the mounted knight. Hallebards and, even more, massed pikes were the arms with which the Swiss peasantry held off and finally annihilated the host of Burgundy. Militarily Morat was one of the great battles of European history; politically it was one of the most decisive. Burgundy dissolved; next year Charles le Téméraire with only 4,000 men tried a last attack; but on the battlefield of Nancy (January 1, 1477) his army was once again beaten and he himself was killed, betrayed by the Neapolitan condottiere, Conte di Campobasso. Only his English mercenaries had managed to give a fairly good account of themselves.

These three battles shook all Europe and filled knights everywhere with a terror of the Swiss. The Confederates themselves were already semi-mercenaries at the battle of Nancy. Duke René of Lorraine had appealed to them for help and offered them 40,000 florins with his duchy as a pledge for payment. The cantons met in a Diet and accepted his terms: each soldier was to receive four and a half florins a month and the contingents were to be led and paid by their own captains but were to follow a simple banner, not the cantonal standard as this was not a cantonal war. In other words, the cantons were already acting as official purveyors of mercenaries. Duke René had called for 5,000–6,000 men but in next to no time 8,000 had arrived.

Already the Swiss were winning a reputation for bravery, ferocity, and ill discipline. When the Rhenish League sent to a canton to hire 400 soldiers, the ambassador told them that the reason the Rhenish League wanted them was 'above all for your terrible war cries, also for your courage, and for the reputation you have like your ancestors for spreading terror and panic when you set out on a campaign.' When these mercenaries captured the Castle of Grammont (which they did without artillery, an exceptional feat), they found a cellar full of wine, 'paddled through the wine up to their knees,' drank it all, and massacred all the defenders of the castle. The neighbouring Castle of Fallon surrendered in terror, and there the Swiss spared the garrison, 'naked in their chemises and with candles in their hands.'

As for the Burgundians, the mere sound of the horns of Uri and Unterwalden set them in a panic by the end. When the Swiss captured the Burgundian town of Saint Nicholas du Port, they amused themselves by tying up Burgundian prisoners and pushing them under water till they drowned, and by planting rows of lances underneath the castle and hurling the Burgundians down onto them from the top of the tower. Even so, before the battle of Nancy they 'fell on their knees and said five paternosters and five ave marias.' After the battle, despising the thought of ransoms, they killed all the Burgundians they could. This cruel, superstitious, and brutal peasantry were the first to indulge systematically in a new and horrible form of warfare in which the law of arms, carefully and laboriously created by medieval Europe and surprisingly often respected, vanished in a welter of atrocities and blood.

A curious episode followed the victory at Nancy. The young peasants, now successful warriors, particularly those from Schwyz and Uri, celebrated Carnival by forming themselves into an anarchical company, setting up as their banner a white flag showing a madman and calling themselves the *Compagnons de la Folle Vie*, Companions of the Mad Life. Seven hundred strong, they marched on Berne, ignoring the orders of the cantons, ostensibly to complain about the division of the booty. Berne, which could put under arms nearly 20,000 men, eventually allowed them inside the city walls. There their delegates made a '*fol et bizarre*' discourse to the Bernese assembly and left, unsatisfied and threatening, to join up with the young rebels of Zug and Unterwalden. Now nearly 2,000 strong, they marched on the free episcopal city of Geneva and threatened it with the sack unless the Bishop paid them 4,000 florins within a week. The town cantons, Berne, Lucerne, and Zurich, decided that high spirits had gone far enough; they armed their men and warned the *Compagnons de la Folle Vie* that it was time to stop. Civil war nearly broke out, but thanks to the restraint of the Bernese, an agreement was reached. Every *compagnon* received five florins and every troop was given four flagons of wine. The Bishop of Geneva promised to pay them 24,000 florins in all for their restraint, and they dispersed in early March when the first of three instalments of this came through.

As a Swiss song of the period went:

> *What is there to do at home?*
> *Suck our fingers and sharpen our fingernails?*
> *We have been in the wars soldiers so faithful*
> *That we have won a lot of possessions*
> *Gold, silver and also subjects and lands.*
> *The lords have had to give us lots of things*
> *In exchange for our precious lives.*
> *That's how we have got into habits*
> *Which we can't get out of now.*

Charles le Téméraire had left as his heiress an only daughter, Mary of Burgundy. Once again the question of an heiress's marriage led to war. Louis XI had imagined that with the death of the Duke he would be able to take over the tottering states of Burgundy. But Mary was affianced to the son of the Emperor Frederick III, Maximilian of Austria.

Maximilian, known as the '*dernier chevalier,*' was slightly less rash but just as knightly as his dead father-in-law. With true chivalric spirit but only two hundred knights he set out for Ghent to rescue his distressed fiancée. Louis XI's ambitions were foiled when the marriage was celebrated, and though ducal Burgundy and most of the lands in France fell into the hands of the King, the Hapsburgs inherited and preserved by this marriage most of the vast Burgundian domain. By 1479 the only important territory at stake was Franche-Comté (capital: Besançon). Louis XI claimed it, Maximilian claimed it, and Berne and the Confederates put in a claim too—but they were bought off by Maximilian for 150,000 florins. In the end Maximilian, who all his life was short of money, failed to pay up and in turn renounced his claim in exchange for a payment from France.

To enforce his rights upon Franche-Comté, Louis XI needed soldiers. He applied to the Swiss. The cantons, however, despite their treaty with France, delayed taking a decision, though at least 6,000 Swiss left to join the French army without cantonal authority[1]. The reason for this reluctance was that Louis XI was in conflict with the Duke of Milan, at that time friendly to the Swiss. Finally at the end of July the cantons held a Diet and agreed to supply troops to France in return for Louis's promise (a) that he only wanted them as a personal *garde de corps;* (b) that they would not be used against the Empire, against allies of the Confederates, or for naval warfare; (c) that he would not separate the contingents from one another; and (d) that he would release them if they were needed by the cantons.

This agreement was typical of the time. It shows how the cantons considered themselves independent and yet united with one another—free to contract alliances and yet still subject to the Empire. It shows how the cantonal governments considered that they alone had the right to supply mercenaries and disapproved of free-lance enlistments by their citizens, and it shows how careful they were to keep the right to call back their little 'armies' if the canton itself was in danger. (The point about no naval warfare is an interesting curiosity, typically Swiss already.)

---

[1] By his edict of 1481, Louis XI showed how highly he appreciated his Swiss mercenaries. He exempted them from all taxes, all garrison duties, all night guards, and all special rules. Commands were given in their own language; they could be punished only by their own officers. They were allowed to buy land and make valid wills (normally the possessions of dead foreigners, will or no will, went to the Crown). The French envied them this privileged position, and centuries later made them pay for it—at the Tuileries on August 10, 1792.

As a result of this Diet, Berne and Zurich each sent contingents of 1,000 men; Lucerne a contingent of 800; Schwyz, Fribourg, and Solothurn (two new cantons) contingents of 500 each; Glarus and Appenzell contingents of 300; Uri, Unterwalden, and Zug contingents of 200; and various subject towns and allies another 790 more—a total of 6,290 men in all. These figures show the relative importance of the cantons and show, too, that the prestige of the Waldstätte, the three original Confederates, depended not on numbers but on a peasant tradition of toughness.

As this was an official cantonal decision, but not a Confederate war, each contingent followed not the cantonal banner but a standard showing the cantonal emblem and marked in every case by a white cross.

One of the reasons for Swiss military success was their ability to mobilize rapidly at a time when it took months to assemble an army. The Diet had been held on July 29, and by August 22 the contingents had assembled and marched out. But when they reached Chalon-sur-Saône, an armistice had already been signed. They were paid and dispersed, though a little town that did not open its gates to them on the way back was stormed, sacked, and burned. At another town, 'where the wine was so good and everything so cheap,' they stayed looting; a Bernese captain, William of Diesbach, tried to repair the damage out of his own pocket.

At about this time the cantonal governments realized that they could not in fact prevent their people from enlisting under foreign princes as individuals or in private bands. A distinction therefore grew up between regular cantonal contingents who were hired out to foreign princes, swore to obey the Confederate military ordinances, and were paid directly by the cantons, which in turn received the bulk sums from the foreign princes,[1] and the free companions who organized themselves (though after the Swabian War of 1499 the cantons tried to control them by

---

[1] And clearly often made a governmental profit: the soldiers were paid four florins a day, but only for so long as their service lasted, whereas the contracts between prince and canton were normally for a minimum period of at least one campaigning season.

insisting they should have official flags and take the official military oath). Military service was compulsory from the age of sixteen to that of sixty. If for any reason a man could not go himself, he had to find and at his own expense pay a substitute or even a foreigner 'who is suitable and well-equipped.' When they took the official oath, the men swore to obey their officers, to be loyal to the banner, to hand in all booty to their captains, to pillage no churches or monasteries, to maltreat no priests or women. Loyalty to the banner at least was observed: the cantonal banners, unfurled only in an official Confederate war, were famous—the crossed keys of Unterwalden, the black bull of Uri, the bears of Berne. All were now marked with a white cross as an emblem of the Confederacy. Behind the cantonal banner many smaller standards followed: Berne's banner was followed, in full array, by forty-eight other standards, each making a special contingent.

Contingents were led by a captain, an adjutant, a banner-bearer, a captain of pikemen on horseback, a captain of hallebardiers on foot, and included an armourer, a cook, a butcher, a priest, a doctor, often musicians and women, and always an executioner. Decisions were always taken democratically by a council of captains; each canton guarded its independence so fiercely that the idea of a general could not be accepted. Amazingly, the system of command worked. In battle the great strength of the Swiss lay in their groups of pikemen, often massed thousands strong, defensively unbreakable by heavy cavalry and formidably terrifying in a slow advance even at this age when artillery was beginning to become important.

In 1481, after a few years of internal disputes caused by new riches and sudden importance, the Confederates on the advice of a hermit, Nicholas Lowenbrügger, revised their constitution. All the cantons were to be fully sovereign and all agreed not to interfere in the internal affairs of other cantons; the Confederates' oath of union and alliance was to be renewed every five years, and so were any bilateral guarantees or promises of assistance among single cantons; booty gained was to be divided proportionately among the active participants in any campaign, but lands occupied by any united or semi-united effort were to be shared equally among the cantons involved. This must be one of the few constitutions in the world in which the division of loot was as important a constitutional principle as internal autonomy: the mercenary nation was defining its main role and *raison d'être* only too clearly.

The great Italian wars in which the modern nation states of Europe were blooded and shaped were now about to begin. For forty years Italy had enjoyed comparative peace, disturbed only by minor wars, the balance of power accepted as a system by Milan, Naples, Venice, papal Rome and the Florence of the Medici. In 1492, Lorenzo the Magnificent, virtual ruler of Florence, died. In January two years later, Don Ferrante, the treacherous but cunning King at Naples died, too, and was succeeded by his son Don Alphonso II, who had a good reputation as a warrior.

In September that year the young King of France, Charles VIII, crossed the Alps at the head of a vast French army, impelled by a craving for military glory, using as a pretext the claim now vested in his person of the House of Anjou to the throne of the Kingdom, and as an immediate excuse an appeal from Ludovico il Moro of Milan.

Ludovico il Moro was, in the words of Burckhardt, 'the most perfect type of the despot of that age, and as a kind of natural product, almost disarms our moral judgment. Notwithstanding the immorality of the means he employed, he used them with perfect ingenuousness. . . . He accepted as no more than his due the almost fabulous respect of the Italians for his political genius.'

Francesco Sforza, in order to reinforce his illegitimate pretensions to rule Milan, had married Bianca Visconti, a daughter of Duke Filippo Maria. By her he had many children, of whom three are important. The youngest, Ascanio, became a cardinal. The eldest, Galeazzo Maria, succeeded his father as Duke of Milan, inherited all the worst Visconti traits from his mother, and was assassinated after ten years. Thereupon the second brother, Ludovico il Moro (so called because of his dark complexion), assumed the regency until his young nephew Gian Galeazzo should come of age. By 1493, however, Gian Galeazzo was fifteen years old and married to a granddaughter of Don Ferrante of Naples, Isabella. The young couple were tired of the regency, and Isabella appealed to her grandfather for support in ousting the regent. But Ludovico il Moro had set up the most luxurious, most profligate, and most cultured court in Europe, now that Burgundy had disappeared; little did he guess that those who had been the ruin of Burgundy were also to be the ruin of him. He was married to the 'high and lointaine' lady, Isabella d'Este, from the ruling family at Ferrara, the most aristocratic in lineage of all in Italy; he had no desire at all to make way for his young nephew. So, to counteract pressure from Naples he thought of the Anjou claim and sent messengers to the King of France, promising his support if the King should care to insist upon this claim. The young couple, Gian Galeazzo and Isabella, were kept under house arrest.

This was just the pretext that the ill-directed military enthusiasm of Charles VIII needed. He decided to enforce his 'rights' and started assembling an army for what was to be the greatest descent that the French had ever made into Italy. Inevitably he sent to the Confederation for troops. His request was turned down formally by the assembled cantons, which forbade any Swiss at all to take part in the invasion. But a certain number of Swiss had served on a small scale under the condottieri in Italy— four hundred in fact were at the time employed by Don Alfonso in the Kingdom—enough in any case had been to and fro for the knowledge of Italy's fantastic wealth to have filtered back into even the most remote mountain hamlet. The new generation, who must have been tired by their fathers' stories of the wealth of Burgundy, saw in the French invasion the chance for loot and plunder on an even more fabulous scale. Golden horizons opened, and no official decrees could stop bands crossing the mountains to join the French army.

The bands, about 6,000 strong, assembled at Vercelli, went on to Alessandria, and finally joined the French at Genoa where they were put under the command of the Bailli of Dijon, Antoine de Buissey. A farcical pursuit by emissaries of the Diet who had orders to fetch them back was foiled at every stage by French and Milanese officials; the emissaries never managed to catch up with the bands and had to return to Switzerland, their mission unachieved.

Here is a description of the French army (roughly 30,000 strong) as it entered Rome. The chronicler was amazed at its size, at its division into different corps, its disciplined but warlike appearance, and above all at its cannon. His reactions must have been typical of the Italians of the time, for the expedition was virtually unresisted.

'Three days later King Charles with his ranks of foot and horse fully armed and drawn up in different sections rode into the City by the Flumentana Gate. The first to enter were the long columns of Swiss and Germans marching by in step to the beating of drums and under their banners, with real military dignity and unbelievable order.

'Their clothes were short, varied in style, and left some of their limbs exposed. All the strongest men wore helmets with plumes and stood out above the rest. Their weapons were short swords and wooden lances ten feet long topped with their metal blades. A quarter of them were armed with long axes from the top of which sharpened points stuck out. They would wield these deadly weapons with both hands; they call them hallebards in their language. About a thousand of them were divided into groups of a hundred armed with arquebuses which fired leaden pellets at the enemy. When they are drawn up for battle, they so despise breastplates and shields and helmets that only their captains and those in the front ranks wear any armour at all.

'Five thousand Gascons followed them, nearly all crossbowmen. This type of soldiers seemed in their general appearance and turn-out a bit deformed by comparison with the Swiss, who certainly stood out the most, with their gleaming weapons and decorative headgear and their fierce looks.'

Two thousand five hundred French knights came next, each knight with his squire, page, and valet, and following them *en masse* the archers, five thousand light horse, 'armed with great fast-shooting wooden bows in the English style.'

Then came the King and four hundred mounted gentlemen of the bodyguard, 'of whom a hundred came from the land of the Scots and were noted for their courage and loyalty to the King by whose side they always rode.'

He was followed by two hundred more knights, the nobles of France, and a swarm of Italian allies: 'There were so many columns of foot and horse not only splendidly and ostentatiously ornamented but also drawn up in as warlike a fashion as if they were about to start a massacre in the City that at the sight everybody found it easy to be terrified. Terror was added to terror because men, horses, banners, weapons all shining and gleaming everywhere, dazzling the onlookers, made their numbers seem greater than they really were. However, people were struck by particular admiration and feelings of fear when they saw the thirty-six cannons (as they are called) which have a barrel as wide as a human head and shoot out iron balls.'

This vast and terrifying army assembled in the early autumn in Piedmont, scared the Medici rulers out of Florence, and reached Rome on New Year's Eve, already renowned for brutality.

'The King retired to his palace, and the soldiers were quartered out in private houses. . . . Two hundred cavalry were barracked in the Campo del Fiori. Riots started spreading throughout the whole City because the Roman people, who have a turbulent and violent character themselves, could not put up with the threats of the insolent French or the harshly accented voices and savage faces of the Swiss. On their side these foreign soldiers spread out through the bars and low dives and through drinking heavily became even more ferocious, and violent quarrels started everywhere. Many of them let their rashness lead them headlong, and as it was night they got lost in the more deserted parts of the

City and were killed by thieves and criminals. A large band of Swiss and Gascons stormed the Banci Palace, killed there some people who had hit a French soldier and struck down Marco Matteo, a nobleman.

'With all this confusion and noise a rumour started and spread quickly that the City was being captured and its palaces sacked by the Barbarians. As the tumult increased, the Roman people began to take up arms—as was only right for those sons of Mars—in order to defend their possessions, their wives and their children. But,' continues the patriotic and pious chronicler, 'on that day the Gods above who watch over the beloved City warded off a grievous struggle and turned aside that moment of supreme danger.' In fact the Pope had in fright taken refuge in Castel Sant'Angelo, but Prospero Colonna, the chief condottiere of the day, who was employed by King Charles, came out and quelled the riot.

In face of such ferocious allies and such formidable enemies, all Italy quailed. Machiavelli, blaming his countrymen's feebleness on the use of mercenary troops and, ignoring the fact that the French army was even more mercenary in composition and spirit, wrote that King Charles was 'able to conquer Italy with his billeting officers alone.' The French army marched into Naples unresisted; Don Alfonso fled to the Castello dell'Uovo and, after making a brief sortie at the head of his four hundred Swiss and Germans, abdicated and fled. The barons cowered abjectly. The Kingdom, which had resisted successfully or unsuccessfully so many French invasions, finally collapsed before a King of France in person with barely a blow struck. Castello dell'Uovo surrendered, and in the late spring Charles began his march back to France leaving a third of his army and a Viceroy at Naples.

General alarm at the fantastic ease of the French conquest had spread not only throughout Italy but throughout Europe. Ludovico il Moro, whose nephew had conveniently 'died,' repented of his rashness and married off Bianca Sforza to

Maximilian. Maximilian was now Emperor-elect; his first wife, Mary of Burgundy, had died from a fall off her horse. A new and important prince joined the league, Ferdinand of Aragon, husband of Isabella of Castile. Family ties, Aragonese pride, and his own interest bound him to his expelled cousins at Naples. The Pope gave his support. Venice adhered.

The League army commanded by the noble condottiere Francesco Gonzaga, Duke of Mantua, tried to cut off the retreat of the French in the north of Italy. But the battle of Fornovo was a half-hearted affair; King Charles only wanted to get home to France, and the Italians were understandably lacking in confidence. Their attack was ruined by the ill discipline of the Albanian light cavalry, the 'stradiots,' the main mercenary arm of the Venetian forces, and King Charles got safely back to France, where he was to die two years later while preparing another Italian invasion.

The Swiss disgraced themselves on the way back at a town called Pontremoli, where a quarrel blew up in which forty of them were killed. In revenge they 'killed all the inhabitants, plundered the houses, set fire to them and burned every living thing and everything else too, including more than ten of their own men who were drunk.' King Charles was furious. He only forgave them when they dragged his famous thirty-six cannon up and down the twisting mountain road at La Spezia—a feat everyone judged impossible but which the Swiss offered to do provided the King would pardon them.

King Charles' cousin, Louis Duke of Orléans, had inherited the town of Asti, not very far from Milan. While the King was down in Naples and relations with the Milanese were deteriorating, the Duke of Orléans claimed by right the town of Novara as well. Louis and Ludovico il Moro both started enrolling mercenaries in the cantons, despite a formal interdiction by the Diet. Men from Berne and Lucerne joined Louis, while Ludovico recruited from the close allies of the Confederates, the leagues of the Grisons and the Valais.[1] On June 10, the Duke of Orléans

---
[1] The Grisons and the Valais did not obtain cantonal status till much later.

captured Novara; three days later he proposed a formal alliance to the Diet, an idea favoured by Lucerne and the Waldstätte, who saw a chance for acquiring territory in the Milanese.

But while the Diet was debating, Ludovico il Moro had allied with Venice, and a combined Milanese-Venetian force was besieging the French inside Novara. The Diet could not agree to a Confederate alliance, but Lucerne, Uri, and Schwyz set up their own expeditionary force to march on Milan. False news came that Novara had fallen, and Ludovico il Moro managed to buy off these formidable enemies with four thousand florins and a small mountain valley as a special *douceur* for Uri.

A month after the battle of Fornovo the besiegers tried an assault, which was repelled by the bravery of the Swiss. King Charles was now close by, about to relieve his besieged cousin. Of his original 6,000 Swiss, he had left 2,000 at Naples, and war, disease, and desertion had almost halved the remainder. But now that he was near Switzerland once more, new recruits started flooding in; 5,000 more men came down from the mountains. Ludovico il Moro's Swiss who had always been reluctant to fight against the Duke of Orléans' Swiss planned to desert, but Ludovico foiled their plans, though many deserted.

While the kings and dukes hesitated, avoiding battle, a wave of enthusiasm for mercenary service such as had never been known before swept over Switzerland. Diets and cantons launched formal prohibitions in vain: when the mercenary fever takes over a nation, no government regulation can stop it. Solothurn locked the city gates to stop the outflow, but men jumped over the walls and sailed out clandestinely in tubs. Over 20,000 Swiss, an unheard-of number, started pouring down from the Alpine passes. They arrived too late to save Novara, which was evacuated under a truce, and their numbers were embarrassing to King Charles, who had to station French officers on the passes into Piedmont to turn back as many as possible.

This unprecedented wave of volunteers, however, gave him great moral support. Ludovico il Moro and the League had to yield before the threat represented by all these Swiss. Ludovico abandoned the League, paid the royal cousins a vast sum of money, and made peace.

But the Swiss, thousands of whom had been enrolled, looked upon themselves as victors and demanded three months' pay, though they had only been serving for a few days. In the end King Charles had to agree: he promised to pay them a month's pay at once and two months' more when they left for Lucerne—a vast total of half a million francs which in fact he did not pay, though the Swiss eventually got it several years later. Meanwhile the original Swiss of the expedition, considering themselves aggrieved as the labourers in the vineyard, seized their old chief, the Bailli of Dijon, and only let him go when they had got fifteen days 'departure money' as an extra payment.

By the end of October all the Swiss mercenaries were back in their cantons. It was a rough journey back over the passes and they arrived in a poor state: the latecomers had won no booty and very little ready cash compared with what they had hoped for, and the survivors of the Naples expedition had all caught the '*mal francese*,' syphilis, which the French army had introduced as an extra boon into Italy. Of the 2,000-odd left as a garrison in Naples, the remnants, a mere 300, returned the following January, physically ruined by this new and raging disease. Not only were these former mercenaries in a very poor way, but they expected the cantons to punish them for disobeying the formal prohibitions on joining the French army. But public opinion was on their side: Berne alone punished a few with fines and short imprisonment. Nevertheless, despite this unpromising start and these disappointed hopes, the Swiss did not lose their enthusiasm for mercenary soldiering. For the next fifty years, whenever there was a battle in Italy, Swiss were fighting on one side or the other.

On May 17, 1498, Louis Duke of Orléans was crowned King of France. Louis XII diverted French aims from Naples to Milan; his grandmother Valentina Visconti had been the sister of the last Visconti duke, Filippo Maria, and the new King considered that this gave him a legitimate right to the duchy of Milan superior to that of the usurping condottiere House of Sforza.

A year after his coronation King Louis prepared for the second royal invasion of Italy by signing an official treaty with the cantons against Duke Ludovico il Moro.

The French army, strengthened by 6,000 Swiss, invaded in mid-summer, and captured the mighty city of Milan almost as easily as their predecessors had captured Naples. Ludovico il Moro fled; but at the end of the year the Milanese populace rose against the French and drove all but the garrison of the citadel out. On February 2, Cardinal Ascanio Sforza entered Milan with 4,000 Swiss mercenaries, and three days later his brother Duke Ludovico il Moro re-entered in triumph himself with an army of 7,000 Swiss and 3,000 Germans. The Emperor Maximilian sent twenty cannon; Ludovico il Moro besieged the French in Novara once again and drove them out, except for the citadel; it looked as if the Milanese triumph was complete.

But French reinforcements under their great general La Tremouille advanced against Novara. The French army had 1,200 lances and 20,000 infantry, including the 6,000 Swiss. A battle seemed inevitable, and for the first time large bodies of Swiss would be facing each other on opposite sides.

This was a situation the cantons had always feared and were not ready to accept. Two weeks previously Zurich had already sent a messenger down to summon the men of the canton on both sides to return home, but they, hesitantly, refused. A Diet was called and on March 31 decided to order the Swiss on both sides not to fight. Messengers from the Diet reached the French camp on April 6, but La Tremouille held them incommunicado and decided to fight immediately before the news of the Diet's decision could become known. Next day, April 7, Duke Ludovico and La Tremouille drew up their opposing forces outside Novara, but the Swiss on both sides refused to fight their fellow countrymen and the battle was no more than an indecisive skirmish.

The Milanese army withdrew inside the walls of Novara, and next day the Swiss captains held a meeting and decided to continue serving till nightfall and then to end an intolerable situation by withdrawing from Novara and abandoning Ludovico il Moro. That evening the Swiss captains in the French army came into the town through the gates guarded by the Milanese Swiss and the two different groups of captains spent the whole night discussing what they should do. The French-Swiss were legally more justified as theirs were official canton-approved mercenary companies, and the Milanese-Swiss captains decided to stand by their decision to abandon Ludovico il Moro. 'We do not want to fight against the Confederates,' they told him. 'We love our country as much as you do yours. If we cause the death of the Swiss in the service of France we will never dare return home.'

For the Duke the position had deteriorated so quickly and unexpectedly that even his political acumen could hardly help him any longer. About to be abandoned by almost his entire army in a small town closely besieged by his bitterest enemies, he must have reflected with *amertume* on the dangers of employing mercenary troops. He spent the next day, April 9, negotiating with a French noble, Ligny, a relative of his, and finally that night agreed to renounce his duchy, surrender, and live in France with a pension of 25,000 francs a year.

But his Swiss, though caught in a difficult enough dilemma, retained enough sense of loyalty to feel ashamed at this utter sacrifice of their employer. They passed the word to the French-Swiss captains that Ludovico had escaped from the city, and on the morning of April 10 came to the Duke and proposed that he should escape with them dressed in Swiss costume and disguised as a peasant soldier. Ludovico, swallowing his pride as the most magnificent ruler in Italy and breaking the treaty he had signed with Ligny on which the ink can scarcely have been dry, agreed.

La Tremouille, however, had never believed the story of the Duke's escape, and had heard from his spies that there would be an attempt to pass the Duke out incognito. When the town of Novara was handed over to him, he made the Milanese-Swiss pass in column, almost in single file, between two ranks of French-Swiss soldiery, certain that thus an intruding Duke would be recognized. What he did not reckon on was the by now strong sense of nationality among the Swiss. The captain in charge of the Duke, Nussbaumer, passed his charge through the French-Swiss ranks and left him with a French-Swiss captain Muller, 'to be handed over to your officers as the common property of the Confederates.'

It must have been an incredible scene: the disguised Ludovico il Moro, semi-booty, semi-romantic hero, being passed from Swiss to Swiss as the word went round and all the Swiss on both sides were let into the secret. The French officers, half realizing what was going on, rode furiously around trying to pin down the one bogus Switzer among so many thousands. The Bailli of Dijon, more subtle than the rest, found a man from Uri named Turmann, handed him a purse of 200 crowns, and had the Duke pointed out to him and arrested. The dramatic attempt at escape was over.

This was the famous, or infamous, '*Trahison de Novara*' which did so much to lower the already low reputation of the Swiss mercenaries. The French-Swiss captains raised an uproar about the arrest of their 'property,' but La Tremouille calmed them by promising that Ludovico il Moro would be regarded as their booty. He did not keep the promise, naturally enough. He bought them off with an extra month's pay in the end, but the Swiss always bore a grudge for this against the French, both for the stain it cast on their honour and for the loss it caused to their pockets.

Ludovico il Moro was imprisoned by the French, and died eight years later in captivity in France. As for Turmann, he did not dare to return to Uri for two years, and when he eventually did return he was at once arrested, tried, condemned, and beheaded.

By the end of April all the Swiss mercenaries were back home, returning from this second French invasion with more profit than from the first—with '*beaucoup d'argent, une honte eternelle mais point d'honneur.*' A few were tried by their cantons for disobedience but only suffered short spells in prison.

* * *

French royalty, with its prestige and extravagant claims backed by Swiss mercenary infantry, was a force too strong to withstand. The popes and the Italians generally were to try to destroy the alliance between the two, only to hesitate fearfully when an abyss loomed before them—the possibility that the Swiss even without France, even despite France, might become masters of Italy. But the Emperor tried a different policy; he set about forming a regular force of imperial infantry which would be able to beat the Swiss on their own terms.

The dukes and electors of the Empire had always looked with suspicion upon any attempt by the emperors to create any sort of standing army, and Maximilian, though direct ruler not only in Austria but also in Flanders and the surrounding territories, never won that prominence over his feudal magnates that the kings of England and France had obtained. The infantry he raised were not a regular force; he assembled them from time to time by giving commissions to minor nobles and professional soldiers to raise regiments. These officers, the '*obersten*,' or colonels, raised infantry that were even more highly organized than the Swiss companies, complete with provosts, disciplinary codes, and an ever growing *esprit de corps*. They were armed and trained on the Swiss model and therefore regarded by the Swiss with peculiar hatred. Even though they began as imperial troops, they very soon realized their own value and hired themselves out to any and every potential employer. In them all the vices of the Swiss mercenaries were exaggerated; they showed no reluctance to fight on opposite sides in the same war. The corps Maximilian had created to save the Empire very nearly ruined it:

> *Wir hab'n kleine Sorgen*
> *Wohl um das romisch' Reich*
> *Es sterb' heut'oder Morgen*
> *Das gibt was alles Gleich.*[1]

---

[1] 'We care little about the Holy Roman Empire. Whether it perishes today or tomorrow is all the same to us.'

These troops are known in the French and English chronicles of the time as lansquenets, a French corruption of their correct title '*landsknecht.*' The title either means foot soldier of the plains (as opposed to the mountain Swiss) or foot soldier of the country. Sir Charles Oman, in his book on the *Art of War in the Middle Ages,* suggests that Maximilian deliberately chose a vague and indefinite word in order to avoid being accused of keeping a regular army. However that may be, no battle was soon to be fought, no army to be complete without its contingent of lansquenets. There was a popular French saying: '*Un lansquenet repoussé du paradis ne peut avoir accès en enfer parce qu'il ferait peur au diable.*'[1] Their ferocity and barbarity outrivalled even that of the Swiss. But despite this the French kings always considered the Swiss just that much better as soldiers—an opinion which they marked in the most practical way by always paying the Swiss half a florin more a month than the lansquenet.

Maximilian tried to use his new military arm in a last attempt to reimpose Hapsburg and imperial authority on the cantons and the string of little leagues now allied to them. At the battle of Dornach the lansquenets, newly formed, were beaten by the Confederates in an official non-mercenary war, the so-called Swabian War. The defeat was by no means crushing, but Maximilian agreed to peace. The Peace of Basel, September 22, 1499, virtually recognized the independence of the Confederacy. The peacemaker who arranged it was none other than Ludovico il Moro, at this stage still reigning as Duke in Milan, and he if anyone deserved the gratitude not the betrayal of the Swiss as the foster father of their national sovereignty.

Shortly afterward three more cantons were admitted to the Confederacy: the cities of Basel and Schaffhausen and the country district of Appenzell. The Confederacy now numbered thirteen cantons, and for centuries no more were to be admitted as full members of the Confederacy.

* * *

---

[1] 'A lansquenet thrown out of paradise cannot get into Hell because he would make the devil afraid.'

For the next half-century the newly formed nation states of Europe fought long and ferocious wars punctuated by bloodthirsty battles over an Italy where condottieri, popes, and republics contrived with surprising success to cling to independence and play off the barbarians against one another. In the end the sombre shadow of Spain spread over the whole peninsula and the fiery pagan spirit of the Renaissance was quenched in the dark but noble waters of the Counter Reformation.

The Swiss and the lansquenets were the ignoble instruments by which the rulers fought their wars until both, reactionary and conservative in their tactics as the condottieri had been before them, went down before the cannon and the arquebuses of the Spanish *tercios*, in their turn the most ferocious, the most courageous, and the most successful infantry in Europe.

But for a brief few years at the beginning of the century the Swiss Confederates, inspired by the success of their mercenary soldiers, nearly created a powerful central European state until they relapsed once more and for ever into their purely mercenary role.

Gradually the cantons turned against their ally and employer, the King of France; slowly Uri and the other Waldstätte claimed and conquered more of the Milanese. Eventually they joined the great warrior Pope, Julius II (della Rovere), who formed the famous corps of Swiss Guards on January 22, 1506, and openly turned against the French. As papal mercenaries they helped to beat the French at the battle of Ravenna and captured Cremona and Pavia.[1] Next year Uri conquered and annexed Lugano and Locarno, and the following year 1513 was their *Annus Mirabilis*. Pope Julius died, Spain and France concluded a truce, and the Confederates fought for themselves alone though nominally for Massimiliano Sforza, son of Ludovico. At the great battle of Novara (June 6, 1513) they came face to face with the lansquenets in the service of France: 'The lansquenets have cried out a great

---

[1] The Guard consisted of 150 men, originally all recruited from the canton of Lucerne, under von Hartenstein. It outshone, at least in numbers, the King of France's *Garde des Cent Suisses*, formed nine years earlier.

cry,' wrote an exultant Swiss on the eve of the battle. 'We have chased the cattle into a pen in which we are going to take our revenge. They have caused us much trouble for a long time; we are not going to forget it; we want to strike them down to death.' Eight thousand lansquenets were slaughtered, though the Swiss lost 1,500 men, the greatest casualties they had ever suffered. 'I place the Swiss above all Kings,' wrote the Florentine, Vettori. 'I can imagine no army to oppose them.' They became the virtual masters of Milan and invaded Burgundy, terrifying La Tremouille, who was defending Dijon. But as always with the Swiss, their mercenary spirit ruined their political enterprises. The French bought them off, the Duke of Savoy bought them off, the Marquis of Montferrat bought them off—and France prepared to take a terrible revenge.

The year 1515 saw a new King on the French throne, the young, bold, and knightly Francis I. It was open war between the Confederates and France and the prize of the war was Milan. In July, Francis led an enormous army over the Alps over the Col de l'Argentière, the only pass that the Swiss were not guarding. The usual nucleus of the army was the regular force of 2,500 lances, but in addition he led 8,000 French infantry, 10,000 Navarrese, Basque, and Gascon mercenaries, and no less than 20,000 lansquenets. Against this the Diet raised first an army of 8,000, then another 14,000, and then decided on a levy of all the remaining strength possible and called up a further 16,000. But this last army did not arrive in time for the battle.

The battle when it came was fought at Marignano on August 13/14, 1515. It began in the afternoon and went on till midnight. It started again at daybreak.

'And you must understand,' wrote King Francis I to his mother, 'that the evening combat began at three o'clock in the afternoon and lasted till between eleven o'clock and midnight when the moon disappeared. . . . I assure you that I saw the lansquenets measure their pikes against the Swiss and their lances against the enemy cavalry; and after this people will not be able to say any longer that our knights are just armed hares, for it was they that did the execution, and it was they—I would not dream of telling you a lie—who in bands five hundred strong, one after the other, made thirty beautiful charges before the battle was won. . . . All night long we remained in the saddle, lances in hand, helmets on our heads . . . and because I was the nearest to our enemies I had to be on watch, so that they did not take us by surprise in the morning. And believe me, Madame, we were twenty-eight hours on horseback without eating or drinking. . . . Never for two thousand years has there been so fierce and so cruel a battle. That's what those who were at Ravenna say—which was only a joust by comparison.'

At the end of the battle 12,000 Swiss, no less, lay dead on the field. This was the end of the great period of Swiss glory, of the mercenary nation-in-arms, which thus lasted from the battle of Morat to the battle of Marignano.

Francis I wisely did not pursue the retreating Confederates. Next year, on November 29, 1516, there was signed the Perpetual Peace which regulated the relations of France and Switzerland until the French Revolution and turned Switzerland into a mercenary recruiting ground for every French king to come.

The Swiss agreed to abandon their claims to the Milanese and never to supply mercenaries to the King's enemies; also to close the cols to the enemies of France in times of war.

The Swiss fought in all the great battles in Italy—Pavia, La Bicocca, and Ceresoles—but never with quite their old success. As regular armies in the modern sense grew up, the traditional spirit of mercenary liberty—the liberty to plunder, loot, and kill— disappeared. The Swiss became disciplined and respectable. Swiss regiments served in the armies of Savoy, Holland, Spain, Austria, and England, but the connection with France was always the most powerful[1] till the massacre of the Swiss Guards in the French Revolution and Napoleon's attack on Switzerland ruined

---

[1] Over a million Swiss served in the French army from the time of Louis XI to that of Louis XVI.

the Perpetual Peace. It was not till after the 1848 Revolution, however, that 'service with foreign armies, military capitulations, and acceptance of foreign decorations and pensions' were formally prohibited, and Switzerland assumed its modern air of vacuous and innocuous neutrality.

5 Mercenaries in the Age of Reason

'He has plundered our seas, ravaged our coasts, burnt our towns, and destroyed the lives of our people. He is at the moment transporting large armies of foreign mercenaries to complete the works of death, desolations and tyranny, already begun, with circumstances of cruelty and perfidy scarcely paralleled in the most barbarous ages, totally unworthy the head of a civilized nation.'
—American Declaration of Independence

THE EIGHTEENTH CENTURY had a great conceit of itself and a great distaste for its predecessors. In the age of enlightenment, the age of Voltaire and the Encyclopedists, ten centuries of European history were considered with supercilious disgust as the mere repository of crimes, follies, and barbarities. That civilization had progressed, was progressing, and would progress uninterruptedly was the leading and almost the undisputed dogma of the age. The prejudices of Voltaire nowhere had—indeed nowhere still have—a greater hold than on the minds of the educated classes in England; he attributed all the misery and suffering of mankind to war and to religion, particularly the Roman Catholic religion, and the enlightened, in England and on the Continent alike, agreed that just as there was nothing worthy of study in the

Middle Ages, *a fortiori* there was nothing deserving of imitation. The atmosphere, the taste of the period, was not conducive to the employment of mercenaries.

Yet the English educated classes found themselves faced with a dilemma. The prevailing system of government in Europe was that of the enlightened despot whose progressive ideas were imposed rather than retarded by the aid of a small standing army. But in England the potential despots, the later Stuarts and the early Hanoverians, were anything but enlightened, and the ruling principle of the English gentry and nobility was to prevent the creation in England of a standing army of any sort at all. Today, when the military power is so entirely subservient to the civil, it needs an effort of the imagination to realize how fearful Parliament was of a royal *coup d'état* and how the ogre of a permanent regular army in England, the only instrument by which a King could once again overawe a Parliament, was constantly present before the minds of all.

Yet wars occurred. Not all French rulers were as enlightened as French philosophers, and throughout the century England considered it her duty (as so often before and afterwards) to teach the French nation, more in sorrow than in anger, how to respect the admirable rules of political behaviour which French thinkers had laid down but which, alas, only the English could be trusted to interpret correctly. At the beginning, in the middle, and at the end of the century England was at war with France, and, most unfortunately, for wars armies were needed.

In the first two great wars, the War of the Spanish Succession, which opened the century, and the Seven Years' War, which marked its halfway point, the English solved their dilemma with great success. England provided the generals and the gold; England's allies provided the troops. Marlborough led hosts of Dutch and Austrians all over Europe; Mr Pitt conquered America on the plains of Germany, with considerable assistance from Frederick the Great; and Clive won India with a single English regiment and a whole army of native sepoys.

But the Dutch, the Austrians, the Prussians were England's

allies. Their own interests were at stake; their own interests were threatened by France. And even if Frederick the Great admittedly made war in order to win glory, he could hardly be termed a mercenary, though his troops were all paid with English gold. The idea was despicable; the term was not applicable; the idea was denied; the term was not used.

But on April 19, 1775, a quarrel that had for years been impending finally broke out in bloodshed. At Lexington nearly eighty British soldiers were killed by rebellious American colonials, and two months later at the battle of Bunker Hill over a thousand men were lost. For the English the third great struggle of the century had begun, but this time the interests of the Dutch, the Austrians, or the Germans could by no stretch of political imagination, by no invention of legal ingenuity, be said to be involved. Lord North's government, only too conscious that the rebellious colonial militias could raise up to 50,000 men in the first flush of enthusiasm, began to wonder where it was to turn for an army.

At this stage the total British regular army amounted to a mere 30,000 men of whom half were permanently stationed in Ireland. In theory the other half were on garrison duty in England and Scotland, but in fact 9,000 of them were in America, of whom the majority were cooped up with General Gage in Boston; and several thousand more were garrisoning Gibralter and Minorca. England was almost denuded of troops, and not the slightest thought of conscription ever crossed the minds of Lord North or his ministers. If there was one freedom to which every Englishman since the end of the Middle Ages was absolutely entitled, it was the freedom not to serve in the army.

England was a nation of traders; the English fought their wars at one remove, by employing Dutch or Prussians or whoever could be persuaded to ally with them, races far more suited to the rough and unenlightened pursuit of war than the English themselves; and if a few hundred reactionary aristocrats chose to be officers and a few thousand semi-criminals volunteered to be cannon fodder, that was their concern and their misfortune—in no way an example to be imitated by the solid mass of the nation. For the navy there was a certain respect; public opinion allowed press-ganging among merchant seamen and likely lads in the port towns. But press-ganging for the army, any form of conscription, would have been considered an assault on the basic rights of the freedom-loving Englishman. And the idea of raising a voluntary force in England for a war that was unpopular with all and loudly condemned by the greatest men in Parliament, including the decrepit but still respected Earl of Chatham himself, was ludicrous—besides being dangerous.

Parliament voted for the enlistment of 25,000 men in a first flush of enthusiasm, but the Government knew that it would be almost impossible to recruit them and that in any case Parliament would soon repent of its imprudence in thus virtually accepting a large standing army. It was not till 11 A.M. on the morning of July 25 that the question became pressing: the news of Bunker Hill reached the Cabinet; Gage was recalled and General Carleton was sent over with Lord North's assurance that he 'hoped to have next spring in North America an army of 20,000 men exclusive of Canadians or Indians.'

But how? The moves that followed that summer are some of the most curious ever made in European diplomatic history.

In August, Panin, the Russian Prime Minister, sent for the British Ambassador, a gentleman by the name of Gunning, to ask him how the rebellion was going. Gunning replied that the situation was under control but asked boldly whether 'in case the circumstances of affairs should render any foreign forces necessary, he might reckon upon a body of Her Imperial Majesty's infantry.' Panin, in a formal reply a few days later made to a request that must have astonished him and Catherine the Great, mentioned Her Imperial Majesty's 'intimate affection for the British nation,' and Gunning took this reply as a promise of support. His dispatch bearing the good news reached London on September 1.

There his message was received with surprising confidence. Suffolk at once dictated a reply telling Gunning to ask for 20,000 fully equipped men to be ready at the Baltic ports next spring to set sail for Canada; he hoped for a reply before October 23 when Parliament was to reassemble. Dartmouth sent messages to Generals Howe and Carleton in America telling them that the Russians would certainly arrive, and a week later Suffolk wrote a second dispatch for Gunning, proposing a treaty with Catherine the Great for 100 years and offering £7-a-head levy money to her per recruit, half to be paid at once and half on embarkation: 'I will not conceal from you that, this accession of force being very earnestly desired, expense is not so much an object as in ordinary cases.'

Gunning, as yet unaware of the enthusiasm his dispatch had aroused, must already have been wishing that he had not been quite so definite and optimistic. On September 10 he had an interview with the Empress, who suggested settling the dispute with the American rebels peacefully. Three weeks later the dispatches from London came in, and he saw Panin, who asked him, 'And could not His Majesty make use of Hanoverians?' but promised, however, that a formal reply would soon be given.

Meanwhile the rumour was spreading around Europe. Vergennes, the French Foreign Minister whose lifelong policy was to take advantage of England's difficulties without embroiling France in another open war, wrote to his Ambassador at Moscow: 'I cannot reconcile Catherine's elevation of soul with the dishonourable idea of trafficking in the blood of her subjects.' In London members of Parliament returning from their holidays were eagerly discussing the news. 'When the Russians arrive,' wrote Gibbon to a friend, 'will you go and see their camp?'

But Catherine the Great's formal reply, possibly influenced by her respect for French views on good taste, had already been delivered to the now highly embarrassed Gunning who found it not 'genteel'.

'I am just beginning to enjoy peace,' she wrote, 'and Your Majesty knows that my empire has need of repose. There is an impropriety in employing so considerable a body in another hemisphere, under a power almost unknown to it and almost removed from contact with its own sovereign. Moreover I should not be able to prevent myself from reflecting on the consequences which would result for our dignity, for that of the two monarchies and the two nations, from this junction of our forces, simply to calm a rebellion which is not supported by any foreign power.'

This crushing but elegant snub reached King George III just before the opening of Parliament and immediately its contents though not its tone became known.

On October 26, King George III made his Speech from the Throne to the Lords. After referring to the 'desperate conspiracy' and saying that an increase in land and sea forces would be necessary, he declared: 'I have also the satisfaction to inform you that I have received the most friendly offers of foreign assistance; and if I should make any treaties in consequence thereof, they shall be laid before you. And I have, in testimony of affection for my people who can have no cause in which I am not equally interested, sent to the garrisons of Gibraltar and Port Mahon [Minorca] a part of my Electoral troops in order that a large number of the established forces of the Kingdom may be applied to the maintenance of its authority.'

The remark about 'the most friendly offers of foreign assistance' was for the time being treated with the scorn it deserved and was ignored, but the news that the King had sent Hanoverian troops to Gibraltar and Minorca aroused the Whig opposition to fury. On November 1, the Duke of Manchester moved a motion in the Lords: 'That bringing into any part of the Dominions of the Crown of Great Britain the Electoral Troops of His Majesty or any other Foreign Troops, without the previous consent of Parliament, is dangerous and unconstitutional.' The debate turned on the interpretation of the Bill of Rights, that second Magna Carta which proclaimed that 'Whereas the late King James the Second by the assistance of diverse evil counsellors, judges and ministers employed by him, did endeavour to subvert and extirpate the Protestant religion and the laws and liberties of this Kingdom ... therefore the said Lords Spiritual and Temporal and Commons ... declare ... that the raising and keeping of a standing army within the Kingdom in time of peace unless it be with consent of Parliament is against the law.' The legal point at issue was whether the phrase 'within the Kingdom' included all the possessions of the Crown of England or literally meant just within the Kingdom of England.

The Duke of Manchester recalled that 'in the late war' Lord Chatham had thought it necessary to raise a regiment of Americans 4,000 strong but had limited the number of foreign officers to 50; he had insisted that all the soldiers be naturalized subjects and Protestants and that their colonel should be a native-born British subject. Lord Lyttelton, taking up this point, remembered how Chatham 'in the very heat of war' had found it necessary to raise a German regiment of four battalions to serve in North America and 'instead of pleading the great strong and justifiable motives of necessity, instead of cavilling on this word or commenting on that, in the full spirit of the Constitution and the full spirit of an Englishman came to Parliament to obtain its sanction,' and Parliament had insisted on two special clauses, first that the Germans should serve only in America and secondly that none of the foreign officers should hold commissions higher than that of lieutenant-colonel. The Duke of Grafton said the spirit of the Bill of Rights, not the letter, was important; he asked the Attorney General whether the King's action was not legally repugnant to the Disbanding Act of William III which limited the standing military force in England to 7,000 men and that in Ireland to 12,000 men? He complained that the Government was too secretive and that Parliament needed information. The Earl of Effingham, whose information appears to have been somewhat out of date, said that he did not want 20,000 Russians in the Kingdom nor did he like the present action of entrusting two valuable fortresses 'to the care of aliens who could never be supposed to be so warmly interested in their safety and defence as Englishmen who, to the duty and prowess of soldiers, would always add the enthusiastic zeal of free men and Englishmen who felt themselves contending for nothing less than the trade, commerce and naval power of the country.'

The Duke of Richmond said that several noble Lords had taken it for granted that hiring foreigners had frequently been practised since the Revolution and that the foreigners had frequently been brought into the Kingdom without the previous consent of Parliament, but the noble Lords were mistaken; admittedly in 1745 and in 1756 the Hessians had not been brought in by an express act of Parliament but both Houses had consented to their employment, in one instance by a joint Address to the Throne and in the other instance by ratifying an existing treaty. He scornfully concluded by a *reductio ad absurdum* of the Government's position: 'I will draw my conclusion as an inevitable consequence of the premises that whenever there is a rebellion in any part of this vast empire, the King can bring into the Kingdom directly without the consent of Parliament any number of foreign mercenaries he pleases.'

Two days later the Commons debated a similar motion. 'Shall we despise the history of all those nations,' asked Governor Johnstone, the proposer, 'from Carthage downwards who have lost their liberty by employing foreign troops and recur to those silly arguments which have always been used as the reason for first introducing them?' He explained the traditional English attitude, recalling how William of Orange had sent a message on March 18, 1688, asking leave to introduce his Dutch troops into the Kingdom and how the House replied that 'they could not consent to his Majesty's request without doing violence to that constitution his Majesty came over to preserve'; and he quoted a contemporary historian who wrote that 'the undue preference given on many occasions to this body of Dutch Janissaries at the expense of the Scots Guards in particular had blunted the zeal of his national troops and almost deprived him of the hearts of his people.' He went on to say that 'the happy predilection every man feels for his native soil is a principle established by God and ought to be strictly adhered to by statesmen even in the formation of armies' and that 'no intelligent statesman ever despised this natural affection or could wish to have recourse to foreigners in the wanton degree the instance before us indicates.' The arguments for employing foreigners were that England had lots of money but few men: if, however, England had lots of money, why was she making a war in order to impose a tax upon America, and if she had few men, the fault was that of her own statesmen. 'How are the mighty fallen since the peace of 1763! What a spectacle for Europe!'

'No man should forget the national tendency of standing foreign troops,' proclaimed Townshend. 'They cannot entertain your laws; they know not your constitution; they cannot respect it.'

All this furore was caused by the comparatively modest administrative action of George III in replacing the garrisons of Gibraltar and Minorca with Hanoverian troops in order to free the British soldiers there for the war in America. The Whigs were disgusted not so much by the use of foreign mercenaries as such as by the threat to Parliamentary control, and in any case the foreign mercenaries were not going to be used to fight against the rebellious Americans. But already the speeches showed a certain distaste at the mere idea of employing foreign troops at all, a growing feeling that only Englishmen should defend English soil or English interests. On their side the Government supporters argued that the King was legally within his rights and that the move was expedient: foreign troops were 'easier to be had and cheaper.' The Lord Chancellor Bathurst said that with rebellion going on, it was no time for 'the quibbles of Westminster Hall and the subtle distinctions of lawyers.' Mr Stanley in the Commons quoted Froissart to show that the use of foreign mercenaries had been 'the uniform practise of the Kingdom since the battle of Newcastle upon Tyne.' And in both Houses the motions of censure were defeated by the practical Tory majority, by 75 to 35 in the Lords and by 203 to 81 in the Commons. Even in those days party lines were more important than the force of argument or the pleas of eloquence.

But the Government's military headaches were assuaged rather than abolished by the release of a few thousand second-rate garrison troops. The debates in Parliament had made it obvious that the country would not stand for the active employment of Electoral troops in America, and in any case many members of the Government agreed privately with the Opposition that this would be to place too much power in the King's hands and too much temptation in his way.

Lord North decided to turn elsewhere. Russia had refused, and Hanover was politically impossible; only the previous year Vergennes had renewed the Perpetual Peace with the Swiss cantons. The list of friendly states which might agree to hire out their troops as mercenaries but under the respectable cloak of alliance was almost closed. But one chance at least remained—Holland.

Why not? said Sir Joseph Yorke, British Ambassador at the Hague. There was a curious and rather special background to the request which might permit the Dutch to show more sympathy than the Russians: nearly two hundred years earlier the Low Countries had pledged to Queen Elizabeth as security for a loan three important fortresses; in 1616 the Dutch had paid up and the garrison had been withdrawn except for one English and one Scottish brigade, both of which had passed into the service of the United Provinces. William of Orange had recalled the English brigade to England, and shortly after the '45 the English Government had withdrawn the privilege of recruiting in Scotland from the Scots Brigade. At the time therefore the Scots Brigade was formed by men of all nationalities, over two thousand in all; its officers, however, were still Scots. This was the force that Sir Joseph Yorke suggested might be released for service in America.

The States General met to consider the English request. Zeeland and Utrecht consented but Holland objected. The delegate from Overyssel, Baron van der Capellan tot dem Pol, argued that Janissaries rather than troops of a free state should be used to subdue colonists. Once again a British Ambassador had underestimated the force of progressive French ideas in Europe. The States General agreed to lend the brigade 'on condition that it should never be used out of Europe.'

This disguised refusal was less offensive to the English Government than Catherine the Great's retort direct, but it was no more helpful. With a certain reluctance the Government fell back on the almost inevitable choice: Germany.

Offers had already been coming in from the minor German princes as soon as they had learned that the English were in the market for troops. The Prince of Waldech wrote offering a regiment of 600 men 'who like their prince will demand nothing better than to find an opportunity of sacrificing themselves for your Majesty.' These princes were the successors of the lansquenet captains; but whereas the great lansquenet captains, the Frundsbergs, the Furstenbergs, and the Schombergs, had led their bands of volunteers into the service of whoever paid them, the princes sent bands of conscripts into the service of whoever paid the princes. They had refined the Swiss cantonal system of official mercenary purveyors to the highest point possible, and many small princes depended for almost their entire revenue upon hiring out their subjects at exorbitant rates. 'This giving commissions to German officers to get men,' complained King George III, 'in plain English amounts to making me a kidnapper which I cannot think a very honourable occupation.' But German troops had a very high reputation; they had fought in all the recent European wars and all over the Continent from Naples to Sweden. In the War of the Spanish Succession three regiments of foot from Hesse-Darmstadt, commanded by their prince, had added lustre to English arms by being the main force involved in the capture of Gibraltar and the storming of Barcelona. Times had admittedly changed; it was not till mid-century that Voltairean ideas became widespread and generally accepted. Frederick the Great, the old ally of England and arch-hypocrite, began to refer continuously to 'this scandalous man-traffic.' But tradition gave a certain cloak, though it would be hard for the Government to pretend that the interests of Hesse and Brunswick were in any way bound up by the fate of the thirteen colonies across the Atlantic.

There was a further objection: the Imperial Diet had forbidden enlistments by foreign powers in any part of the Empire. Vienna sent messages throughout the Imperial territories saying that Britain 'has no more connections with the Empire than Russia or Spain, neither of which powers is permitted to recruit within its limits.' But the Thirty Years' War had almost completely destroyed the Emperor's power outside Austria and the Hapsburg domains. British recruiting agents set up offices unhindered in the territories of the Prince Bishop of Liège and the Elector of Cologne; British diplomats in Germany were instructed to give all possible aid to these recruiting agents without implicating the Government.

Suffolk sent out as his main recruiting agent and plenipotentiary an army officer named Colonel Faucitt. Already a few open rebuffs in reply to open approaches had come through; the Elector of Saxony had refused to hire out his troops, as the suggestion 'affects too nearly my pastoral tenderness for my subjects,' and the English decided to rely on the smaller Protestant princes. It is noteworthy that the two states which finally supplied most troops, Brunswick and Hesse-Cassel, were precisely those two states which alone were still fighting for the Protestant cause at the end of the Thirty Years' War.

Colonel Faucitt went first to Brunswick. The reigning Duke, Charles, was a bankrupt who had lavished all his money on French dancers, Italian opera singers, and his efficient little army. The Duke's brother, Prince Ferdinand, however, was a famous general who had served under Frederick the Great; he was a great friend of the English, and the husband of Augusta, King George III's sister. He was also co-regent; George III was later to choose Ferdinand's younger daughter Caroline as a fitting wife for the Prince of Wales. With such close connections very little difficulty was to be expected.

Faucitt spent two days wrangling with Feronie, the first minister, about the annual subsidy to be paid to the Duke, but his instructions from Suffolk were to get as many men as he could as quickly as possible without worrying too much about the expense. Agreement was soon reached: Brunswick would supply 4,000 foot and 300 light dragoons—a total of one-sixth of all the able-bodied men in the duchy—under the command of Colonel Riedesel who would be given the rank of major-general.

Colonel Faucitt hurried on to Cassel. The Landgrave of Hesse-Cassel, Frederick, was also connected by marriage with the English royal family but less happily so: he had married a daughter of George II who, sickened by his brutalities, had fled back to England for protection. The Landgrave was a lout, but a cultured lout—he had abolished torture, built an opera house and a theatre, and corresponded with Voltaire. More important, the Hessian troops were the finest and best disciplined in Germany; the Landgrave took a special pride in the appearance of his crack regiments, such as the Blue Hussars. The hussars were spectacularly turned out in jackets and colimans of sky blue and white, set off by red trousers; their officers wore silver hats embellished with a bunch of heron feathers. As usual, pride in appearance was matched by pride in performance. To obtain Hessian troops was the most important part of Colonel Faucitt's mission. As opposite number he had to negotiate with General Schlieffen; the negotiations were hard and the treaty was not signed until New Year's Eve.[1]

By its terms the Landgrave received 20 per cent more levy money per head than the Duke of Brunswick; he obtained the right to provide his own hospital and his own clothing, unlike the Brunswickers, and to receive extra payments from the British as a set-off. He revived and insisted on a scandalous claim for £41,000 owing for hospital expenses incurred in 'the late war,' and he insisted that the British pay should be paid into the Hessian treasury rather than directly to the troops. As the British rate of pay was higher than the Hessian rate of pay, the reason for this was but too clear. Colonel Faucitt rather feebly urged that the Hessians in the field should be paid as much as the British. 'They are my fellow soldiers,' said the Landgrave; 'do I not mean to treat them well?'

---

[1] The full text of the treaty is given in Appendix II. It is a very fine combination of bombast and bargaining.

But the greatest Hessian triumph was the subsidy money. Subsidies were a lump annual sum paid to the princes in addition to levy money, pay, and the rest, for the right to levy troops in their territory. The normal system at the time was for the government hiring to pay an annual subsidy to the German ruler, but the annual subsidy continued to be paid for four years even if the war the troops were hired for was over in one campaign. The Hessians asked for a double annual subsidy to be paid merely for the duration of the campaign; the English were confident that the campaign would last only one year and agreed, thinking that in effect they would thus be saving two years' subsidy money. In fact the treaty continued in force for ten years; never was such an expensive miscalculation made by any mercenary-hiring government.

The terms were so much better than the Landgrave had hoped to obtain that he offered not the original 5,000 men asked for but 12,000 foot, plus 400 Jägers armed with rifled guns, plus 300 dismounted dragoons, plus 3 corps of artillery—the double subsidy to be paid on all. Four major-generals, none distinguished, were to command this army. Suffolk had written to Colonel Faucitt that 'delay will mar the expected advantage,' and the Landgrave agreed that his thirteen battalions should march for the ports on February 15. Many desertions were expected, particularly on this march, but in fact vague hopes of plunder and loot induced most of the Hessian troops to go willingly.

Colonel Faucitt, having closed a bad but substantial bargain, went on to Hanau; the hereditary Count in person went round to choose recruits—they only amounted to a few hundred from this small territory—and accompanied his regiment in person as far as Frankfurt.

In early February the Fourteenth Parliament of the United Kingdom assembled again after the Christmas recess; on February 20 the treaties between His Majesty and His Most Serene Highness the Duke of Brunswick and Luneburgh, between His Majesty and His Most Serene Highness the Landgrave of Hesse-Cassel, and between His Majesty and His Most Serene Highness the Hereditary Count of Hanau were presented to both houses.

On this occasion the Commons was the first to debate the treaties. Lord North, the Prime Minister, put to the House these questions: 'Whether the troops hired were wanted? Whether the terms on which they were procured were advantageous? Whether the force was such as might be deemed fully advantageous to effect the operation for which it was intended?' His answers were obvious; to the third question he replied, with a depth of miscalculation rarely equalled by a British Prime Minister, that the force would be enough 'in all human probability' to compel submission, possibly without any shedding of blood.

It was the second point, however, on which the Commons fastened with near fury. Lord John Cavendish pointed out that the troops were entering into pay even before beginning to march, an unheard-of procedure, and that the levy money was at too high a rate, as were the subsidies also. Burke complained that the pretence of cheapness was abandoned: 1,000 foreigners would cost as much as 1,500 natives. Sir George Savile also complained of the incredible expense: he had 'never known so disgraceful or dear a bargain.' The Government was driven onto the defensive: Grenville admitted that the expense was heavy and the terms hard but said that it had to be done, and Lord George Germaine, Secretary of State for the Colonies, defended the treaties on the grounds of necessity.

Lord Irham attacked them also on practical grounds but from a different angle. He argued that the Landgrave, the Duke, and the Count were feudatories of the Empire; that the laws of the Empire only allowed troops to be sent out of the imperial territories provided that they could be called back to its defence if the Emperor was attacked or involved in a war. 'Now, Sir,' he said, 'if this is the true state of the privilege these princes now enjoy, can it be fairly inferred from thence that they can merely for lucre and pecuniary considerations transport their vassals to the East or West Indies, nine parts in ten of whom will hardly ever return; and thus by depopulating their territories deprive their lord paramount of the succour which he has a right to expect from them . . . to support a cause in no shape whatsoever connected with the Empire and which must render it vile and dishonourable in the eyes of all Europe as a nursery of men reserved for the purposes of supporting arbitrary power whenever grasped at by those who have more money though not more justice than the others whom they can pay for oppressing?'

Lord Irham's marathon rhetorical question was on too technical a point to interest the Commons, who as always cared very little about European opinion. But it met an echo in Europe where Faucitt was still flitting from court to court and disgust was growing. The Elector of Bavaria wanted to hire out troops but was too ashamed to speak of his desire to his own ministers. Frederick the Great wrote to Voltaire: 'Do not attribute his [Hesse-Cassel's] education to me! Were he a graduate of my school, he would never have . . . sold his subjects to the English as they drive cattle to the shambles. He a preceptor of sovereigns! The sordid passion for gain is the only motive of his vile avarice.'

Only two speeches in the Commons rose above the level of mere practical criticism. Hartley attacked the whole war, the lies of the Government, its conduct and its character. 'Sir,' he protested, 'my opposition to this unjust American war is so total and absolute against every part of it that I hardly know in what terms to express my aversion to any one part more than to every other; yet I think, Sir, if there could remain any measure exceeding every preceding one in disgrace and barbarity, it is this of introducing foreign troops. . . . I call it a fatal measure; because when foreign powers are once introduced in this dispute, all possibility of reconciliation and return to our former connection is totally cut off. You have given a justification to the Americans by your example if they call in the assistance of foreign powers.'

Yet even Hartley was attacking the treaties on grounds of expediency rather than principle. It was left to a back bencher, a typical squire of the shires, to express with bumbling incoherence what was probably the true feelings of nine-tenths of the House; his name was, extremely fittingly, Bull.

The desire of the Government for Protestant blood, said Mr Alderman Bull, 'cries aloud to Heaven for vengeance.' He was astonished to see 'how much professions of patriotism are become a subject of ridicule.' His peroration is a masterpiece of insular art, its tone so often to be echoed in later centuries in the chamber in which it now resounded: 'Let not the historian be obliged to say that the Russian and the German slave was hired to subdue the sons of Englishmen and of freedom; and that in a reign of a prince of the House of Brunswick, every infamous attempt was made to extinguish that spirit which brought his ancestors to the throne and in spite of treachery and rebellion seated them firmly upon it.'

By contrast the debate which followed in the Lords a few days later was conducted on a far higher level. It is unlikely that at any time or in any place were the principles of mercenary soldiering and the right of a government to hire mercenary soldiers submitted to such searching and profound criticisms. Politically the debate was notable for an intervention by the King's brother, H.R.H. the Duke of Cumberland, who in a short speech said: 'My Lords, I lament to see Brunswickers who once to their great honour were employed in the defence of the liberties of the subject, now sent to subjugate his constitutional liberties in another part of this vast empire.'

Morally the initial object of attack was the terms of the treaties, particularly the Hesse-Cassel treaty.

'The tenor of the treaties themselves,' said the Earl of Suffolk, defending the Government, 'is filled with pompous high-sounding phrases of alliance; but I will be so ingenuous as to confess to the noble duke that I consider them merely in that light'—an extraordinary defence, which cannot have made agreeable hearing when it was reported back to the Landgrave of Hesse-Cassel. Very few governments ever admit openly that their treaties are full of high-sounding and meaningless phrases, desirable though such an admission may be.

The noble duke referred to was the Duke of Richmond who

moved an address in these terms: 'We beg leave humbly to represent to your Majesty the sense we entertain of the danger and disgrace attending this inconsiderate measure; when it has been judged necessary, in the first exertions of Great Britain to subjugate her colonies, to hire an army of foreign mercenaries, acknowledging to all Europe that these kingdoms are unable, either from want of men or from disinclination to this service, to furnish a competent number of natural-born citizens to make the first campaign.' On the treaty: 'We may say with truth that Great Britain never before entered into a treaty so expensive, so unequal, so dishonourable and so dangerous in its consequences.' It was 'a downright mercenary bargain for the taking into pay of a number of hirelings who are bought and sold like so many beasts for slaughter. There is no common interest which mutually binds the parties; and if there were, the conduct of the foreign princes would be the most extraordinary that was ever known.'

Richmond supported his speech by a thorough review of the various treaties made since 1702 with the Landgraves of Hesse-Cassel who 'never failed to establish the former extortion as a precedent for the basis of the succeeding treaty, always taking care to make some new demands upon this country.' The Duke of Manchester raised the tone again after Suffolk's unhappy intervention. Manchester was very worried by the whole train of events, with foreign troops coming in everywhere: 'An abridgement of British, as well as American, liberty would not be disagreeable to some of our present rulers. . . . I doubt this country is very near that crisis when she will passively surrender all those rights her ancestors held most dear.'

He analyzed the war situation: 'Let us consider the means we have to prosecute this war. The British troops, we find, fail not, my Lords, in point of courage but they show an honest backwardness to engage against their fellow citizens. To Germany we have recourse for assistance: 17,000 German mercenaries are at last obtained; with these and a small British army, many of whose regiments consist entirely of recruits some of whom are of the worst description—for I have been told that even the prisons have been ransacked to augment their numbers—is this country to engage a nation who are enthusiastic in their case, have no hopes but in success, are united in every tie, have every stimulative to courage that shame or ambition can give an army of brothers?' Machiavelli never put the advantages of a citizen army so well. 'The mercenaries we employ,' continued the Duke, 'for they may be justly called so since that man must be deemed a mercenary soldier who fights for pay in the cause in which he has no concern,[1] are a motley barrel of various nations who are yet in Germany, are yet to be conveyed across the Atlantic; some will perish on the way, some desert, but I will suppose the remnant landed on the American shore. Will conquest immediately follow? Impossible to expect it.'

The war, forecast the Duke, would become a 'war of detail, of partizans,' and one impossible to win.

Viscount Townshend disagreed: 'I know of no method so probable to ensure success to our operations as that now adopted by us. By it we procure an immediate supply of men—men trained to the use of arms and of course fit for immediate service. And I have no reason to doubt that the measures being pursued will put an end to the war in a single campaign.'[2]

The Duke of Grafton, the third duke to attack the Government in the debate, demanded angrily whether or not all the British forces in America would be 'under the absolute command of a foreign mercenary at the head of 12,000 hirelings.' On this point, which worried many other members of the House, Suffolk was for once able to give a reassuring answer. The Hessian generals would always be under the command of a British commander-in-chief.

The Earl of Shelburne stated official policy only to attack it. The policy, typical of any rich state that decides to employ mercenaries, was to keep the native population at home engaged

---
[1] Perhaps a better definition than Larousse's. See page 17.
[2] Every war has its pathetic optimists—almost invariably cabinet ministers and generals. Between the noble Duke and the noble Viscount history has judged.

in industry and agriculture and to employ foreigners to fight abroad. 'Is this, my Lords,' he asked, 'a language to be endured?' He pointed out that 'in the late war' trade and manufacture had been better than ever, even though a huge number of the population had been serving in the army. Lord Lyttelton, following him, was one of the few government supporters to speak; he attempted to steer away from the inflammatory topic of mercenaries to general grounds of policy—the need for firmness followed by generosity. In the mood of that debate such a diversion could not be successful.

Finally, Lord Camden made what was probably the best and most eloquent of all the fine speeches heard by the Lords that day. He attacked the treaties: 'To give this bargain the appearance of what it really is not, the whole is stuffed up with pompous expressions of alliance founded on reciprocal support and common interest, as if these petty states were really concerned in the event of the present contest between this country and America. Now, my Lords, I would appeal to any of your Lordships if the whole of the transaction be not a compound of the most solemn mockery and gross imposition that was ever attempted to be put on a house of parliament? Is there one of your lordships who does not perceive most clearly that the whole is a mere mercenary bargain for the hire of troops on one side and the sale of human blood on the other; and that the devoted wretches thus purchased for slaughter are mere mercenaries in the worst sense of the word . . . ? But, my Lords, even this measure, hazardous and impolitic as it is, is not what presses most forcibly on my mind in the context of this wanton, cruel and diabolical war.'

For the argument in favour of the treaties amounted to this: that men were not to be had within the Kingdom. If true, it proved that all England's boasted wealth and power were held under 'precarious tenure' dependent upon her 'worthy mercenary allies on the Continent.' This could not be so; if it were, it would be England's end as a sovereign state and a free people.

'The history of all ages and nations proves the fatal effects of calling in foreign auxiliaries, but more particularly mere mercenaries, to fight their battles. . . . I cannot better express my disapprobation of employing foreigners particularly to fight our domestic quarrels than by quoting the opinion of that great man, Sir Walter Raleigh. In his *History of the World* he says that they are "seditious unfaithful disobedient devourers and destroyers of all places and countries whither they are drawn as being held by no other bond than their own commodity." Yes, that which is most fearful among such hirelings is that they have often and in times of great necessity not only refused to fight in the defence of those who have entertained them but revolted to the contrary part, to the utter ruin of those princes and states who have entertained them!'

Despite the eloquence, the passion, the arguments, and the logic of the Opposition, the treaties were approved, by 242 votes to 88 in the Commons and by 79 to 24 in the Lords. Only in a Committee of Supply did Colonel Barré, a protégé of the young Whigs, manage to have a resolution passed: 'That an address be presented to his Majesty humbly to recommend that he will be graciously pleased to use his endeavour that such Foreign Troops as are now, or may hereafter be, employed in his service, be clothed with the manufacturers of Great Britain.' If not, Colonel Barré argued that he did not doubt that 'the sale of human blood would turn out as advantageous to the woollen manufacturers of Brunswick and Hesse, in the clothing branch, as it was already likely to become lucrative to their respective sovereigns.' Even this amendment, however, was only a dubious improvement in practice. British clothing contractors proved to be at least as unscrupulous as their Brunswick or Hesse rivals, and a furious general later accused the contractor who supplied the Brunswickers' boots of providing 'fine thin dancing pumps.'

These debates in Parliament have such a modern ring about them that only the superior eloquence, the finer turn of phrase, the more cultivated background of the speakers would distinguish them from any debates that might take place should a similar suggestion for the use of mercenaries to crush a rebellious colony be made in Parliament at the present time. There are the same evasive and optimistic replies from ministers; the same demands for information, the same prophecies that the end of the parliamentary system is at hand from the Opposition. The Commons tends to be practical and worried more about money than about principles; the level of debate and ideas in the Lords is far higher. But when the votes come to be counted, the Parliamentary system showed as many sheep then as it does now; all the most progressive arguments appear to have been on the side of the Opposition whose speeches indicate both how unpopular the war against the Americans and how repellent the idea of employing mercenaries were; yet practical reasons dictated, as always, the action of a pragmatic British government and the votes of their loyal and robot-like supporters.

It comes as something of an anticlimax to have to record that the German mercenaries were neither as effective in the field as the Government had hoped, nor as seditious, disloyal, and dangerous to employ as Lord Camden and his fellow peers had feared. The Americans found that the Germans behaved much the same as the British troops, and surprisingly few accusations of atrocities or looting were made throughout the course of the war. The truth appears to have been that the old unruly mercenaries of the lansquenet days had been organized into tight regimental units whose discipline was good but whose courage was limited by the general reasonableness of the time.

The first great shock to the British government came in the winter of 1776 when after a moderately successful summer campaign nearly 1,000 Hessians were outmanoeuvred by Washington and surrendered. 'All our hopes,' said Lord George Germaine, 'were blasted by the unhappy affair at Trenton.'

The news of the surrender stunned a Europe that had expected rapid and inevitable success from the British effort, backed as it was by these professional soldiers. Pleasure at the British discomfiture soon exceeded the initial surprise. 'Throughout Germany,' wrote Niebuhr, 'the news of the capture of German troops by Washington in 1776 excited universal joy.' Kant condemned the mercenary trade; Goethe expressed his disapproval of the Hessians; Schiller's poetry was influenced by the struggle for freedom in America; and Lessing, though employed by the Duke of Brunswick, wrote: 'How came Othello into the service of Venice? Had the Moor no country? Why did he hire out his own arm and blood to a foreign state?'

Public opinion thus being aroused and spreading quickly from the intellectuals to the rulers, the indefatigable Colonel Faucitt found his efforts to hire new and larger numbers of troops largely unsuccessful. 'If that Crown,' wrote Frederick the Great, 'would give me all the millions possible, I would not furnish it two small files of my troops to serve against the Colonies.' The Emperor agreed with the electors of Mentz and Treves to throw a slur on the system; that year free passage through those territories was no longer granted. The Prince-Bishop of Treves removed eighteen Hessians from the new recruits that were passing through the bishopric; at Coblentz, Metternich reclaimed his subjects and sheltered deserters. Of the new recruits from Brunswick, Faucitt wrote, 'I hardly remember to have ever seen such a parcel of miserable ill-looking fellows collected together.' Three thousand were expected from the Duke of Wurtemberg who had visited England in search of a contract, but he was unable to raise them. The Catholic princes of the Empire banded together to condemn the system. Charles Augustus of Saxe-Weimer, though only nineteen years old, refused an almost open offer for the use of some of his battalions. His secretary noted: 'Serenissimus himself posted the letter.'

In this unpropitious atmosphere Colonel Faucitt was reduced to buying reinforcements from the princes already committed (though the Landgrave of Hesse-Cassel, for instance, could only raise about a thousand more that season) and to turning to some of the less reputable rulers. The Prince of Waldech escorted a disarmed regiment with mounted Jägers to the embarkation port and thus managed to prevent deserters. The Margrave of Anspach-

Bayreuth did the same, but even so was himself summoned in haste to quell a mutiny in a vineyard and in Holland escorted the men on board ship in person, 'going through the ships with them,' as Sir Joseph Yorke notes, 'marking their beds, giving out every order which was recommended to him and seeing it executed, with but little assistance indeed from his own officers.'

The half-mad Prince of Anhalt-Zerbst was billeted with six hundred hounds and other princes of his family at Dessau when an overture was made to him, which he accepted. He wrote, 'At the first crack of the huntsman's whip or note of his hunting horn the dogs come together like troops at the beat of the drum, and they begin to run down the beasts of the forest; it would not be bad if we could run down the Americans like that.'

But from his exile in Holland, Mirabeau was already raising the wild cry of liberty: 'What new madness is this?' he protested. 'Alas miserable men, you burn down not the camp of an enemy but your own hopes! Germans! What brand do you suffer to be put on your foreheads?'

Some figures: nearly 30,000 mercenaries came over to fight in America of whom nearly 13,000 never returned. Only 548 were killed in battle though almost as many again died of wounds. The incredible total of over 6,000 died of diseases, natural causes, or accident and the remaining 5,000 deserted. Most of the deserters settled in with the German colonists already established in the thirteen colonies.[1]

Of the 30,000-odd, the Landgrave of Hesse-Cassel supplied nearly 17,000 men, the Duke of Brunswick a little over 5,700, the Prince of Waldech about 2,000, the Margrave of Anspach-Bayreuth about 2,350, and the Prince of Anhalt-Zerbst just under 2,000.

The mercenaries fought at Fort Washington, at Red Bush, and at Yorktown, in particular. A large number surrendered with Burgoyne at Saratoga Springs. They were supplemented by

---
[1] So much for clause XIII of the Treaty. (See Appendix II.)

various hordes of American Indian mercenaries whose help proved equally indecisive in the attempt to suppress the rebels and whose use was severely criticized in the Commons.

Let the final word remain with Lord Chatham, who made one of his last speeches in the Parliament opened by the King on November 20, 1777.

'My Lords,' he said, 'you cannot conquer America. In three campaigns we have done nothing and suffered much. You may swell every expense, accumulate every assistance you can buy or borrow, traffic and barter with every pitiful little German prince that sells and sends his subjects to the shambles of a foreign power. Your efforts are forever vain and impotent, doubly so from this mercenary aid on which you rely; for it irritates to an incurable resentment. If I were an American as I am an Englishman, while a foreign troop was in my country, I never would lay down my arms; never, never, never.'

6 The Myth of the Legion

March 9, 1831: Marshal Soult, Minister of War, signed a decree forming *'A Legion of foreigners to be known as the Foreign Legion for service outside France.'*

HAD THE FOREIGN LEGION not been invented, it would not have been necessary for it to exist. This is not true in the strict sense; there were reasons both historical and practical for the existence of a body of foreign mercenaries in the French army. But there were no reasons at all for the growth of the mythology of the Foreign Legion—unless indeed every myth is by a hidden law of nature invented to satisfy a subconscious need of the human race and must therefore inexorably be invented whether the human beings apparently concerned in its invention wish it or not. Perhaps France herself had to be invented to satisfy a subconscious need of the human race; barely any other explanation would suffice to explain the rashness of the human race in imposing upon itself so turbulent a myth as France. But that is another question—though not altogether.

There was no particular reason why the Foreign Legion should have become more distinguished than any other of the groups of foreign mercenaries which throughout its history had served in the French army. Indeed there was every reason why, at a time when the French felt themselves to be still the best soldiers in Europe, the foreign mercenaries in their army should be looked upon as the lowest of the low, as just extra manpower. Moreover, the idea of employing mercenaries was discredited; it had become even more repugnant after the volcanic nationalism of the French Revolution than it had been a decade earlier in the Europe of the enlightened despots. And yet the myth of the Foreign Legion gradually grew and swelled out of all proportion until no single military unit in the world—and there were many both more picturesque and more heroic—was as well known and as admired.

This was a counter-sense, almost a non-sense. The Legion, at least to start with, was not even of any particular military importance or value. The French government at the time needed extra manpower, and the Legion began as a corps of second-rate infantry, its soldiers despised, as mercenaries at that time were despised. In England the King's German Legion was soon to be disbanded and at that no romantics shed a tear. But the Foreign Legion in some way was different; it is interesting to speculate why. Gradually the myth became the reality and the reality became the myth, until the Foreign Legion had a more real existence in the imagination than it did in cold fact. The myth established itself in the minds of millions of inhabitants of the globe, particularly at a certain period when it inspired and was inspired by a literary cult; more surprisingly it gripped the French too. Edith Piaf sang *Mon Légionnaire* with a catch in her voice and millions of Frenchwomen appeared to envy her the personal possessive pronoun. At the annual military parades in Paris on July 14 the greatest volume of cheers and applause invariably greeted the Legionnaires. And the myth produced the reality: portrayed as heroes in fiction, the legionnaires died heroically in fact. But the reality had also produced the myth.

Theoretically in modern times every man of good character is prepared to die for his nation, just as every man of good character was prepared to die for his lord in medieval times. But that a man should be prepared in an age of nationalism to die for another country, for a country to which he owed no duty, appeared paradoxical. The sentiment did not, in fact, occur in the general body of men and very rarely in the individual.

Nations, however, like women, inspire devotion in varying degrees. Foreigners who have in the course of history been prepared to die for England or Germany or Belgium or Sweden are few. Some have been ready to die for Greece, more for Spain, and quite a number for Ireland. But for no country have so many foreigners died so willingly and so joyfully as for France. The idea of France is a potent myth, intoxicating and heady. That Frenchmen should become inebriated with patriotic fervour appeared to their fellow countrymen as only natural; it had always been so. When the cry of '*Vive la République!*' was added to the cry '*Vive la France!*' the myth became even more powerful and the idea of dying for the myth even more tempting. But that foreigners should die for France in the same spirit appeared almost supernatural; it was as if a legend were consecrated by a reversal of the natural law, by a miracle, and the French recognized with awe that the idea of *la France* was potent even far beyond its geographical boundaries. Naturally they were flattered, and they esteemed these foreigners all the more because by the standards of patriotic nationalism, their behaviour was inexplicable. Adjutant-Chef Mader, in the First World War, killed his own countrymen on the Western front and became the most decorated NCO in the history of the Legion and a Chevalier of the Legion d'Honneur. By nationalistic standards this was treason to the Reich; by neo-feudal standards, to the Kaiser. But by semi-mythical standards it was fit homage paid to the overriding ideal of *la France*, the idea of a nation that while remaining itself inspired all mankind. Therefore France took her mercenaries to her heart.

Tears stood in my eyes and my voice broke as I concluded quoting:

> *'Soldats de la Légion,*
> *De la Légion Etrangère*
> *N'ayant pas de Nation*
> *La France est votre Mère.'*

The loyalty of these mercenaries was, like Caesar's wife, above suspicion. It was not a case of free companies nor even of Hessians. Like the Hessians, the legionaries may have been hired only for a few years, but the mark of the legionary, like the mark of the priest, was indelible. It was almost the soul of the legionary that was hired, and if France were a devil, the legionary would be a Faust.

> 'Then read this form and sign it,' he said with a distinct sigh. 'Remember, though, that as soon as you have done so, you will be a soldier of France, entirely amenable to martial law, and without any appeal whatsoever. Your friends cannot possibly buy you out, and your Consul cannot help you for five years. Nothing but death can remove you from the Legion.'

The Foreign Legion being a mercenary corps bound to its employers by loyalty to the myth of France, its mercenaries thus lose immediately one of the stigma that attach to mercenary troops. Their loyalty is—and was—almost above question, and as a professional soldier, the legionary satisfied that vague demand that public opinion imposes upon professional soldiers: loyalty over and above the mere minimal loyalty to an employer.

The other stigma, however, remains, at least in theory and in the marching songs of the Legion:

> *Tiens, voilà du boudin, voilà du boudin, voilà du boudin,*
> *Pour les Alsaciens, les Suisses et les Lorrains,*
> *Pour les Belges il n'y en a point*
> *Pour les Belges il n'y en a point*
> *Car ce sont des tireurs au flame.*

Boudin: blood sausage, the Legion's traditional festive dish. But butin: booty, would perhaps be more appropriate in sense and no less appropriate in rhythm, for loot is the traditional motive of the mercenary; and the idea, though more of an aspiration than a practice, links the Legion with mercenary tradition.

It is not the only link. There is a surprising continuity in mercenary history. Just as the Hessians can be traced back to the lansquenet, so the Foreign Legion can be traced back to the peasants of the Waldstätte; for the Swiss regiments, after the interlude of the revolutionary period, had come back into French service with the restoration in 1814. Four Swiss Regiments of the Line, two Regiments of Swiss Guards (and one German—the Hohenlohe Regiment) were incorporated in the revived Bourbon army. However, they were disbanded in January, 1830, the year of political upheavals in France. The July Revolution put Louis-Philippe on the throne; next year the Legion was formed.

At first it was organized into seven national battalions: the 1st, 2nd and 3rd were German, their officers and NCO's mainly Swiss; the 4th was Spanish; the 5th Italian; the 6th Belgian and Dutch; the 7th Polish. Their first commander was a veteran Swiss officer, Colonel Stoffel, and the battalions, as soon as they were formed, were sent to Algeria. France's first colonial venture of the modern era had begun the preceding year with the landings at Sidi Ferruch. There began the long connection of the Legion with its 'home,' Sidi-bel-Abbès, and with the Sahara—the visual picture that the word legionary still calls to most minds.

> Life at Zinderneuf was not really life so much as the avoidance of death—death from sun-stroke, heat-stroke, monotony, madness or Adjudant Lejeune.
>
> *Cafard* was rampant; everyone was more or less abnormal and 'queer' from frayed nerves, resultant upon the terrific heat and the monotony, hardship and confinement to a little mud oven of a fort; many men were a little mad, and Adjudant Lejeune, in the hollow of whose hands were our lives and destinies, was a great deal more than a little mad.

A tradition had begun, but the Foreign Legion had not particularly distinguished itself. It was the next campaign, in which the Legion fought under the command of French rather than mercenary officers, which was decisive for its reputation.

In June, 1835, Louis-Philippe decided to hire the Legion out to the legal government of Spain and to its head Queen Cristina.

The first Carlist War—first of a long series of Spanish civil wars—aroused as much passion in Europe as the last civil war did in its time. As always in Spain, ideologies rather than interests were in conflict. The Carlists were—still are—reactionaries of a special sort; the Cristinos, as the legitimists were called, passed for liberals. The war, fought over the north and northeast of Spain, was vicious, epic, and ill organized. France and Britain supported the liberals rather more effectively than in the last civil war. The Cristinos were aided not only by the French Foreign Legion but by a semi-official body of British mercenaries, the British Auxiliary Legion, raised and led by a liberal Member of Parliament, Sir de Lacy Evans. These British mercenaries proved to be militarily almost useless, politically embarrassing, contributed little and gradually disbanded themselves. But the French Foreign Legion virtually won the war for Queen Cristina. Don Carlos, the rival Pretender, had in his turn raised a Carlist foreign legion; at the battle of Barbastro in June, 1837, the rival foreign legions almost obliterated each other while the Spaniards on both sides paused to look on. Five thousand legionaries had come to Spain; 875 fought at Barbastro; of these 160 survived the battle. This was the last great battle of rival mercenary armies, equal in its ferocity if not its scale to those of the landsknecht and the Swiss.

Here, properly, began the mythology of the Legion, created by its original commander in Spain, Colonel Bernelle. First the ingredients had to be restirred: if national regiments were retained, national pride would subsist—at the expense of France. Bernelle mixed the nationalities by forming thoroughly heterogeneous battalions—the first and last time that this has ever been persistently done in mercenary history. The experiment succeeded: when Marshal Lyautey asked a soldier at an inspection in Morocco what his nationality was, the man replied, 'Légionnaire, mon

Général.' It was at this time, too, that the tradition started that a recruit's past and correct name were no concern of the Legion's. No other single rule in any army has ever become so famous and so successful: the past is so encumbering both in its misdeeds and its loyalties that many dreamed of joining the Legion who would never have done so in practice. Bernelle also added those touches of eccentricity that marked the Legion as different: he formed the platoons of bearded sappers that always lead the Legion parades. Above all he instituted the system of ferocious discipline that has always been the mark of the Legion.

> ... Colour Sergeant Lejaune,[1] a terrible and terrifying man, who had made his way in the Legion (and who made it further still) by distinguishing himself as a relentlessly harsh and meticulous disciplinarian, a savagely violent taskmaster, and a pushing non-com of tremendous ability, energy and courage ... ; at times he was undoubtedly mad, and his madness took the form of sadistic savagery.

Bernelle's successor in Spain, Colonel Conrad, stamped the Legion with its other distinctive marks. He was a Frenchman who prided himself on that unusual accomplishment among the French, an ability to speak many languages; he was known to the German legionaries as '*der alte Fritz.*' As a commander, he had the reputation of knowing only one word of command—'Charge!' He died, suitably, at Barbastro leading a bayonet attack. From his period in command sprang the reputation of the Legion for military *élan*.

> With 100 rounds of ammunition in our pockets, joy in our hearts and a terrific load upon our backs, we swung out of the gates to the music of our magnificent band, playing the March of the Legion, never heard save when the Legion goes on active service.

---

[1] Lejaune had been a sergeant in the Belgian army and a Congo rubber-station overseer, but 'his brutalities and atrocities there had been too much even for good King Leopold's merry men!'

Captain Danjou had a wooden arm; on such details myths are built. The Legion was in Mexico. On April 30, 1864, Captain Danjou, commanding a detachment of the Legion fifty-nine strong, was surrounded at a farmhouse in the hamlet of Camerone by thousands of Mexican troops. From early morning until dusk the legionaries resisted all assaults and contemptuously rejected all summons to surrender. All the officers and most of the men were killed; those who fell prisoner were severely wounded. The Emperor Napoleon III erected a memorial stone on the site:

> Ils furent ici moins de soixante
> Opposés à toute une armée
> Sa masse les écrasa
> La vie plutôt que le courage
> Abandonna ces soldats français.

The rescue column arrived too late. But its commander detached Captain Danjou's wooden arm from his body and it was taken to the Salle d'Honneur in Sidi-bel-Abbès. There, on Camerone day, the great annual feast of the Legion, it was carried onto the parade ground and 'took the salute'; to the parading legionaries an account of the battle was read by the most decorated officer present.

Camerone became the epic of the Legion. At Dien Bien Phu in 1954 legionaries noted in their diaries the gloom of a Camerone day spent without the traditional wine and blood sausages. At Bukavu in 1967 on the day of the final assault one of Schramme's mercenary captains asked: *'Qu'est-ce que je pouvais faire avec cinq gars contre la bande qui nous encerclait? Qu'est-ce que je pouvais faire? Camerone?'*

At Bukavu the mercenaries retreated. At Dien Bien Phu, where five out of the original twelve infantry battalions were legionaries, a final sortie, bayonets fixed—a Legion tradition known as the *baroud d'honneur*—was attempted. When the war ended at the Geneva conference that year, over ten thousand legionaries had died in French Indo-China in eight years of war. Dien Bien Phu was a Camerone on a large scale, with a less glorious ending.

Here he sat on a log and absolutely thrilled us to the marrow of our bones by tales, most graphically and realistically told, of the Spahis, the French Foreign Legion, the Chasseurs d'Afrique, Zouaves, Turcos and other romantically named regiments.

'I'm going to join the French Foreign Legion when I leave Eton,' announced Michael suddenly.

'So am I,' said Digby of course.

'And I,' I agreed.

The end of every war in Europe brought new recruits to the Legion, particularly from among the conquered. Thus the original proportion of Germans (who formed three of the first seven battalions) remained almost consistent: there have always been more Germans than any other nationality in the Legion. But political upheavals too caused jumps in recruitment—the Russian Revolution of 1918 was followed by a period when many of the Legion's officers were members of the Russian nobility. A recruit who had been an officer in another army and could prove it began at the rank of corporal rather than as a simple *Légionnaire Deuxième Classe;* the rise to the rank of officer was long and difficult but it could be accomplished: Colonel Prince Amilakvari, a Georgian, commanded the famous 13th Demi-Brigade, the one regiment of the Legion which rallied to de Gaulle and Free France in the Second World War. He was probably by then a French citizen, for a legionary has the right after five years' service to be naturalized as a French citizen.

The Legion had its heroes; it had its piquant character, its admiring enemies, its minor deities; but no gods or heroes reach their full mythological stature until they are sung. The Olympians would be almost uninteresting without a Homer; the Gods of Valhalla without the Eddas; the Legion without P. C. Wren.

Beau Geste was published in 1920; since then, in British editions alone, it has sold roughly 1,700,000 copies. Any number of films, serials, and comic strips have been based directly or indirectly on that silent fort at Zinderneuf manned by a company of dead legionaries, every man carefully propped up with his rifle at the firing position. *Beau Geste* was the first of a trilogy; it was followed by *Beau Sabreur, Beau Ideal*, several other novels and collections of Legion short stories by Wren, and a whole host more by his imitators.

Glamour and brutality are the common stuff of romantic novelists. It is, as always, the realism of the details that establishes the myth: the 'dirty little' *Bureau de Recrutement: Engagements Volontaires* in the Rue Sainte-Dominique in Paris; the description of the unvarying food—*soupe*, served twice a day in tin basins called *gamelles*, no knives and forks, with unsweetened milkless coffee from a pail. The daily training routine—05.15 reveille, 05.30 the recruit, the *bleu*—parades in white uniform, knapsack, rifle, belt, and bayonets, ready for the incredibly long route marches at the unvarying pace of five kilometres an hour. The continual talk of desertion—*faire la promenade;* the absolute power of the NCO's. The moral rules of the Legion: 'Theft in that collection of the poorest of poor men was the ultimate crime, infinitely worse than murder,' and punished according to 'Legion law' by a bayonet through each hand.

The heroes may be dated and conventional, in keeping with the correct idea at the time of Englishmen, Americans, women, and others, but the villains and their language ring true still.

> 'Cré bon sang de bon Dieu de Dieu de sort,' swore Lejaune, 'and I'll deal with you after this *chien d'une revolte* ... If you don't both die en crapaudine, by God, you shall live en crapaudine.'

Wren had been a legionary, and he had a power of description, a mastery of slang, and a touch for the ingenious plot almost equal to that of Kipling. The French authorities publicly denounced his books, furious at the powerful myth of sadistic NCO's and barely tolerable conditions. He clothed the bones of the myth in flesh and added the necessary feet of clay to the near superhuman. Mythical heroes are never so popular as when they are portrayed heroic indeed at a crisis but banal at all other times; the Legion became a world-wide symbol of romance, with just enough vestige of the old anarchic mercenary tradition to season the monstrous brutality of those years of imperialist conquest and inevitably successful colonial wars. Curiously enough, it is this same anarchic tradition to which Larteguy has returned in his best-selling novels about the modern French *paras*, whom he is continually referring to and comparing with mercenaries or (in his purpler patches) to condottieri. Larteguy is, for the French, an up-to-date P. C. Wren, spicing his colder brutality and darker glamour with sex and politics, but for all that less of a realist and less successful as a myth-maker. Both these popular novelists, however, have one very important point in common: they both treat of a section of an army, and in both cases that army is the army of France.

Why was it that other mercenary forces never became as popular and as well known as the French Foreign Legion? The British had their King's German Legion; it was hardly known. The Spaniards still have their Foreign Legion; mythologically speaking, it does not exist. Other European countries had their brigades of native or mercenary troops; these troops, too, probably had their heroic last stands, but obscurity enfolds them. The Gurkhas certainly have served if not England at least the King-Emperor with as much devotion and more heroism, but the attempt to create a myth around them, noticeably by John Masters, has been only half successful.

It is perhaps this question of armies. The French army is different from the other armies of the West; it has always been marked by a different spirit. It is not a question of military glory or efficiency. It is not a question, either, of militarism, in the South American or neo-African sense; the army of France has never been just a passive tool to be used by a military dictator. The French army has known ignominious defeats by the side of its great victories, although even Dien Bien Phu, like Waterloo, was a triumph of a sort. The French army has managed to keep, for centuries, a different sort of spirit from other armies. This spirit is semi-feudal: orders are generally but not necessarily obeyed and the criterion at a grave moment of crisis is honour—

what de Vigny describes as *la conscience exaltée*. French officers (and even soldiers) are not the blind automata of a German army obeying the High Command, the Kaiser, the Führer, or of a British army obeying the civil power. Yet they have never, not even in defeat, lapsed into the lethargic inefficiency of certain other European armies whose discipline is equally irregular.

They have preserved that quality which Cyrano de Bergerac preserved to the last: their *panache*. There is and always has been a kind of anarchy of spirit about the French army which has kept it closer than any other army in Europe to the feudal array—bold, rash, efficient, but independent-minded soldiers. In that way the Foreign Legion is typical: the anarchic tradition is combined with military virtue in war and with loyalty both to an idea and to the direct commander but not to a political leader.¹ The French army has always remained mercenary in spirit; that is to say, it has remained sceptical and independent. In that sense Larteguy's paratroopers have replaced Wren's legionaries as the new type of mercenaries whom the state, their employer, will one day have to destroy.

---

¹ The 1ᵉʳ Regiment Etranger Parachutiste was solemnly disbanded in 1961 on the orders of the Army Minister, Messmer, for the leading part it had played in the anti-Gaullist Generals' *putsch* of April 25. The regiment had occupied Algiers, following without question the orders of its acting commander Elie de Saint-Marc, who was later court-martialled. The year before its then colonel, Henri Dufour, had been condemned to three months' close arrest for insubordination.

This regiment had had a short but extraordinarily dramatic history. Shortly after the end of the War, in 1948 and 1949, two Legion paratroop battalions were formed, despite fears—later to prove justified—that they might come to consider themselves an élite within an élite. The 1ᵉʳ REP was wiped out at Cao Bang in 1950 (90 per cent losses including the commanding officer). Disbanded, it was reformed in March 1951 only to be wiped out again at Dien Bien Phu in 1954 (576 killed out of 700—of the French troops at Dien Bien Phu only one in five was a native-born Frenchman). Reformed again, the regiment took part in the Suez expedition before being posted to Algeria—where, on May 7, 1958, its commanding officer was killed in action. In 1960 the 'Battle of Algiers' was won for the French by the 1ᵉʳ REP; in 1961 the regiment was ignominiously expunged.

The 2ᵉ REP has had a rather less dramatic history, though it too fought at Dien Bie Phu. However, at the moment of writing (late 1969), the last paragraph of this chapter no longer applies: the 2ᵉ REP is back in the traditional décor, in the Saharan desert of Chad. (Incidentally, on the other side of the Sahara the Spanish Foreign Legion, 20,000 strong, is based, as always, at El Aiun). Just as Louis Philippe sent the Legion to help Queen Cristina against the rebel Carlists in Spain, so, over a century and a quarter later, General de Gaulle has sent the Legion to help President Tombalbaye against the Muslim rebels of Chad. This secretive war, unpopular both in France and (apparently) with the Legion, is beginning to attract attention. It is a bizarre example of history repeating itself.

The old mercenaries are fading away, for Wren's setting, that picture of the fort at Zinderneuf, was right. A Legion of sorts still exists; it is based in Corsica. Its Salle d'Honneur has been transferred from Sidi-bel-Abbès to Provence. It is as if the gods of Olympus had taken refuge in the Massif Central.

For myths cannot be exploded like old mines, or discarded like old clothes. But, like old soldiers, they can fade away. The Foreign Legion was a period piece, a drama played out before the world in a traditional décor. But the décor no longer exists.

7 World Opinion and Twentieth Century Mercenaries

'C'est la faute des journalistes si nous sommes si mal vus dans le monde.'—Lt Gouhaux, a mercenary officer, as quoted in *Le Figaro*

IT CAME AS A SHOCK when mercenaries suddenly reappeared in the Congo in 1960. The word itself had fallen out of use, and the idea appeared utterly anachronistic, distastefully medieval. For the world had become used to conflicts of ideologies fought between nation states; the mercenaries who still existed were disciplined troops incorporated in national armies and never referred to by that term. 'Military advisers' was another category —officers and NCO's lent by a government for political reasons to advise and occasionally to lead the armies of underdeveloped countries. These were mainly seconded officers; even when (as in the case of Glubb Pasha, commander of Jordan's Arab Legion) they retained no official ties with their army of origin, it was an understood thing that their basic loyalty was still to their nation of origin. These 'military advisers' were admissible and admitted. But 'mercenaries,' 'adventurers,' 'soldiers of fortune'—public opinion, shocked as always by the unusual and the unexpected and resolutely progressive at that stage of African history, turned against them from the first. There was little attempt to take a detached view and to see in their apparition a historical phenomenon reviving. Furthermore, in the confusion of the Congo, in that early medley, villains and heroes were needed, both by politicians and the public. The heroes tended to change (or to die) with confusing speed. But the faceless villains were successfully found: the mercenaries and, behind them, the sinister capitalists of Katanga, the Union Minière.

Later the trend was to be reversed. The time was to come when the mercenaries, no longer faceless, became cult heroes of a sort; the halo of respectability floated vaguely around their heads, and the rite of beatitude was finally conferred seven years later when a mercenary leader, Hoare, signed a leader-page article in *The Times* (London) calling, with solemnity, on the British government to take steps to halt the Biafra war. But in the early days, the Katanga days, this was inconceivable. It was well known that the mercenaries were a handful of paid killers drawn from the gutters of Europe and it was felt in a vague but passionate way that by exterminating them the United Nations would be doing the world a service and probably clearing up the Congo mess as well. The United Nations itself and the Security Council followed rather than led public opinion. The tone of their debates and resolutions suggested that wise men of every complexion agreed that once the Congo was rid of its serpent, the mercenary plague, it would become again that Garden of Eden for which nature had so obviously designed it. It may be that when a situation is too complex, men, even wise men, refuse to admit that nothing can be done except by time and they fasten on a tangible part of the problem in preference to the intangible whole. At any rate, the Security Council passed resolutions condemning the separation of Katanga 'caused by the lawless acts of mercenaries,' and the Afro-Asian press fulminated.

The reactions of the Western press, however, were more ambivalent. Many journalists instinctively recognized the framework for a new myth. Perhaps the West was tired of over-organization and had a longing for the sweet pleasures of anarchy;

perhaps people recognized that war was chaos, particularly in the Congo; perhaps they even believed, remembering the past, that rationalization in war is far more frightening than the chaotic. In any case a line was invented, adopted, and generally followed: the mercenaries were paid killers, yes, and in general bad and to be condemned; at the same time they were interesting psychological studies and so worth writing about. The popular press, for its part, found that they were irresistibly photogenic; the larger and more colourful the picture, the shriller grew the accompanying text. There was a period when it was hardly possible to open a Western magazine without coming across technicolor photographs on the theme, backed by technicolor prose.

The attitude varied, of course, from country to country, and inside countries from newspaper to newspaper. Gradually a new tendency took shape, led perhaps by *Le Figaro* in France and *The Daily Telegraph* in England. This line was: paid killers, yes, but almost despite themselves defenders of Western civilization and values. The colour issue complicated the question: the mercenaries were white and superior as fighters to their enemies; their enemies, however, were mainly black. Praise of the mercenaries, then, appeared to be racist; contempt for the mercenaries as people—it soon became impossible to despise them as soldiers—was a sign of liberalism. The lines were drawn, and both sides sharpened their adjectives.

'They are the world's last soldiers of fortune, outdated relics of the past. They are outcasts from the modern world which expelled them or from which they fled—on the lam from an infamous past, a burnt-out adventure, a dead faith. They are all ex-something[1]: ex-SS officers from Germany, ex-CIA pilots from Cuba, ex-students from South Africa and Southern Rhodesia. Some follow a macabre ideal of glory and adventure; some believe they are fighting a last-ditch battle against communism; some are known as Les Affreux, the Horrors, who just love war.'

Probably the purple prosodists of this sort came out best. The

---
[1] It would have been somewhat surprising if they had been ex-nothing.—A.M.

deadpan reporting of the pro-mercenary press with its careful attribution of 'Colonels,' 'Majors,' and all the correct military titles to the mercenary leaders and with its factual front-line accounts of tactics and strategy as though from the Western Desert never rang very true. The sophisticated and would-be impartial drawing-room style—'Old Harrovian Alastair Wicks added a touch of elegance to often bloody proceedings'—seemed equally out of place. On the other side moral indignation was the note most often struck: the mercenaries' military achievements were minimized; a nasty touch of gloating emphasized their difficulties, defeats, or deaths; and the utter depravity of their character and actions was constantly kept before the public's eye. The inevitable ravings of African leaders and newspapers—'human vermin,' 'ignoble mercenaries,' 'gangsters in the service of Western imperialist capitalism'—graded away to such comments as that of the *Guardian* (under the heading 'No Orchids for Colonel Schramme'): 'The Mercenaries are being ignominiously stripped of what spurious glamour they used to have. . . . Their plight will cause relief far beyond the Congo—for mercenaries have become a symbol of chaos and of neo-colonialist meddling, wherever trouble brews in Africa.' And, a few days earlier: 'Mercenaries are a double bogy in Africa. Like vultures, they hover where trouble brews.' Occasionally, however, even the ranks of Tuscany. . . . A long article on the situation in the Congo at the end of 1964 by a *Guardian* correspondent was headed 'Fanfare for an Army of Mercenaries.'

On television the mercenaries invariably came out well, if only because their enemies always appeared to be fleeing in the opposite direction when direct action sequences were shown. In television interviews, neither their hands nor their consciences appeared particularly bloodstained. *Le Monde*, praising a programme about them under the heading '*A la Gloire des Mercenaires*' asked whether it was necessary to present them as '*de sympatiques héros menant un juste combat.*' But in fact, visually, it would have been difficult to present them in any other way.

One particular interview caused a stir of sorts in England. In it Hoare recounted how as a matter of discipline he had once shot the big toes off a mercenary guilty of an atrocity; the man was a professional footballer and the punishment therefore severe. To many this punishment seemed in itself an atrocity, and it was particularly repugnant to two regular British army officers who confronted Hoare in a later television programme. One of them, Brigadier Peter Young, described the act as 'orthopaedically unjustifiable', but their main objection to Hoare, very interestingly, appeared to be not that he had served in a foreign army[1] but that he had not stuck to the British military code of behaviour and justice. After this, those newspaper critics who noticed the programme all more or less agreed that no one who had seen it could retain the slightest respect for mercenaries. However, the letters which the programme producer received afterward were all without exception from men who wanted to know how they could join the mercenaries.

This is more than just a symptomatic detail. The opinion of the general public in the West never really accepted the moral condemnation of the mercenaries by the leaders of opinion. At first, admittedly the general public was shocked, disgusted, and ready to believe the worst; when the mercenaries were fighting the United Nations in Katanga there was no general sympathy for them at all except in France and to some extent in Belgium. It was their second flourishing, during the Simba war, that led to feelings of uneasy admiration, for there were a handful of white mercenaries routing thousands of black savages and rescuing white missionaries from appalling tortures. The admiration remained uneasy because the whole situation seemed a hundred years out of date. After all, 1960 had been the *annus mirabilis* of Africa, marking almost the end of British, French, and Belgian colonial rule in black Africa, with all the euphoria of a fresh start for a new continent. But people became confused by the Congo, not merely by the actual political situation (though that was confusing enough) but by its implications: that chaos, savagery,

---

[1] Brigadier Young had been in the Arab Legion. The other officer, General Alexander, had commanded Nkrumah's army. The pots could hardly call the kettle black.

and tribalism lay just below the surface and that the former colonial masters had not really succeeded in imposing their ideas and manners on these well-dressed, well-spoken, new African leaders. To understand was too great an effort, and so the mercenaries became the projection of an instinct, the rather guilty instinct of white superiority and unity.

In Rhodesia and South Africa, naturally enough, the feeling of guilt was absent. There the Congo massacres of Belgian settlers in 1960 and the victory of the white mercenaries in 1964 merely reinforced existing ideas: viz, that the munts had just come down from the trees and that one white man was worth a hundred kaffirs. On the other hand, people saw the mercenaries at close range; they knew that many of them were on the verge of the criminal classes or else often young louts of the 'poor white' class. Occasionally a returned mercenary would be arrested; now and again there was a scandal, once a murder, in which returned mercenaries were involved. The two governments tolerated them but always with reserve, for in the closely organized white communities of those parts the mercenaries were an uncontrollable element and could not be allowed to assume too much moral or material importance. Almost instinctively the ranks of the white middle classes—the mass of society—closed against them.

In the rest of the white world, however, the cliché took over as the mercenaries became personally better known and the names of Hoare, Schramme, and Denard, of Faulques, Wicks, Peters, and Mueller, replaced the confusion of Umbus and Ubus in the popular mind. Accordingly the mercenaries were defined. The French were fierce but malevolent; any French mercenary by definition had been with the OAS[1] and was involved in tortuous political intrigue. The Englishman was an officer and a gentleman, slightly distorted; the South African an illiterate tough there for the pleasure of killing kaffirs; the German a sinister former SS officer. The Belgian was less defined but was held to

---

[1] Organisation de l'Armée Secrete, the anti-Gaullist terrorist movement in Algeria.

be generally despised by his fellow mercenaries. To add colour, the odd Pole or central European, usually minus teeth and invariably drunk, was thrown in.

In time this hotchpotch of characters overflowed from the magazine article and the television programme into the novel and the film. They featured in a gargantuan intellectual monstrosity, an excursion into fiction by a Quondam Fellow of All Souls, Oxford, entitled *The Decline of the West*. Jean Larteguy took Colonel Trinquier's misadventures in Katanga as the basis for yet another book glorifying the French military tradition (and incidentally, rancorous enough toward the Belgians), *Les Chimères Noires*. A very shoddy novel, *The Mercenaries*, published in South Africa and written by a Rhodesian, Wilbur Smith became the basis of a rather good film. It dealt with the first mercenary venture, the Baluba war, and under the title *Le Dernier Train du Katanga* the film had a great success in Europe, though less so in the Anglo-Saxon countries. Claude Lelouch's *Vivre pour Vivre* was the first French film in which mercenaries appeared momentarily—an excuse for romantic pastiche with the usual hint of moral superiority. It was becoming almost a rule that any film of any pretensions on Africa should have at least one sequence showing white mercenaries.

Clichés are the blurred image of truth. The stock characters existed, or almost existed, but very few were as two-dimensional as they were portrayed to be. To take one example, the former SS officer was a cliché produced by the photographers and invented by the writers. It started with one of the mercenary officers of Five Commando, Siegfried Mueller, who insisted on wearing an Iron Cross (which he had won on the Russian front, with the Wehrmacht SS) at all times; he was even rumoured to wear it with his pyjamas. A few photographs were all that were needed to start that particular myth. In fact, Mueller, so far from being a sadistic former war criminal on the run, was part showman and part intellectual. He was not a particularly good soldier but he was a decent enough man. Attached to the English-speaking mercenaries, he was treated with a certain affection in which a note of mockery was discernible.[1] The French, on the other hand, seemed to run truer to type; a lot of them had been involved with the OAS in Algeria and those who had not liked to give the impression of slightly murky pasts. But they were not all good fighters by any means. The English-speaking mercenaries despised their French-speaking companions as an inefficient and disorderly crowd; Hoare, in his article in *The Times*, wrote that he[1] was convinced that a small well-led force of white soldiers could sway the war in Biafra but that they must be the 'ghurka type, not *les affreux* such as have been making a spectacle of themselves recently in Bukavu and Katanga.' The French speakers for their part played down the role of the English-speaking mercenaries whom they implied to be hopelessly naïve politically. It was extremely curious to see how the English-speaking press and the French-speaking press both exaggerated, whether in praise or blame, the importance of their own compatriots.

Surprisingly, all the novels, major and minor, that had appeared by 1969 were limited to the Katanga period. No fiction writer had yet taken as his background the Simba war or the rebellion of the French-speaking mercenaries. On the other hand, a series of chronicles had appeared, written largely during one or the other of these two episodes and so naturally tending to be pro-mercenary and biased. Rather more interesting were the 'memoirs' written by former mercenaries: Siegfried Mueller wrote (or had written) a very windy account of his life, philosophy, and Congo adventures including an apologia for the incident that ruined his military reputation in the Congo—an ambush of a convoy he was leading at Bafwasende. Dr Hans Germani, a writer who joined the mercenaries as their doctor for a period, wrote a far more entertaining and informative book, unfortunately published only in South Africa and Germany, entitled *White Soldiers in Black Africa*.

Hoare and Schramme have so far been the only mercenary leaders to write their own accounts. Hoare's *Congo Mercenary* is

---
[1] Having shared a villa with Siegfried Mueller in Stanleyville, the author came to know him quite well.

a simple chronicle of the military campaigns of Five Commando; it is accurate as far as it goes but studiously avoids the awkward and interesting questions of motive, ambitions and concealed pressures. It is a disappointing book, almost an exercise in whitewashing, in the sense that it gives an impression of the Congo as being just a gigantic playground for *Boys' Own* heroes. Schramme's *Le Bataillon Léopard* is an annoyingly ridiculous fanfaronade, bombastic and inaccurate, stuffed with extraordinary claims, unanswered questions, and just enough information to infuriate.

It is a great pity that neither of these men could bring themselves to write a critical self-appraisal and a full account of the facts; for, in a purely historical sense, their achievements have been far from negligible. It is to be hoped that someday they will bring to light that valuable source material which alone will prove how far foreign governments or international business were involved in the whole affair. Denard's memoirs could, when they finally come out, be the most fascinating of all—but 'confessions' would probably be a more suitable title for the genre than 'memoirs'.

On the other hand, it is natural enough that mercenaries writing about the recent past should be discreet; the arrest of Schramme in June, 1968, shortly after his return to Belgium, on the charge of having murdered a fellow Belgian in the Congo a year earlier showed how dangerous it could be for anything like the whole truth to leak out.

Schramme was arrested under a Belgian law that makes the murder of a Belgian citizen by *another Belgian citizen* a crime over which the Belgian courts have jurisdiction, whatever the part of the world in which the alleged crime may have been committed. There is an article in the Italian criminal code which by contrast makes the murder of any other human being of whatever nationality wherever it may take place, by an Italian citizen a crime over which the Italian courts have jurisdiction. The most notorious *cause célèbre* indirectly connected with the mercenaries arose from this article.

Jacopetti was an Italian film director who made his name and fortune in the late fifties by producing a film called *Mondo Cane*—

scenes from all over the world, apparently genuine, showing man's cruelty to man and such gruesome national habits as the Japanese practice of chopping off fingers to be used as charms. The film had an immense success all over the world, and after a sequel to it Jacopetti decided to set off in a slightly new direction by making a film on independent black Africa. It was to be entitled *Africa Addio;* its theme was to be savagery, the more photogenic the better; and the director and his camera crew filmed massacres of Arabs in Zanzibar, of Watutsi in Rwanda, of elephants in the game parks, and of standards in Kenya. Clearly they could not avoid the Congo, particularly as the Congolese were famed and loathed in Italy for the killing and eating at Kindu in 1961 of thirteen Italian civil airmen who had been lent to the United Nations force.

Possibly Jacopetti therefore imagined that no cruelties inflicted on the Congolese could possibly outrage the Italian public. But at the same time as he was in the Congo, there arrived a special correspondent sent out by the left-wing Italian intellectual review *L'Espresso;* his name was Piero Gregoretti, and on his return to Italy he wrote a series of articles in one of which he accused Jacopetti of having arranged the shooting of two Simba boys by the mercenaries especially for his film.

Gregoretti's article created an enormous scandal in Italy. Jacopetti denied the allegation; Gregoretti repeated it. The issue, inevitably in Italy, quickly became political. The Communists and Socialists called for an inquiry and the public prosecutor announced that Jacopetti would be tried for alleged homicide under the article in the criminal code mentioned above. Justice was no speedier in Italy than anywhere else, and the film was out before the initial inquiry was completed. *Africa Addio,* beautifully photographed but horribly one-sided, roused a furore all over the world; wherever it was shown, African embassies protested, and in some countries left-wing demonstrators broke up the theatre. It won the Golden Lion at the film festival in Palermo, traditionally presented by the Italian Minister of Culture, who, however, refused to do so at the last minute on the grounds that he could have nothing to do with so racist a film. The mercenaries in the film were presented as cold-blooded but efficient, degraded but not nearly so degraded as their African allies or enemies.

The moral of this story is difficult to draw; perhaps the only conclusion is that film-makers are fanatically devoted to their films. It promised to be a sensational trial but at the last moment Jacopetti admitted that the incident of the boys being shot had been staged with actors and was not really a documentary excerpt. He had risked very serious charges and penalties before he was finally forced to admit this—an admission, of course, which took the wind out of his opponents' sails but completely destroyed the value of *Africa Addio* as a document. Jacopetti had again and again claimed that it was all true, none of it staged; after this admission, nobody was likely to believe him or to take the film seriously. But by that time it had already been launched.

All this immense publicity of and about the mercenaries led to a curious but significant episode in May, 1968. This was the month, as all the world knows, when the students of Paris occupied the Sorbonne, with all the repercussions that followed. Toward the end of the occupation the rumour got about that a group of former mercenaries calling themselves *les Katangais*— 'the Katangese'—had installed themselves in part of the Sorbonne and were trying to take over its running from the student organizations. It appeared that the 'Katangese' had, during the barricades, acted as shock troops on the side of the students against the police and that they were a bunch of unsavoury desperadoes. By the beginning of June the students had almost lost all popular support and the French government was obviously encouraging press and news reports of these 'Katangese' in order to give themselves an excuse for reoccupying the Sorbonne with the CRS, the riot police.[1] However, the students anticipated them and in what the French papers described as a 'pitched battle'

---

[1] The story also produced bizarre side effects. The Congolese Ambassador in Paris protested solemnly against this misuse of the name of the inhabitants of a peaceful Congolese province.

threw the 'Katangese' out themselves. The band dispersed, and a series of robberies and the murder of 'Jimmy' their leader by some of his companions far outside Paris eventually brought out the truth: the 'Katangese' consisted of a band of young thugs aged between eighteen and twenty-five, plus their girlfriends, who had helped the students against the police and then attempted to give themselves an importance which they did not merit. The only 'ex-mercenary' of any description was a twenty-two-year-old Italian who had deserted from the Foreign Legion.

The significance of this comparatively minor episode was that these young thugs should themselves have chosen the title of 'Katangese' and boasted of being former mercenaries and also that the press should have used this ridiculous boast as a way of frightening public opinion. It implies that by 1968 'mercenaries' were recognized almost as a class in Europe and that in a situation of disorder and confusion it was feared by some and hoped by others—but in any case came as no surprise—to learn that 'ex-mercenaries' had taken charge and, inevitably, on the side of the revolutionaries against the existing government. Once again a historical phenomenon was reappearing: the Black Prince had known difficulties with former free companions, the Swiss cantons with their own cantonal former mercenaries. Public opinion, which had concentrated on the role of mercenaries as fighters abroad, began for the first time to notice the role of former mercenaries as a novel, minor, but preoccupying class in their countries of origin.

8 What the Mercenaries Did in the Congo

THE CONGO IS AN EMPIRE, not a nation. It is larger than Europe, inhabited by hundreds of tribes, with no common language or common culture. The three principle cities are—or, to be accurate, were—Leopoldville, Elizabethville, and Stanleyville. General Mobutu changed their names in 1967 but in order to avoid confusion and save space I intend to refer to them by their original nicknames—Leo, Eville, and Stan.

The history of the Congo since independence has been, to say the least, bewildering. It is very difficult to disentangle the mercenaries from the history; but perhaps certain guidelines will help wanderers through the maze.

First, then, the cities. Leo, in the west near the sea, is the capital of the country, the seat of the government, held since 1960 by government forces. Eville in the south is the capital of the mining state of Katanga, incredibly rich in resources and dominated by the great mining capitalist society the Union Minière. Stan is an outpost in the wild territory of the northeast and has as often as not been held by rebels or breakaway leaders. No normal roads or railways join these three cities; the only real link is by air.

Next, a man: Tshombe. Tshombe proclaimed and led the

independent state of Katanga which gave the United Nations so much trouble. After a short period in exile he was called back as Prime Minister of the whole country and succeeded in crushing the Simba revolt. He was ousted again at the end of 1965 and went into exile once more. There were continual plots involving or based on his restoration. On June 30, 1967, he was kidnapped on board a private aircraft and flown to Algiers where he was thrown into jail; there he died, two years later[1] to the day. Tshombe was the man whose name is linked with the mercenaries; he employed them while President of Katanga and re-employed them while Prime Minister of the Congo. During his exile they plotted against the state and used his name as a rallying cry.

Third, a force: the ANC, the Armée Nationale Congolaise, formerly known as the Force Publique but renamed at independence. Its mutiny sparked off the whole melodrama of the Congo. Its strength has always been in the region of 30,000, and its general tendency has been towards indiscipline and panic on most occasions. Its commander-in-chief almost since independence has been General Mobutu, who staged a first half-hearted coup in September, 1960, very soon after independence, and a serious coup in November, 1965. After the first coup he proclaimed his intention of giving up power six months later; he did so. After his second coup he declared he would hold power for five years; he has not yet done so but he has lasted longer than seemed possible. He is supported by the Americans and in particular by the CIA.

Fourth, a rule-of-thumb division. From the mercenary point of view, the history of the Congo falls conveniently into three periods: the Katanga Secession, from July, 1960, to January, 1963; the Simba War from July, 1964, to the end of 1965; and a period of Plots against Mobutu, from early 1966 till November, 1967.

Fifth and last, a brief summary of the events of mid-1960:

---

[1] Even the most obstinate rationalists (few of whom, admittedly, are attracted to the study of the Congo) must be tempted to stoop to superstition when confronted with the importance of this date in Congolese history. Independence: June 30; U.N. troops leave: June 30; Tshombe kidnapped: June 30; Tshombe dies: June 30. Is it not, one asks oneself, yet another plot?

June 30	The Congo becomes independent.
July 5	ANC mutinies.
July 10	Belgian troops flown in to rescue Belgians.
July 11	Tshombe proclaims the secession of Katanga.
July 12	President Kasavubu and Prime Minister Lumumba appeal to the United Nations for help.
July 14	The first United Nations troops flown in.

THE KATANGA SECESSION

President Tshombe of the newly independent state of Katanga needed an army. Three threats posed themselves. First, the northern half of Katanga was inhabited mainly by the Baluba tribe, whose leader, Jason Sendwe, was Tshombe's chief political opponent inside Katanga and head of the opposition political party, the Balubakat. To start with, the political game complete with assembly, elections, and votes of censure was played, but the Balubas were not prepared to be dominated, and bands of their youths, armed mainly with sharpened bicycle chains, were already forming into those gangs known as 'Jeunesse' which later became such a title of terror. The second threat came from the central government at Leo, which never accepted the independence of Katanga and which eventually was to 'invade' Katanga on several occasions with units of the ANC. The third and at that time still more remote threat came from the United Nations forces, for from the very beginning the United Nations condemned the secession.

Tshombe had help at hand; there were a large number of Belgian troops still in Katanga, at the enormous military base of Kamina which the Belgians had designed as a bastion of NATO in Africa. On the night of July 9/10 the ANC at Eville, at Camp Massart, mutinied, but the Belgian paratroops quickly suppressed the disorders and only 300 of the original 2,800 ANC were retained; the rest were disbanded. Among those retained was an ancient sergeant-major, Norbert Muke, who was promoted to colonel and appointed commander-in-chief of the Katangese gendarmes; for Tshombe decided to form not his own army as such but his own gendarmerie. To all intents and purposes it was the same thing, and the Katangese troops even when they were later integrated into the ANC were still always referred to as 'gendarmes'. This then was a new army of a new state, starting from zero. Its officers and NCO's were (apart from the commander-in-chief and other titular leaders) Belgian regular soldiers who were, in effect, seconded to Katanga. Their *eminence grise* was Colonel Guy Weber who had arrived in Katanga on July 10 with a paratroop brigade and who stayed on as Tshombe's military adviser (known as 'the Shadow') for almost a year; he was recalled by Brussels on June 17, 1961.

Tshombe, however, wanted his independence; he was too agile a politician not to realize that other countries besides Belgium would be interested in Katanga, and he seems right from the first to have chosen a policy of playing other interests off against the Belgians without, however, risking on any occasion a total break with Belgium. Very soon, too, the war against the Balubas in north Katanga turned savage and bitter, and it became known throughout the Federation of Rhodesia, Tshombe's neighbour to the south (then ruled by Sir Roy Welensky who was to become Tshombe's friend and supporter) that there was a well-paid opening for police officers in the Katanga gendarmerie. The occasional English-speaking mercenary began to appear in Eville.

By the end of the year Lumumbist troops—ANC deserters who had gone over to another separatist state, Gizenga's regime at Stan—were invading north Katanga and helping the Balubas, while isolated detachments of United Nations troops held various strongpoints and attempted to keep out of trouble. At this stage Tshombe took a more important decision: he made a move to enlist French officers and NCO's to reorganize and lead his army.

The whole of this episode is still obscure, and the following account may be wrong in several details as it is pieced together from various sources. It seems that Katanga made a formal but secret request for aid either to the French government or directly to the French Ministry of War. At any rate, Colonel Trinquier, a well-known soldier in the French army, a specialist in 'revolutionary warfare', veteran of Indo-China, commander of the *3ᵉ Régiment de parachutistes coloniaux* in Algeria, and a leading figure in the coup of May 13, 1958, received a letter at Nice on January 5, 1961, offering him in effect full control of the Katangese gendarmerie. It seems that the Rue Sainte-Dominique (the War Ministry) had considered both General Massu and Colonel Trinquier but had preferred the latter; the Quai d'Orsay objected to the whole scheme. In any case, whether the motive of the highest authority in France was to replace the Belgians in Katanga or to get rid of dangerous elements in the army or to kill two birds with one stone, Trinquier flew to Eville on January 25 with—he claimed in a letter to *Le Monde* of October 1, 1966— 'the full accord of the French government,' the only stipulation being that he had had to write a letter of resignation from the French army, to be accepted when he took up his post in Katanga. Trinquier was accompanied by various French officers, including Commander Roger Faulques; and others, for example the future OAS chief Colonel Godard, had asked to be sent with him.

Trinquier's mission was to see how the land lay and write a report for Tshombe. He presented his report in February. Its tenor was that the enemies of Katanga were preparing to overthrow the state by using the techniques of revolutionary warfare which had been successful in Indo-China and Algeria and that the main threat to Tshombe would come from subversive cells organized in Eville. This diagnosis of Trinquier appears to be yet another example of a specialist duped by his own speciality—the eventual force that overthrew Tshombe was the very conventional troops of the United Nations using the techniques of traditional warfare. However, in order to combat this supposed threat Trinquier demanded control of the Katangese armed forces for five years, with virtual control, too, of the ministries of Information and the Interior, the full support of the President, the support of the Belgian officers of the gendarmerie, and permission to recruit 'fifteen to twenty French officers, broken into the methods of modern warfare.' 'Alone, in fact,' he wrote, 'I will be of no use to you. It is necessary, then, on this point at least, that I should obtain the aid and support of the French government.'

Tshombe accepted Trinquier's report enthusiastically and the Colonel flew back to France to enrol his twenty officers. There his troubles began. He opened an office of sorts, after reporting to Messmer, the Minister of War, and Couve de Murville, the Foreign Minister. It appears, however, that there was a certain disaccord, not unknown at other times, between different branches of the same government. His office was searched, though not closed, by the police after stories had been leaked to the press, and the Colonel blamed the journalists for their *propagande intempestive* which, he claimed, contributed to foil his mission—a mission which *'était bien dans l'intérêt de la France et du Congo.'*

It was not, however, only at Paris that Colonel Trinquier's plan for a virtual take-over of Katanga was meeting with difficulties. Back at Eville, Colonel Weber had inevitably got word of it and was doing his best to stop French expansion into this Belgian preserve. It seems that Tshombe promised both Weber and Trinquier his full support, and the whole idea came to an almost farcical ending, typical enough of the Congo, when Trinquier, flying back to Katanga in March with his twenty French officers, was refused permission to land at Eville and had to meet Tshombe's Minister of the Interior, Munongo, at Ndola in northern Rhodesia. In any case, between Trinquier's first and second visits Lumumba had been murdered in Katanga[1] and the

---

[1] Probably on January 17, 1961, though his death was not announced till February 12. According to certain accounts mercenaries were responsible for the deaths both of Lumumba and of Dag Hammarskjold in 1961. However both allegations were rejected, more or less completely, by the official U.N. commissions of enquiry, which would have been only too happy to add these to the list of mercenary crimes if there had been any real evidence. Even Conor Cruise O'Brien, whose descriptions of the ghastly French mercenaries and of the sinister Godefroid Munongo are a literary joy, does not really hold to these accusations, although he does describe how Munongo hired a mercenary for an unsuccessful attempt to assassinate his successor, Urquhart.

It may possibly be true that a Belgian mercenary administered the *coup de grâce* to

[*Footnote continued on next page*

Devotion to war – the mark of the mercenary

Above Sir John Hawkwood (Giovanni Acuto), leader of the Free Companies in France and Italy, and almost the only mercenary leader of the time to die peacefully of old age
Below The Battle of Crécy. The Genoese crossbowmen who survived English arrows were finished off by their enraged French employers

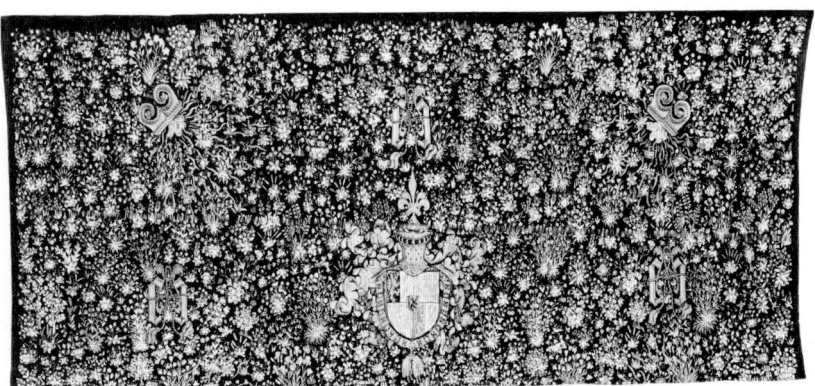

Above Landsknechts (or Lansquenets) engaged in one of their many mutual massacres. Not a very attractive profession but it had its rewards
Below The 'Booty of Burgundy': the Hundred Flowers Tapestry decorated with the arms of Charles le Téméraire, part of the fabulous loot acquired by the Swiss at the Battle of Grandson. On show at Berne's Historical Museum, part of the collection still known as 'die Burgunderbeute'

The Battle of Marignan, from the bas-relief on the tomb of King Francis I. Note the formidable phalanxes of Swiss pikemen

Employer, victim, and mercenary. *Above* Pope Urban VI whose mercenaries defeated those of Pope Clement VII so decisively at the Battle of Marino. *Below left* Ludovico il Moro, Duke of Milan, in the end betrayed by his Swiss mercenaries at Novara. *Below right* Gattamelata, Venetian captain-general and condottiere. No native of Venice was ever permitted to lead the Republic's land-forces

The great Federigo da Montefeltro, reading in his library at Urbino – the most civilized and cultured mercenary leader of all time

The Foreign Legion: myth and reality. *Above left* That famous fort at Zinderneuf. *Above right* A 'stepson of France' in all his anonymous glory. *Below* Legion *cuisine:* the *soupe* and the *gamelles*

Death in the Congo. *Above* The first two casualties of 5 Commando: two German mercenaries killed by the Simbas. *Left* Atrocities, however, were common on both sides

Life in the Congo: 5 Commando at Stan. *Above* Homage to Tshombe. A 'guard of honour' at the airport, drawn up in best 'British Army' style. *Below left* Homage to Lumumba. All Orientale was dotted with these shrines to the dead 'hero'. *Below right* The 'battle honours' of 'the gallant men of 53 Commando'.

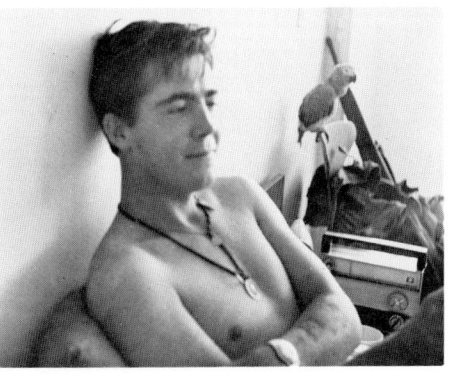

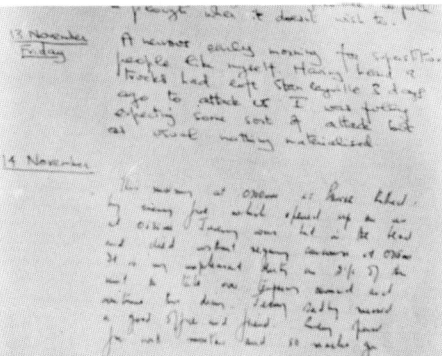

Top On the banks of the River Congo. Mercenary on duty. *Above* In a 'liberated' villa. Mercenary very much off duty. *Right* A 'jungle bunny'. *Below* Two entries in the unit diary of 56 Commando. (See pages 223-4)

The mercenaries' revolt: success. *Above* The capture of Bukavu – arrival of Schramme's mobile column. *Opposite page. Top* The defence of Bukavu – Katangese gendarmes led by white mercenaries 'dig in'. *Middle left* The siege of Bukavu – the perennial problem of provisions

The mercenaries' revolt: failure. *Middle right* After the fall of Bukavu, the white mercenaries fled across the Shangugu to Rwanda where they were interned – and eventually, much to their relief, flown out to Europe. *Bottom* Meanwhile, Denard's 'invasion' of Katanga had failed – perhaps understandably given his means of transport

Moise Tshombe, employer of the mercenaries in the Congo. He revived the 'profession'

'Colonel' Jeremiah Puren, *left* one of Tshombe's faithful henchmen.

Mike Hoare of 5 Commando. Irish origin, British character, South African nationality

Siegfried Mueller, an officer, and German, of 5 Commando

Bob Denard, best-known figure among the French mercenaries

Jean Schramme, a Belgian planter, leader of the mercenaries' revolt

Rolf Steiner, the former legionary who fought for Biafra

Count Carl Gustav von Rosen, the Swedish idealist who flew for Biafra

Death in Biafra. *Left* 'Taffy' Williams giving orders for the attack on Onitsha (10 November 1968) to the Flemish mercenary Marc Goosens. The meditative mercenary sucking a straw is Armand Ianarelli. *Below* Minutes later Goosens has been killed. His men bring back his body resulting scandal apparently shook the desire of all or any of the French ministries to become even semi-officially involved. The ANC-Lumumbists at the time were launching an offensive which captured Manono, the chief town of north Katanga; Colonel Weber threatened to cut off all Katanga's Belgian-supplied ammunition; the U.N. delegate Khiary, a Tunisian, showed himself bitterly anti-French, it being the period of the Bizerta crisis; Tshombe tergiversated. And so in the end Colonel Trinquier flew ignominiously back to Paris, where his resignation from the army had been accepted, and his only consolation was to sue Tshombe before the Seine tribunals for 20 million *francs anciens* for breach of contract. It seems, however, that later on he was allowed back into the French army.

The Trinquier affair, however, was not without importance. Most of the twenty French officers who had come with him stayed on, and Faulques became the real leader in the fighting against the United Nations. Faulques had been an officer in the Legion, one of the few officers of the 1ᵉʳ REP[1] to survive Cao-Bang and the Vietminh prison camps. Presumably he rejoined his regiment after being liberated in 1954. He later became one of its battalion commanders but had to leave Algeria, I was told because of the '*triste affaire Audin*'—a scandal which blew up following the death in mid-1957 of a French schoolteacher in Algeria who was suspected of being a rebel sympathizer. Was he then involved in the OAS? Possibly not. He was scarred, publicity-shy, ruthless, and much admired; it appears that he left Katanga early in 1962, swearing that he would never again accept orders from Africans, and went to the Yemen to train forces for the Imam el Badr. He was rumoured, and—later known, to have been in Biafra,[2] but he remains the most obscure of the well-

---

Lumumba, though it seems more likely that he was beaten to death by his ANC escort. But if a mercenary pilot did manage to shoot down Hammarskjoeld's plane in such a way that it could be taken as an accident, it was an example of unparalleled efficiency. This was the period when nearly all commentators were tempted by the conspiracy theory of Congolese history.
[1] See footnote, page 141.
[2] See pages 257, 260 ff.

known mercenary leaders and also the most respected by those mercenaries who fought with him.

In any case, this was the beginning of the French mercenary involvement in the Congo—a failed semi-official mission. Other French officers and NCO's, including Bob Denard, later to become famous, followed their friends to Katanga, particularly after the purge of the French army that followed the 'Generals' Coup' in Algeria in the early summer of that year.

Meanwhile the English-speaking mercenaries were forming themselves into a separate group, and rivalry and mutual mistrust among the French, the English, and the Belgian mercenaries was already making itself felt. It was an odd and ever-present factor on the mercenary scene, well shown in the following report by a United Nations official, Dr Mekki Abbas, after a confused skirmish on April 7 near Manono, where for the first time mercenaries clashed with United Nations (Ethiopian) forces. Several Ethiopians were killed and about thirty mercenaries were taken prisoner. Their commander was Captain Richard Browne, an Englishman.

'Although the apprehended personnel claimed different nationalities,' wrote Dr Abbas, 'they all enlisted for service as mercenaries while they were in South Africa, Southern Rhodesia or Katanga. Most of the personnel questioned were ex-Servicemen. They were physically fit, had a soldierly bearing and showed a sense of discipline. They came from various walks of life and the motives for enlistment given ranged from financial reasons, domestic troubles and lust for adventure to a desire to serve what they considered a good cause. Most of them claimed to have been under the impression that they were enlisting for police duties and not for active warfare. . . .

'The following is a condensed summary of the information obtained through the questioning of the apprehended personnel.

'*Recruitment:* The existence of two recruitment centres, one at Johannesburg, the other at Bulawayo, was established beyond reasonable doubt. There are indications that the second one has run into difficulties with the local authorities and is not operating.

The Johannesburg recruiting office is directed by Mr Carlos Huyghe, Belgian adviser to the Katangese Ministry of Defense, and by Mr Russell Cargill, a resident of South Africa. . . . There also existed a recruitment centre in Salisbury which was operated by Mr Cargill, who, however, was forced to leave and to transfer his activities to Johannesburg.

'Recruits were lured by advertisements in [South African] newspapers . . . which called for ex-servicemen looking for an interesting and adventurous career but did not mention Katanga. The recruits were called for an interview at which they were told that they were to serve as policemen and given a free ticket on scheduled Sabena or UAT flights from Johannesburg to Eville. Requirements for acceptance were previous military service and physical fitness. Contracts were for 6 months, renewable for further periods. Conditions offered included pay ranging from £100–£180 a month, plus a "danger allowance," family allowance, insurance and a free vacation after one year. Most recently the service contracts were not issued at Johannesburg but only after arrival at Eville, to avoid compromising the recruiting drive by a chance discovery of the contract prior to the recruit's induction into the Katangese forces.

'*Military:* The group of mercenaries commanded by Captain Browne had been organized in a unit called the *Compagnie Internationale*[1] . . . consisting mainly of ex-soldiers recruited from South Africa. Its present strength has been reported as approximately 200 officers and other ranks. When fully operational, it would consist of 5 platoons. The *Compagnie Internationale* was armed and equipped by the Katangese gendarmerie and wore the same uniforms. . . . The unit to which the apprehended personnel belonged was used as a spearhead and fought through to Manono which its men were the first to enter. . . . The information obtained confirmed that the non-Congolese military personnel . . . formed the backbone of the military operations in Katanga and were instrumental in carrying out the recent offensive of the Katangese forces. In particular the *Compagnie Internationale* commanded by

---
[1] Echoes of the Spanish Civil War.

Captain Browne and composed of experienced and disciplined soldiers seemed to have supplied the élite necessary for this type of military operation.

'*Discipline:* Captain Browne maintained that his unit observed throughout the operation strict discipline and the recognized rules of military combat. He admitted inflicting casualties during the advance on Manono and while clearing a road-block but claimed that his unit fired only at military personnel opposing him, when military necessity so required. In this connection he and some other members of his unit were sharply critical of the methods used by the Katangese gendarmerie units led by Belgians and *Les Affreux* whom they accused of burning habitations indiscriminately and firing at people who were not offering resistance. Towards the end of the operation, friction appeared to be developing for this and other reasons between the *Compagnie Internationale* and other units of the Katangese forces. One of the factors contributing to this friction was the disillusionment of the mercenaries as regards the type of service demanded from them. . . . '

This seems to be a fair and accurate report, from a source naturally hostile to the mercenaries—though Dr Mekki Abbas was obviously something of an Anglophile and appears to have swallowed a certain amount of guff from Captain Browne. Browne was the brother of the Tory M.P. for Torrington, which caused embarrassment at Westminster. From other sources it seems that Browne was more often to be seen at the bars than in the field; he was renowned for his drinking and for his size. He was expelled after this 'apprehension' by the United Nations but kept coming back into Katanga from northern Rhodesia and then being expelled again.

What is out of proportion, however, is the importance accorded in this report to him and to the other 30 mercenaries—the remaining 170 of the ephemeral *Compagnie Internationale* sound more fictional than factual. For most of the other mercenary leaders who were later to become famous or notorious were also active in Katanga. Alastair Wicks, who had emigrated after the War to Rhodesia, certainly fought in the Baluba war; he was later to become Hoare's second-in-command, a position for which he was ideally suited. Jeremiah Puren, an obscure Afrikaner, was appointed titular commander-in-chief of the Katangese air force for reasons obscurer still. Hoare was also there, though he seems to have played a comparatively minor rôle. He had known Katanga from pre-independence safari expeditions; and the story goes that he was hired not as a mercenary but on a sort of freelance basis by a South African millionaire named Anderson whose son had been reported missing in North Katanga. Sometime in 1961 Hoare led an expedition of half a dozen mercenaries out into the bush only to find that the missing son and a Scotsman had been ritually murdered by the Baluba; whereupon Hoare sacked and burnt the village of Kalamatadi. This seems to have been his only major exploit, and he apparently left Katanga before the major battle that marked the end of the year 1961, the Second Battle of Katanga.

Schramme, however, took part in this battle. Jean Schramme was the son of a highly respectable Bruges lawyer; at the age of eighteen he had come out to the Congo to run a family plantation near Bafwasende to the north-east of Stan. He fled, like so many other Belgian *colons*, during the troubles following independence and in early 1961 ended up in Katanga after having taken refuge in Uganda. There he was enrolled as a training officer at Kamina base; and, after taking part in the fighting at Eville as one of Faulques' subordinates, he was sent to Kansimba in North Katanga where he recruited fifteen and sixteen-year-olds from the local tribes and formed his 'Leopard Group', officered by himself and one or two other Belgian ex-planters. In Katanga he did not cut much of a figure; he was reputed to be shy and rather nervous, though eager to please.

Denard was just the opposite—what the French call a *baroudeur*, physically large, colourfully dressed, moustachioed, and a Gascon —a contrast to Hoare and Schramme who were both small and rather precise men. 'Bob' was too flamboyant a figure for the

English-speaking mercenaries to take seriously, and was viewed by the Belgians (as Schramme's later attitude indicates) with a mixture of uneasy admiration and deep suspicion. Denard had been an NCO in the French marines and later a policeman in Morocco and Algeria. He seems to have acted as a sort of right-hand man for Faulques; he too was apparently involved in extreme right-wing activities, directed particularly against Mendès-France. When Faulques left, he took over command of the mercenaries for the last battle against the United Nations. It was there, at Kolwezi, that he won that reputation for personal bravery and loyalty which his later activities were to do nothing to justify.

But at the time of the capture of the *Compagnie Internationale* the mercenaries were still fighting the Balubas, not the United Nations forces. Dr Abbas reported that they were astonished when told about the Security Council's resolution of February 21: Captain Browne said that they had been under the impression, for so Belgian officers had briefed them, that there would not be any conflict between them and the U.N., only between them and the rebel Balubas. 'Sold up the river' was the phrase Captain Browne used to give vent to his feelings, and he suggested piously to his interrogators that the United Nations should take steps to warn mercenaries of their true position.

This resolution of February 21 was the direct cause of almost all the fighting that was to follow in Katanga. It authorized the United Nations forces to use force if necessary in order to prevent civil war. Whereas previously the Security Council had limited the U.N. forces in the Congo to strictly defensive police actions, this resolution allowed them to go on the offensive more or less as they judged necessary. It also demanded that all foreign 'advisers' and military and paramilitary personnel should leave Katanga. There were by mid-1961 about 20,000 United Nations troops in the Congo, commanded by an Irishman, General Sean McKeown.

The special representative in Katanga of the Secretary General,

Dag Hammarskjöld, was also an Irishman—Conor Cruise O'Brien—and an Irishman of very decided political views. On August 28 he organized 'Operation Rumpunch'—the arrest, by United Nations troops, of all the foreign military advisers who were still in Katanga.

There were 512 'foreign military or paramilitary personnel' in Katanga, according to the United Nations; about half of them were Belgian regular army officers. Operation Rumpunch was a success; by the end of the day all but a hundred-odd of the original five hundred had been arrested, without a shot being fired. Those who escaped the net, however, were the fighting officers (including eleven of the French) out in the field with their units. Among those who did not escape were Wicks and Schramme. Wicks was expelled and does not appear to have returned. Schramme, according to his own account, was arrested at Kamina and was one of four mercenary officers sent to Leo as prisoners of the ANC—if his story is true, this was to almost certain death. He was helped by a friendly chaplain to escape from prison, flew out from Leo to Brussels, and then took almost the first plane back to Eville.

Expulsion was not a particularly efficient way of dealing with the mercenaries; the main result of Rumpunch was to clear out the regular Belgian army officers from Katanga—they lost a good deal of face by the rapidity with which they surrendered—and to leave the control of the Katangese gendarmerie in the hands of the three elements who formed the original mercenaries, that is to say, the English-speaking police officer type, the French paratrooper type, and the local Belgian settler type. Thus the end of Operation Rumpunch marked the real beginning of the mercenary period in Katanga, and these hundred-odd mercenaries formed the hard core, both as types and as individuals, of all future mercenary activity in the Congo. Although the core was expanded, it never grew to any great size. It is doubtful whether at any one time there were ever more than five hundred mercenaries in the Congo. More likely, their strength, continually changing, wavered around the two to three hundred mark.

Compared to their historical predecessors, this was a surprisingly small total.

The rest of the history of the independent state of Katanga is that of a struggle between the United Nations and Tshombe which finally ended in Tshombe's defeat but only after a series of dramatic reversals of fortune and the death of the Secretary General. Three times the struggle burst into open battle between the United Nations forces and the Katangese gendarmerie led by the mercenaries.

The First Battle of Katanga: September 13–21, 1961

Following the easy success of Rumpunch, Conor Cruise O'Brien decided to launch a United Nations *coup d'état* in Katanga, with the aim of ending the secession.

September 13	United Nations troops under Brigadier Raja seize control of key points 'in order to prevent civil war.' Conor Cruise O'Brien announces (prematurely) 'Katanga's secession is ended.'
September 14	Katangese counterattack. Their two aged Fougas give them control of the air. Heavy fighting in Elizabethville and elsewhere.
September 17	Irish U.N. garrison at Jadotville, 184 strong, surrenders to Katangese led by the French mercenary Michel de Clary.
September 21	Ceasefire.

This was a stalemate, in fact a virtual victory for the mercenaries and a military disgrace for the United Nations forces. Dag Hammarskjöld had died in an aircraft over Northern Rhodesia three days before the ceasefire; his successor U Thant recalled Conor Cruise O'Brien and General Sean McKeown. A U.N. air force was formed: Sweden and Ethiopia each gave four jet fighters and India gave six jet bombers. A new Security Council resolution on November 24 gave the Secretary General legal authority for taking the offensive.

The Second Battle of Katanga: December 5–21, 1961

This followed only six weeks later. It was really a face-saving operation, pretty repellent whatever one's views on the rights or wrongs of an independent Katanga. The keepers of the peace seemed to have no more scruples than any warmonger in seizing on the flimsiest pretexts as an excuse for launching an attack.

The *casus belli* was a document captured by the United Nations —a plan for the defence of Katangese territory, generally attributed to Faulques, in the event of a combined ANC/U.N. attack. The territory of Katanga was divided into five military zones: Albertville under Major Jacques, Kongolo under Major Bosquet, Manono under Commandant Protin, Kamina under Major Barvaux, and Kamiama under Major Faulques. In the case of a combined attack, the plan called for 'harassing of the United Nation garrisons,' with counterattacks on the U.N. bases at Eville and Kamina.

December 5	U.N. Gurkhas assault a Katangese roadblock. U.N. air force destroys Katangese air force on the ground at Kolwezi.
December 5–11	U.N. softens up resistance by mortar and air attacks on centre of Eville. On the ground mercenaries hold three key points against probing attacks.
December 13	U.N. Swedes attack Lido Hotel.
December 15	U.N. troops, roughly 5,000 strong, occupy half of Eville.
December 19	U.N. Ethiopians occupy Union Minière headquarters.
December 21	Kitona Agreement. Ceasefire.

This was a victory for the United Nations, although given their overwhelming numbers and equipment, it had taken

Brigadier Raja far longer than it should have done to capture Eville. Politically it looked like the end of Tshombe and Katanga. In fact, however, a year of political manoeuvring followed: there were continued reports that the last mercenaries had left or were leaving, but the reports were untrue.

The Third Battle of Katanga: December 28, 1962–January 21, 1963

Nearly a year later, at the end of November, U Thant's military adviser General Rikhye left New York to inspect the U.N. forces in Katanga, now well over ten thousand strong. Two weeks later the United Nations delivered an ultimatum to Tshombe; in his turn Tshombe alleged that the United Nations was planning to arrest him.

December 28	U.N. troops moved in on Eville in overwhelming numbers before dawn.
December 29	U.N. in control of Eville. Resistance elsewhere in Katanga.
December 30	U.N. in control of Kipushi and Kamina.
January 3	U.N. occupies Jadotville.
January 13	U.N. occupies Shinkolowbe.
January 21	Kolwezi, the last bastion of Katangese resistance, falls.

Bob Denard was in command of the mercenaries at Kolwezi and carried on resistance in an obviously hopeless struggle. The mercenaries threatened apparently to blow up the great hydroelectric installations there—which would have ruined Union Minière's installations—and only a direct appeal from Tshombe stopped them. Schramme is reported to have set out with a large convoy in north Katanga and to have joined Denard after a dangerous journey across U.N.-controlled territory. Together they retreated, with perhaps a hundred mercenaries and several thousand Katangese gendarmes, across the border into Angola. The policy of the Portuguese authorities has always been to allow mercenaries and gendarmes to take refuge or regroup in their territory, to help them as little as possible, and to deny to the whole world that any mercenaries have so much as set foot on Portuguese soil. The permission irritates the Congolese, the lack of help irritates the mercenaries, and the denial irritates everybody; but Portugal does not seem to have suffered particularly from this general irritation.

In any case, this marked the end of Katanga. On February 6, Lieutenant General Norbert Muke took the oath of allegiance to President Kasavubu, following which he was demoted to Major.

THE SIMBA REVOLT

On June 30, 1964, a year and a half later and four years after independence, the last United Nations troops left the Congo and Tshombe returned to Leo from his exile in Madrid. A totally new menace was shaking the whole country: a revolt against the central government had started in the province of Kwilu, led by a former minister, Pierre Mulele. '*Mai Mulele*' was the rebel war cry—'the water of Mulele.' Pierre Mulele had won fame as a schoolboy by forming an anti-Immaculate Conception society which had ramified throughout the Catholic mission schools. He adapted Catholic doctrine at this stage by baptizing his followers with his own water, a baptism that protected them against their enemies' bullets. Shrines to the dead Lumumba were set up and '*Mai Lumumba*' alternated with '*Mai Mulele*.' Before the Lumumba monuments all the enemies of the revolution—all the Congolese with any book-learning—were sacrificed, as the movement spread through many parts of the Congo. It spread like wildfire, and the ANC, terrified by the '*dawa*'—the fetishes—of the rebels, fled like rabbits or joined the Simbas. Swahili for 'lion', Simba was the title that the Mulelist warriors chose for themselves; the most feared of all were the 'Jeunesse,' the young Simbas aged from ten to fourteen, who invented some of the foulest tortures.

The Simba revolt was decolonization in its purest form. Many African leaders had proclaimed that it was not enough to get rid of the colonial masters or even the neo-colonial economic powers, but none except the Simbas actually put into practice the idea of 'the African solution' and 'negritude.' It was instinctive but not unidealistic; it spread quickly into the provinces of Kivu and Orientale which had always been violently anti-European. Various exiled Congolese politicians saw their opportunity, and as the revolt spread, a triumvirate appeared in the northeast— Gbenye, Kanza, and Soumaliot. Mulele himself stayed in Kwilu; at the time it was not known whether he was dead or still alive; in any case his name and his supernatural powers were more important than his person.[1] The Chinese saw in the revolution a chance of increasing their influence in central Africa; from their heavily overstaffed embassies in Congo-Brazzaville and Burundi they gave moral and, increasingly, material support to the triumvirate and the Simbas. Chinese action brought an American counteraction; the Americans politically though not economically were playing an ever greater part in Congolese affairs. Their policy was to fill the gaps left by the Belgians. Militarily this meant that they set about forming a Congolese air force, supplying planes and pilots who were generally anti-Castro Cuban exiles, and also providing the large C130 transport planes which were vital to supply and move the ANC. It was from this period that it is fair to say that Mobutu was the Americans' man in the Congo: though perhaps not precisely a puppet, he certainly broadly followed the lines that pleased the American government, and the CIA, for their part, were to support him faithfully.

Politically, both for the Belgians and Americans, Tshombe was the only live leader whose prestige could possibly counteract that of the dead Lumumba and the divine Mulele. A week after he returned from exile he formed a government. At first he attempted a plan of 'national reconciliation'; it failed. On August 5 the Simbas captured Stan and the triumvirate proclaimed His Excellency Christophe Gbenye President of the Popular Republic of the Congo. The Stan government was recognized almost at

---

[1] In fact he was shot on the orders of Mobutu on October 9, 1968, after accepting a treacherous offer of amnesty. He had been living in Congo-Brazzaville, though for how long is unsure. His death led to Congo-Brazzaville breaking off diplomatic relations with her powerful neighbour.

once by most of the Communist and anti-Western Arab powers. It looked as if nothing could stop the Simbas: Albertville, Baudoinville, Kindu, Uvira, Coquilhatville had fallen to them; invaders from Congo-Brazzaville had opened a new front threatening Leo; and only at Bukavu did the ANC, led by Colonel Mulamba, fight back and finally beat off their attack.

These were the circumstances in which Tshombe turned again to 'his' mercenaries. He summoned Mike Hoare and Jeremiah Puren from South Africa and gave them a commission to form a group of white mercenaries to be known as Five Commando. The reasons for which he chose Hoare and Puren rather than any of the many other mercenary officers who fought in Katanga are obscure. Admittedly Puren[1] had kept in continuous contact with Tshombe and had often flown back and forth between Jo'burg and Madrid, apparently at his own expense. No sooner was Tshombe designated prime minister than he contacted Puren by cable; Puren then phoned Hoare in Durban; and the pair of them flew into Leo on June 30.

Hoare, born in Dublin, was an accountant by profession. He is said to have fought with the Chindits in Burma and to have been on Mountbatten's personal staff. Two years after the War he emigrated to South Africa and in addition to his practice as an accountant became the sleeping partner in a used-car business and an active safari-organiser. His background and connections are none too clear; in any case he turned out to be the man for the job.

A few days later Schramme and the Katangese gendarmes, over 8,000 in all, crossed the border from Angola and re-entered Katanga. (Denard, unlike Schramme, had not waited idly in Angola; he was by this time out with Faulques in the Yemen and

---

[1] 'A shabby figure but one of the faithful' was how a personal acquaintance described him. He married a Belgian girl whom he had met in Katanga, and justified his former titular command by learning to fly during Tshombe's period of exile. It is tempting to consider him as an *eminence grise*—particularly since, according to various accounts, this was a temptation to which even the high and mighty succumbed: the South African government considered him to be the secret emissary of Tshombe and Tshombe considered him to be the secret emissary of the South African government.

does not seem to have reappeared in the Congo until the following year.)

With the return of Tshombe, the Belgian military mission in the Congo resumed its importance. The Belgians controlled the administration of the ANC; supplies of weapons and ammunition depended on them as well as the running of the base camp at Kamina and of headquarters at Leo. The Belgian officer of most importance during this time was Colonel Vanderwalle who took command of the Fifth Mechanized Brigade, of which Five Commando was a part. Vanderwalle was the strategist who planned the moves that eventually led to the defeat of the Simbas; he was backed up by a large number of Belgian military 'technical advisers.' Their rôle was to assist Congolese officers of the ANC in planning and administration; technically, they were forbidden to take part in actual combat. This difficulty, however, was surmounted either by ignoring the rule or by the practice of attaching a Belgian 'mercenary' as assistant to a Belgian regular officer. The normal ANC battalion then would have a Congolese colonel, with a Belgian regular army captain as his adviser and a Belgian mercenary lieutenant as the actual combat leader; Belgian NCO's helped with the technical side and the advanced weapons while the Cuban CIA 'mercenary' pilots gave air support.

This stiffening worked quite well, but Five Commando, composed entirely of white mercenaries, was the spearhead of all the ANC attacks. Hoare was its commander in the field, Puren was the liaison and administrative officer in Leo, and Wicks was the second in command. The mercenaries were recruited openly in South Africa and Rhodesia and flown to Kamina where they were trained for two or more weeks before being committed to action. The terms of the contract were those referred to in Dr Mekki Abbas' report on the *Compagnie Internationale*. Technically the recruits were meant to have some military experience, but a lot of them were young men in their early twenties and the former soldiers were a minority. At first chaotic conditions reigned: no barracks, uniforms, or weapons were ready for the new recruits at Kamina; no contracts were drawn up and no money appeared. A large number of them insisted on being sent back to South Africa where the press published their tales of disorganization. Hoare's first attempted action, a lake-born attack on Albertville with a handful of mercenaries, ended in ignominy and the first deaths: two German mercenaries.

Shortly, however, with the support of Vanderwalle, Hoare managed to get his base organized. The second batch of recruits found themselves being trained and drilled according to strict British army precedents and commanded by officers, most of whom had served either as regulars or national servicemen in the British army. The rank and file was formed mainly by young Afrikaners; and the NCO's by men such as John Peters who had been NCO's in the British army or the British colonial police.

Five Commando never numbered much more than two hundred men. Hoare divided it into small units of approximately thirty men and two officers, known as 51, 52, 53, 54, 55, 56, 57, and 58 commandos. Each of these units could and did operate separately as completely independent commands. When they were operating at a distance, Hoare's control over them was remote and occasionally nonexistent, to such an extent that some of his men claimed that he got undue credit for military successes which he had had nothing to do with. However, there seemed to be a general respect for 'the Major' (or 'the Colonel' as he later became), and the various attempts at mutiny, almost all started by mercenaries finding out that no money had been paid into their bank accounts at home, tended to die down when Hoare appeared.

Five Commando's first success was the recapture of Albertville by Lieutenant Gary Wilson, a South African who had served in the Blues. After that the commandos were flown all over the Congo and invariably succeeded in recapturing towns held by the Simbas. In the autumn Colonel Vanderwalle drew up a master plan for an attack on the Simba capital at Stan; Five Commando was to form the spearhead of the main motorized column, Lima One, which was to advance directly from Bukavu northwards. A second column, Lima Two, under Colonel Liegois, was to support this advance; as spearhead of Lima Two, Vanderwalle assembled a group of French-speaking mercenaries to whom he gave the title of Six Commando. Six Commando was placed under the command of another Belgian regular army colonel, Lamouline, assisted by the mercenary Commandant Protin. But at this stage it had something of an artificial existence, because the French-speaking mercenaries who were now technically part of Six Commando were mainly spread out in small groups among ANC companies and battalions. They never formed an all-white unit, as Five Commando did.

The rebel government at Stan panicked, and the events that followed held the world's attention. All the whites still alive in Simba territory, mainly missionaries, were rounded up and held as hostages. Gbenye wildly appealed for help to all African leaders of goodwill and announced: 'We will make our fetishes out of the hearts of Belgians and Americans and clothe ourselves in the skins of Belgians and Americans.' As Lima One advanced from Bukavu, the Belgian government supported by the British and the United States governments decided to drop paratroops on Stan and Paulis in order to rescue the white hostages. Hoare's advancing motorized column was delayed by ambushes during the night of November 23/24, and when it reached Stan next day, it found the city almost totally in the hands of the Belgian paratroops.

The rebel government had lost its capital, and at first it looked like the end of the rebellion. The Belgian paratroops were flown back to Belgium amid furious protests from the Afro-Asian world at this neo-colonialism; and indeed the motives of Brussels might be suspect but for the fact that Stan would certainly have fallen to Vanderwalle's columns even if no paratroops had been dropped. However, the reaction particularly in North Africa was strong; the Egyptians and the Algerians began sending modern arms and weapons down to the Simbas mainly through the Sudan, and there were continual rumours (never substantiated) of

Arab and even Chinese 'advisers' leading the rebel forces. In the following months Hoare from his base at Stan continually sent out his commandos to the towns and villages in Orientale province and succeeded in saving the lives of literally scores of missionaries and in closing the Sudan border. The Simbas' new arms and improved tactics, however, had made them more formidable enemies, and a column of forty vehicles commanded by Siegfried Mueller was badly ambushed and most of the vehicles were destroyed. But in spite of defeats and deaths which lowered at times the morale of this mercenary force, Hoare succeeded in defeating the rebellion in the northeast.

One rebel redoubt remained—the wild Fizi-Baraka area to the east of the province of Maniema where Schramme, back from Angola, was pacifying the area where he owned plantations. His 'Leopard Group' was now dignified with the title of Ten Commando.

The Fizi-Baraka area was inhabited mainly by the robber Wabembe tribe, aided at this time by bands of roving Watutsi warriors, the giant exiles from Rwanda. It was a mountainous plateau, and the only road approach led up the Lulimba escarpment, an absolutely impregnable position. Hoare prepared with great care a 'combined operation' on land and water, with air support. Wicks led the land group and blocked the road out at the foot of the Lulimba escarpment. Hoare himself led the rest of Five Commando in a water-borne night assault from Lake Fizi. The mercenaries suffered heavy casualties, particularly among the officers, but resistance faded away once they had captured the lakeside town of Baraka, and with the success of this operation in October, 1965, the Simba revolt was virtually over.

With its collapse, the old political struggle resumed in Leo. Tshombe and President Kasavubu began a power struggle— which was ended by General Mobutu's coup on November 25. Kasavubu retired to a farm, and Tshombe to exile. Tshombe's fall involved the fall of his friends; within two months Vanderwalle had been replaced by a new Belgian military adviser, General Delperdange. Lamouline and Protin of Six Commando were ousted by the French mercenary Bob Denard, and Hoare, shortly followed by Wicks, resigned his command.

The new colonel commanding Five Commando was John Peters, who had started as a sergeant under Hoare and had been rapidly promoted to officer because of his extraordinary bravery. Peters had been a regular British soldier but had deserted from a Yorkshire regiment and gone to South Africa. When he took over, the duties of Five Commando were inevitably changing: the mercenaries became more of a police force, and both the glamour and the hopes of booty had disappeared. Peters had a fanatical prejudice against the British officer class and soon got rid of the remaining mercenaries of the Hoare style; the new mercenary officers were usually Afrikaners of the NCO type, such as the young George Schroeder, who could barely speak English. Peters, by contrast to Hoare, had a reputation as a killer and as a very cold man; he was, however, equally respected and even more feared. Five Commando's mercenaries were still scattered around the northeast, under the remote control of Denard at Stan.

PLOTS AGAINST MOBUTU

The year 1966 opened with rumours of a conspiracy to restore Tshombe. A revolt that eventually failed broke out in Stan on July 23. The following account is, once again, likely to be only as near the truth as one could hope to get at this time.

The main mover in the plot was René Clemens, a professor in sociology at Liège University and an old supporter of Tshombe. With the help of another conspirator, Mario Spandre, he had been responsible in the Katanga days for drawing up the Katanga constitution. On the military side, the plotters probably had at least the advice of Colonel Vanderwalle, who still retained contacts in Six Commando.

The conspirators planned that rebel units should seize simultaneously Stan, Eville, Bukavu, and Albertville. For the leader of the revolt, they intended to call Hoare out of his retirement. But the plan almost immediately went wrong. The South African government showed no interest, and Hoare telephoned Peters, who was on leave in Rhodesia, to warn him that the conspirators planned to approach him next.

This they did. Peters was offered £15,000 in cash if he would attack Eville; he refused. Fearing that he would be kidnapped, he hurriedly left Rhodesia, flew to London for the World Cup finals and then back to Leo where he told Mobutu as much as he knew about the plot. Meanwhile the conspirators had contacted Wicks, who first accepted the offer but then backed down, after having himself been in touch with both Hoare and Peters.

The conspirators, having failed with Five Commando, turned elsewhere. About half the 8,000-odd Katangese gendarmes had, after their return from Angola, been reorganized by Vandewalle into one regiment forming part of the ANC: the titular commander of the Baka Regiment was a Katangese officer, Colonel Tshipola, but, as always, the operational commanders of the four battalions composing the regiment were mercenaries. The 11th Commando was led by a Belgian, Wauthier; the 12th by a Frenchman, Gouault (or Gouhaux); the 13th by another Frenchman, Bruny; and the 14th by a Bavarian, Wilhelm, whose 2 i/c was 'Frenchie' Delamichel, another mercenary who had won a reputation for rashness in the fighting against the United Nations in Katanga. Commandant Wauthier had also been in Katanga; expelled at Operation Rumpunch, he had later acted as liaison officer between Tshombe in exile and Schramme in Angola. He was the lynchpin of the plot and is said to have been a member of the Belgian secret service.

The Katangese had been dissatisfied since Tshombe's fall; they particularly loathed the élite ANC paratroops, Israeli trained, and the paratroop Colonel Tshatshi, military commander of the Stan area and of the Fifth Motorized Brigade.

Meanwhile in Leo there were rumours that General Delperdange would be replaced by Colonel Marliére. On July 16, Delperdange and Mobutu had an interview, at which they allegedly discussed the difficulties of Five Commando. Possibly Mobutu feared that Peters was playing a double game.

One week later, on Saturday, July 23, the revolt broke out. In Stan the Katangese gendarmes killed Colonel Tshatshi and occupied the airport and the radio station; their plot to kill all the ANC officers at a christening party failed, and the ANC paratroops held the right bank of the river. Denard, who apparently knew nothing of the plot, quickly ordered his mercenaries of Six Commando to occupy the post office and the bank and to remain neutral; by occupying the post office Denard was the only man in Stan who could get direct telephone contact with Leo. He did so, told Mobutu that there was a mutiny and that the situation was confused, and demanded that Colonel Mulamba, 'the hero of Bukavu,' now Mobutu's Prime Minister, should be sent to negotiate with the mutineers.

Meanwhile Wauthier attempted to move on Stan with his troops. He told the mercenaries with him that a *coup d'état* had already taken place in the capital. He was not believed. A quarrel followed and Wauthier was shot; Lieutenant Piret then suggested flying Wauthier's body to Leo as a sign of good faith. Piret eventually did this and was rewarded for his pains by being interned in Camp Kokolo.

Wilhelm shortly afterwards descended on Paulis, which he and his men captured in a quarter of an hour and put to fire and sword. When they left Paulis, however, to march on Stan, they were ambushed by a well-armed party of Simbas. Sixty out of the six hundred Katangese were killed, and ten of the twenty-one white mercenaries were wounded. It seems that Wilhelm either died of his wounds afterwards or was caught and killed by the ANC. In any case the rest of the battalion, now under Frenchie Delamichel, did not reach Stan till August 15, three weeks too late.

The plot had failed, largely due to the conspirators' error in underestimating the importance of Six Commando, actually in Stan, and therefore of the attitude of its leader, Denard. After tortuous and confused negotiations that dragged on for two months, the 3,000 mutinous Katangese broke away from Stan and fled towards Punia in Maniema, the area controlled by

Schramme. Peters and Five Commando blocked the escape route south but did not apparently attack them. The rôle of Schramme, who had been sitting on the fence and avoiding any commitment, is obscure; according to his own account he acted as peacemaker and protected the Katangese until a truce was arranged, but according to other accounts he too was preparing to attack them. In any case the Katangese were promised an amnesty and surrendered. Their reward was death. They were all, incredible though it seems, massacred. 'Most of the mercenaries grouped around Colonel Bob Denard at Stan,' Radio Leopoldville announced, 'have remained loyal to the Republic. It is thanks to them that the plot formed against the government both inside and outside the country has been discovered.'

The precise manner of the massacre is obscure. Did it follow a surprise attack by Denard on the disarmed Katangese, as certain accounts allege? Or was it the direct responsibility of Mobutu and the ANC? Questions that will probably never be answered ... such nightmarish bloodshed and treachery ends by arousing more disgust than curiosity.

For 1967, President Mobutu had offered his capital as the meeting place of the fifth OAU heads of state congress. It was important for his prestige and position for the offer to be accepted: it would amount to a recognition by all Africa of his success in establishing himself as ruler of a united Congo.

It seems that other African leaders were reluctant to accept the hospitality of a fellow African who employed white South African mercenaries; against the French-speaking mercenaries no such general rancour was felt. Mobutu therefore decided to disband Five Commando and, if possible, to disband or at least to reduce the numbers and importance of the remaining mercenaries by September when the heads of state were due to arrive. Peters gave up his command at the end of February and returned to England, having been forbidden by the South African government to go back there. George Schroeder, aged twenty-four, took over as commander of Five Commando for the last three months till it was finally disbanded without incident toward the end of May.

Disbanding Five Commando was a rash move on Mobutu's part in the still tense atmosphere of conspiracy. No doubt he counted on the proven loyalty of Denard.

The following report sent by Schroeder to General Bobozo, titular head of the ANC, gives an idea of the situation in the spring of 1967. It was dated March 17, from Albertville.

> Mon Generale,
>
> First I would like to assure you of my co-operation and sincerity towards the Congolese government and yourself and extremely appreciative of the confidence you have shown in appointing me as Commander of Fifth Commando unit and will strive to give you the type of security and strength that is so badly needed to rebuild the Congo.
>
> My initial orders to this unit were based on the obvious need for reconstruction and resettlement, as well as the security necessary for the local population to settle back into a productive way of life. We have embarked on projects lying close to the roads: rebuild bridges, repair schools and many other things essential to regain normality in the Republic.
>
> The areas not clear of rebels, small patrols are harassing them continually so that the native population is spared the atrocities so common to rebel occupation. After the rainy season is finished, we shall progress much more rapidly in opening the Nmoya Nakalitza Enemendi complex to the normal civil administration.
>
> I have assigned certain of my best qualified men to establish an intelligence unit designed to detect any form of opposition that might be detrimental to the best interest of the Central Government. It is my good intention to provide you with an intelligence report periodically in the near future.
>
> The following points have come to my attention which shall be pointed out to you at this time.
>
> 1) Arms and ammunition are coming in approximately three kilometres south of the C.L.F. harbour. This fact was confirmed from information received from several civilians.
>
> 2) The arms and ammunition are brought in by local fishing

fleets from the Tanzania side of the lake. The arms and ammunition are being carried in fishing nets under the water. When our naval force investigated these fishing boats they cut the ropes with the result that no proof can be produced.

3) The amount of arms and ammunitions already in Albertville is unknown to us but I do know it is quite a substantial amount.

4) A Greek by the name of Sporof went to fetch these arms and ammunitions on a number of occasions.

5) A local shop-owner by the name of Klanthonides Leonadis came approximately ten minutes after the beach droppings into the harbour. Furthermore we suspect that a house in the village contains a very strong radio set but we cannot do anything until we have more proof. We do know further that four ex-rebels are having a meeting in this house every second or third night.

We also suspect that arms and ammunition are coming in in bags and in foodstuffs to the docks. We do know furthermore that there are between three hundred and four hundred here possibly originating from Somalia. They are here without permissary documents. We checked on this point with the local police saying that we are looking for a certain Arab we had met before and that we now believed he is in Albertville. We requested them to go through their records to confirm this and supply us with his residential address. They informed us that this would be impossible owing to the fact that few of them have legal documents. We have checked with different civilians and they agree that there are quite a lot of Arabs in Albertville.

6) I suspect that they are here for one of the following reasons (a) starting a new rebellion, (b) mutiny in the army and police, (c) preparation for Tshombe.

On 16.3.67 one of my officers was doing investigation work and came across a group of fifteen men with rifles having a meeting. Unfortunately he could not understand much, due to the fact that they were speaking Arabic but he could follow that there was an argument in the group. The name of General Mobutu was used, as well as my own name and that of one of my officers who was working in this intelligence force. While listening in on this discussion, two armed guards attacked him and tried to overpower him. Only through fast reaction and good capability he managed to get away, with only cuts on his hands.

The report of this incident immediately reached me. If I may give my opinion I suspect that it starts the local rebellion on the shrewd movement of the Tshombe group. We all know that President Mobutu[1] is arriving at my position tomorrow, 17.3.67.

If I could inform you I suspect it would be a great opportunity for opposition forces to start off with an assassination of the President, which I would like to prevent as far as possible from my side. At the same time they will attempt to knock off other high authorities which will leave the Congo without leading men. They will also attempt to eliminate me and my officers. This would leave Five Commando for a short time in a position where they cannot act to protect Albertville properly. After this it would be easy for a ship to enter the harbour with arms and ammunition, since our navy could only operate for a certain time, and then have to return to harbour for re-fuelling and re-loading purposes. Should the navy stores be taken by rebels it would be impossible for them to carry on with operations.

I have only a few men in the position. You will appreciate that if you would give me orders to withdraw some of my men from the field to protect Albertville from what could well be a very serious situation.

I would like you to send immediately a special security force to investigate these matters of arms and men coming into Albertville. I do think this matter is more serious than what anyone would like to believe at this stage.

Furthermore, we know that Tshombe is supposed to be in jail in Southern Arabia for high treason. This could be a bluff and these Arabs could be working in conjunction with him. This information about him could only be to take us off the hook.

Once again, Generale, I wish to thank you for your confidence and I hope you do believe and trust my motives. I can assure you my duties are only to serve you and the President. Rest assured that the Fifth Commando will be loyal to the Republic of the Congo as long as I am in command.

This report shows, no doubt, the political naïvety of the South African mercenaries; the naïvety is balanced by an obvious loyalty to their immediate employer. If this is the report of even a potential

---

[1] Mobutu cancelled his visit.

pro-Tshombe conspirator, it would be a Machiavellian work of art.

Would Five Commando have remained loyal to Mobutu had it still been in the Congo when Six Commando revolted? By that summer Schroeder was back in South Africa running a travel agency; he had a list of all the former mercenaries of Five Commando and claimed that he could raise two thousand men in a week. He appeared to be without direct news from the Congo and waiting for a summons that never came; and my personal impression is that the summons he was expecting and hoping for would have come from Mobutu, not from Denard—that is to say, that he was perhaps ready to lead South African mercenaries against the Belgians and the French.

The revolt of the mercenaries in 1967 was a highly dramatic affair which at one time looked as if it would topple Mobutu. Its background is dealt with more fully in a later chapter; here just a condensed summary of what happened will be given.

May	Five Commando repatriated.
June 3	Public hanging in Leo of the 'Pentecost Conspirators'—four politicians including former Prime Minister Kimba accused of plotting against Mobutu. World opinion is horrified.
June 12	Blowing up of the Lubudi Bridge in Katanga—an act of sabotage which cut the copper exports.
June 14	Three mercenaries condemned to twelve years' penal servitude for holding up a bank in Goma. They claimed not to have been paid.
June	Congo-Belgian relations deteriorate sharply, particularly after a Belgian planter has his fingers and ears cut off for alleged participation in the Lubudi Bridge sabotage.

June 30	The seventh anniversary of independence. Tshombe is kidnapped on a private flight to Majorca and flown to Algiers. Mobutu demands his extradition.
July 5	The Congolese Radio announces that a mutiny has broken out at Stan and elsewhere; two plane-loads of foreign mercenaries have landed. Until August 10, almost the only information comes from the Congolese radio, most of it false. Mobutu decrees a state of emergency and general mobilization and appeals to the Security Council.
July 7	The radio reports a 'great victory'. No more is heard of the foreign airborne invasion. It seems that Denard and Six Commando have mutinied. But Denard is wounded.
July 10	Twelve wounded mercenaries including Denard fly to Rhodesia in a stolen DC3. It looks as if the mutiny, headless, is over. There are fears for the safety of white civilians held as hostages in Stan. *Le Monde* writes, '*La rébellion des mercenaires serait terminée.*' The radio announces that the horde of *affreux* is in flight. On President Johnson's initiative the Americans send three C130's to transport ANC troops to Stan.
July 12	The mercenaries in fact pull out of Stan on this day. The Red Cross announces that the 'hostages' (including thirteen journalists) are safe, though the mercenaries have taken other hostages with them.

July 13–26	The mercenaries disappear in the northeast of the Congo, apparently fleeing for refuge toward the Central Africa Republic. For the first time the name of Schramme is mentioned. Finally they are reported south of Stan, at Punia; apparently they have changed direction and are fleeing south. A 'Congolese source' in Leo announces a violent clash at Itibero.
August 3	The radio announces a battle at Walaikili nearer Bukavu. The 2,000-strong European population starts fleeing from Bukavu across the river to Rwanda.
August 7	ANC troops, with special orders from Mobutu to 'annihilate' the mercenaries, are stationed along the Rwanda border to stop them fleeing across.
August 9	The mercenaries led by Schramme descend on Bukavu and capture the city with ease. The ANC due to annihilate them flee across the Shangugu to take refuge in Rwanda, handing in their weapons to the frontier guards under the gaze of astonished television cameras. The whole situation is dramatically reversed, the obviously vanquished having become the potential victors. World opinion is extraordinarily confused.
August 10	Schramme gives interviews to press and television in Bukavu. He gives Mobutu a ten-day ultimatum to negotiate and threatens to descend either on Katanga or Leo. A Katangese colonel with him, Monga, announces the formation of a Provisional Government of Public Safety

in Bukavu. The white 'hostages' with the Schramme column turn out to be civilians who of their own free will had chosen to be escorted by Schramme to the Rwanda frontier and safety. News leaks out of a massacre of mercenaries in Leo on July 6. (It is later proved true. About thirty mercenaries, on administrative work in the capital, were rounded up by the ANC and killed.)

August 11   The Congolese Foreign Minister appeals to the Security Council for aid.

August 13   Belgian Embassy in Leo sacked.

August 15   Mobutu in his turn gives the 'ignoble mercenaries' a ten-day ultimatum to leave Bukavu.

August 16   Schramme sends an ultimatum to Colonel Micombero, President of Burundi, threatening to cut off all the electricity in Burundi (which depends on Bukavu's hydroelectric works) if Burundi continues to allow free passage to ANC troops. Burundi demands that Belgium should 'assume her responsibilities.' Belgium disowns the mercenaries.

August 24   The Congolese Foreign Minister announces, 'There never has been and never will be negotiations between Schramme and the Congolese Government.' Schramme announces that he is aiming at the fall of Mobutu. Two Belgian civilians are killed by the ANC in Eville.

August 26   About half the ANC, 15,000 strong, are grouped around Bukavu. Schramme has roughly 150 mercenaries and 800

Katangese gendarmes. There is a forty-eight-hour truce.

A strange pause in activity followed. No-one knew what Schramme's intentions were and why he did not march on Katanga and spark off a general uprising. There were continued rumours that Denard, who had left his hospital in Rhodesia, was about to open a 'second front' by organizing an invasion from Portuguese territory. Meanwhile both the Congolese Radio and Schramme's Radio Bukavu announced that the Simbas were joining in the revolt; and Bukavu that a column of mercenaries had captured Goma. This the Congolese Radio denied—and claimed, with heat, a record of objectivity.

On September 11 the OAU heads of state met, after all, in Leo, though only twelve of the thirty-eight total roll call attended. President Kaunda of Zambia proposed a peace plan, and the OAU appealed to the International Committee of the Red Cross to arrange the mercenaries' evacuation.

On September 24, Schramme told Radio Luxembourg that his men were '100% idealists' and announced that he had got enough arms and ammunition to hold Bukavu for months. By mid-October it looked as if he was deliberately dragging out negotiations with the Red Cross in the hopes that Mobutu's ever-weakening situation would get worse and worse. The three universities of the Congo were closed and the general economic situation was deteriorating; there were stories of food riots in Katanga.

Meanwhile Denard, the most ingenious if the least successful of the mercenary leaders, had not been inactive. Godefroid Munongo, Tshombe's former minister of the interior and a tribal leader of great importance in Katanga, was one of Mobutu's few opponents to have escaped hanging, shooting or assassination. He was mildly imprisoned on an island in the Congo estuary; Denard set about organising his rescue. In mid-September one of Denard's assistants, a mercenary recruiter named Moreau, began hiring men in Paris. Eventually thirteen mercenaries, of whom six were

French, set out from their base in Angola and attempted a canoe-borne commando raid on the island of Bula Bemba. They would have done better to have been more superstitious; the raid ended in a farcical failure.[1]

This attempted *coup de main* took place on the night of October 28/29:

October 29	ANC launches a violent attack on Bukavu.
October 30	Battle rages.
November 1	Lull at Bukavu. At 0400 hours a column led by Denard invades Katanga from Angola—the long-awaited second front. The Congo appeals to Security Council.
November 2–3	Lull continues at Bukavu. No real news of the Denard invasion.
November 4	The ANC launches a final assault from all sides on Bukavu. Schramme's ammunition stocks fall to almost nothing. After day-long combats the mercenaries and

---

[1] The basic idea behind the raid was, however, admirable—with Tshombe immobilized in Algiers the mercenary revolt needed a well-known figurehead. It leads to an interesting question: were there any attempts to rescue Tshombe from his prison in Algiers? Apparently so—though not at this time—according to an extraordinary account published two years later in the *Evening Standard*, shortly after Tshombe's death. This rescue plot was organized, or so he claimed, by the 'Black Eagle' of Harlem, Colonel Hubert Fauntleroy Julian—a gentleman now in his seventies—who had flown for Haile Selassie against the Italians (a curious coincidence here with another aged adventurer, the Swedish Count von Rosen) and thereafter led a suitably rocambolesque life. He eventually became part of the wide variety of fauna attracted to Katanga; where, apparently, he would boast of million-dollar arms deals one moment and casually request the price of a taxi-fare the next.

The details of the Tshombe rescue saga are not unbreathtaking. Originally it was to cost Tshombe six million dollars, mainly in bribes to Algerian officials. But then at the end of May 1969 an independent and quite separate attempt was made by a group of mercenaries unknown to the Black Eagle. This raid ended in failure and the death of several mercenaries; but as a result the price demanded for bribes and flight organization rose to a total of fifteen million dollars. Nevertheless the Black Eagle had everything arranged and set up, only to be foiled once more by the news of Tshombe's death.

This melodramatic farrago might just possibly have some basis of truth—at least in that not-improbable report of a failed mercenary raid, which bears the Denard touch. And then, that other question: how did Tshombe die? The Algerian government collected a batch of doctors to certify that his death was due to natural causes. But scepticism it almost unavoidable; and, if it should ever be proved that there was a rescue attempt shortly before, would become entirely justified.

November 5   Katangese fall back toward the bridge leading across the Shangugu to Rwanda. Bukavu falls. Schramme and the rearguard retreat into Rwanda. 'His people'—130 surviving mercenaries, 800-odd Katangese men, and 1,500-odd women and children—interned by the Rwandese authorities.

November 7   The Denard column retreats ignominiously back into Angola.

This was the end of the actual revolt, but not quite the end of the affair. In mid-November a special mission of the OAU visited the internment camp and persuaded the Katangese, including Colonel Monga, to accept Mobutu's offer of 'amnesty' and 'resettlement.' 'Thus,' said the annual report of the International Committee of the Red Cross, 'at the end of the month of November began the repatriation of the Katangese gendarmes to the Congo—organized by the Congolese authorities alone and without the Red Cross having been invited to lend its assistance.' Previously the Red Cross had said that they were ready to help in transporting the Katangese, 'on the condition that the free choice of individuals should be verified under their control and on a new basis guaranteeing the interested parties effective freedom of choice.'

This scepticism appears to have been more than justified. The Katangese departed, singing, it was reported, mournful songs in which they expressed their desire to die in their own country. Monga, according to a reliable eyewitness, left with the first planeload for the Congo and then returned voluntarily to the camp in Rwanda to persuade the rest of the Katangese to accept the offer of amnesty and resettlement; he then of his own free will went back into the Congo. How he, who had publicly proclaimed Mobutu a bloodstained thief and a traitor, could have hoped to survive passes all comprehension. No more was heard of the Katangese for several months; intermittent attempts by the Red Cross to obtain information met with vague but reassuring replies. Then on April 25, 1969 a brief official statement announced that Monga, Nawej and six other officers had been executed a fortnight previously at Camp Kokolo in Leo. A few days later Monga's widow held a press conference in Brussels at which she claimed that her husband and the other officers had been tortured for thirty-four hours before being killed, and also that over six hundred of the Katangese gendarmes who had accepted the offer of amnesty had also been killed. She accused the secretary general of the OAU, Diallo Telli, of breaking the guarantee underwriting the amnesty which the OAU had given. Her allegations were treated with a certain scepticism by the Red Cross. But no more has ever been heard of the Katangese.

The repatriation of the mercenaries to Europe was not so swiftly achieved. First Mobutu demanded a monetary indemnity from the governments of their countries of origin for the damage caused by the revolt. Next he demanded their extradition and announced that they would be tried in Leo for war crimes. Finally, in January, he broke off diplomatic relations with Rwanda, 'the protector of assassins.' The OAU leaders who had guaranteed the Red Cross their support did not keep their word, and it was not till April 23, 1968, that two Dutch DC6 jets hired by the Red Cross took off from Rwanda with the 123 remaining mercenaries. One of the planes flew to Pisa, Zurich, and Paris: at Pisa, seventeen mercenaries including three Greeks and one Israeli got off; at Zurich, four South Africans including Puren (who immediately caught a plane back to Johannesburg) and one Swiss (who was immediately arrested); and at Paris, twenty-five French, two Germans, and four Britons. The other plane flew directly to a military airport near Brussels; the Belgian authorities took extraordinary precautions to keep the time and place of arrival secret because they feared a hero's welcome for Schramme. Sixty-one mercenaries disembarked, of whom two were immediately arrested for past crimes.

Schramme retired to his family mansion at Bruges, apparently having been warned by the authorities to make only the briefest of declarations to the press. On June 27, shortly after a private visit paid by Mobutu to Brussels which marked yet another Belgo-Congolese reconciliation, Schramme was arrested on the charge of murdering at Yumbi in May, 1967, a Belgian planter, Maurice Quintin. In his deposition Schramme admitted the charge: Quintin had come to him proposing a pro-Tshombe revolt; when Schramme refused to discuss it, Quintin threatened to inform Mobutu that Schramme had agreed. 'I could not run the risk of reprisals against my men and myself,' declared Schramme. 'It was my duty to prevent Quintin from putting his plan into action. I shot him and ordered Rodriguez [a mercenary barman, accused together with Schramme] to finish him off and to throw his body into the Lowa.'

This charge and this admission ruined Schramme's reputation as an idealist and a hero in Belgium. Had the mercenaries' revolt succeeded, it would probably have not been held against him. As it was, not even the fairly convincing account he gives in his book of the reasons and formal justification for this killing without trial could justify him in the eyes of his compatriots. Furthermore it became obvious that in spite of his often-declared attachment to 'his' Katangese, he had in fact left them to their fate while he and the surviving mercenaries saved their own lives.

Once Schramme's aura had been destroyed, the Belgian judicial authorities showed no particular haste to press the charge against him. In August he was released pending trial. In the spring of 1969 the trial was still pending, and he applied for authorization to visit Brazil in order to investigate buying a plantation there; 'consideration having been given to the state of the investigation,' stated the official Belgian communiqué, 'the competent judicial authorities gave him this permission.' And so this possible murderer had his passport restored.

The authorities then learnt with amazement that Schramme had never arrived in Brazil but had assumed a false name and had flown out elsewhere, in all probability to Angola. A minor diplomatic incident between Belgium and Portugal blew up and as quickly blew over. Schramme's subsequent whereabouts and activities were, at the end of 1969, still not definitely known.

9 Strength and Weaknesses of the Mercenaries

'Ils ne ressemblent en rien à la Légion Etrangère avec ses traditions de discipline et d'obéissance aux chefs.... Ce sont plutôt des bandes opérant à la façon des Grandes Compagnies et fort chatouilleuses sur le point d'honneur.'—Max Clos in Le Figaro

THE MERCENARIES WERE EXTRAORDINARILY SUCCESSFUL as soldiers, and why this should have been so remains puzzling. There were never more than several hundred in the Congo and yet they had more direct success and indirect effect than the Ten Thousand Greeks in Persia. When they were finally beaten—in the third battle of Katanga and at the end in Bukavu—it was by forces enormously superior both in numbers and equipment.

The mercenaries fought first the Balubas, secondly the United Nations troops, thirdly the Simbas, and fourthly the ANC. In each particular war it is possible to explain away their military success by citing the faults or weaknesses of their opponents. But the implication then is that the mercenaries themselves did not suffer from the same or even worse military weaknesses, and this is untrue. How untrue it is, the following detailed account of their only ignominious defeat—Denard's 'invasion' of Katanga in support of Schramme—will show.

Denard's invasion force consisted of 110 mercenaries and 50 Katangese. Strategically, Schramme was 'fixing' half the ANC total strength at the siege of Bukavu and Denard's aim was therefore to make a lightning invasion of Katanga (where the restless population was held in check only by the remaining ANC garrisons), seize one or more key points, and set off a general insurrection.

For this, by Congolese standards, his force was large enough. It was reasonably well armed, consisted of experienced mercenaries, and Denard planned to strike into that part of Katanga which he knew well, the Kolwezi area, from his old base in Angola. The Portuguese, however, were cooperative only to a certain extent; they transported Denard's band to the frontier but refused to supply him with any vehicles.

Wednesday, November 1. Denard's force crossed the frontier shortly before dawn and took the border village of Luashi defended by two ANC soldiers who, naturally enough, fled.

Tactically, Denard's first task was to obtain transport for this force. The enemy, the ANC, had a garrison of six hundred at the town of Dilolo, a stronger force at the mining city of Kolwezi and a military base and planes at Kamina. Denard, however, had at least temporarily the advantage of surprise and his obvious task was to seize either Kolwezi or Kamina as a prelude to a general uprising and the capture of Eville.

Denard divided his force into three platoons. Half a platoon under Major Piret took the only transport available, fifteen bicycles, and set off on the road to Kisenge where there was a manganese mining company centre and a platoon of ANC. This operation was a success; Piret seized six lorries and two jeeps and the ANC fled. Nevertheless, even with the bicycles, it had taken the whole day largely owing to Piret's reluctance to 'requisition' these European-owned lorries. In any case the Denard force was now motorized and capable of making a rapid attack.

Thursday. The tactical objective was either Dilolo or Kolwezi. Kolwezi was the more important, but local Katangese were already flocking in to join Denard, and the capture of an ANC barracks would mean arms to distribute all round. By the end of the day two to three thousand Katangese had joined Denard and there were only twenty old Mauser rifles to distribute among them.

Denard moved out and took Kasagi, a deserted town, which for the next few days was his headquarters. He sent one platoon to Kisenge as the first move against Dilolo. This platoon arrived at the same time as an ANC company; both sides exchanged fire and then fled.

Friday. Denard changed tactics and sent two platoons off to capture Kolwezi. The leaders of this attack thought this was too tall an order and set up an ambush before Mutshasha to catch the ANC counterattack which they felt sure must come along that road. By late afternoon no counterattack had materialized, so they pulled back to Kasagi, leaving Frenchie Delamichel and twenty men still in ambush.

The invasion was now three days old and had accomplished nothing. That night Denard harangued his men, said that there would be no more divided efforts, and sent off two platoons to attack Dilolo.

Saturday. The attacking convoy went slowly through the night and at dawn was ambushed unsuccessfully by an ANC company. They tapped the telephone wires and intercepted a message saying that an air attack was coming from Kamina. By the time the two T-28 Congolese jets appeared, the lorries were off the road and camouflaged. Two hours later this menace had disappeared and the column resumed its advance.

Not far outside Dilolo the ANC had set up a second and more efficient ambush supported by cross fire, mortars, and a Ferret scout car. This was the decisive engagement. The commander of the mercenary force panicked and ordered his men to abandon their lorries and escape back through the bush to Angola. However, a lieutenant took charge and eventually got all the vehicles turned round even though under fire. The engagement lasted two hours and ended with the mercenaries retreating at full speed. Their casualties were three wounded.

Meanwhile the ANC had discovered Frenchie Delamichel's ambush near Mutshasha and he also pulled back (without orders)

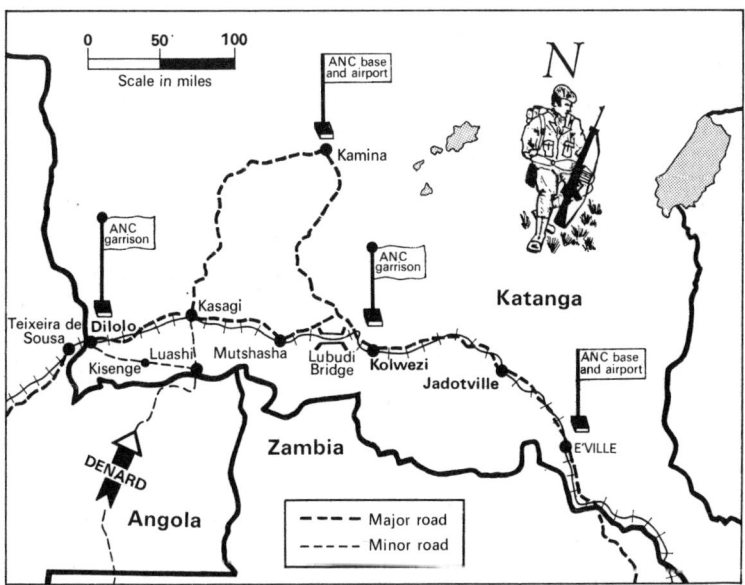

The Mercenaries' Revolt: Denard's 'Invasion' of Katanga in support of Schramme.

to Kasagi. There the whole mercenary force reunited that evening and furious discussions began. 'Denard was arguing like a woman,' wrote a mercenary afterward. The Congolese Radio announced that Mobutu had had flown down (in the remaining American C-130's) his crack 1st Para Regiment from Leo and that the ANC were about to attack from Kamina, Dilolo, and Kolwezi. In an atmosphere of near panic the mercenaries pulled back that night to Luashi. They suffered their first and last casualties in that retreat: three of them were killed as they drove back by another group who had set up a rear-guard ambush and mistook them for ANC. A fourth was crushed to death when his lorry overturned at a river crossing.

This was the day of the final combats at Bukavu.

Sunday. The mercenaries regrouped at Luashi. There was a near mutiny and some desertions.

Monday. ANC advanced into position around Luashi. The mercenaries remained inactive.

Tuesday. In the afternoon the ANC attacked fiercely with well-directed mortar fire and encircling infantry movements. Denard was already over the border in Angola, and Piret directed the defence. At dusk Piret led his men back over the frontier, where the Portuguese disarmed them.

Naturally enough, there was talk of treachery and suspicion that Denard had been playing a double game. However, this seems a less likely explanation than sheer muddle and confusion. Denard had to stay at Kasagi rather than lead the attacks personally in order to maintain radio contact with Schramme at Bukavu and contact of some sort with the Portuguese; he later claimed that the Portuguese had promised him 2,000 rifles to arm Katangese volunteers, and even if this was not true, it is obvious that he hoped for arms and supplies from Angola once he could show that things were going well. At the same time he had promised Schramme that a flying boat loaded with arms and ammunition would land on Lake Kivu at this time. He had, in fact, a lot to coordinate, and in any case Kasagi, at the junction of three roads, was a tactically suitable headquarters for the control of the invasion operations.

The whole episode is a fine example of the disadvantages of a mercenary force. Mercenaries are easily discouraged by setbacks and by very slight casualties; mercenary officers tend not to obey orders and to take their own decisions; in defeat, furious arguments rage and accusations of treachery are hurled about. A mercenary leader has to show personal courage and to lead his men in attacks; otherwise he is quickly despised. There is no way to prevent desertions, particularly when a frontier is nearby, and mutinies can only be stopped by a sense of self-preservation in the face of the enemy.

Denard's invasion was ruined by cowardice, inefficiency, and disorder, by bad leadership, time-wasting, and lack of administrative planning and clearly defined strategic aims. It was not untypical of the mercenaries in the Congo: all their groups and all their operations suffered, in varying degrees, from the same inevitable weaknesses. Their command was never united, their administration never efficient, and their courage never superhuman. It is all the more extraordinary and all the more inexplicable that, apart from this episode, they either won or, if beaten, lost with distinction.

*   *   *

The Baluba war gave the mercenaries the chance to develop the tactics which they later used so successfully in the Simba revolt. Basically they relied on speed and firepower. A mercenary attack would be a lightning affair; the commando in jeeps would drive at full speed into an enemy position or village and open up with heavy machine guns and automatic rifles. Against the Baluba tribesmen, who hardly had a modern weapon among them, these tactics were invariably successful. Against the Simba hordes, particularly after the capture of Stan, less so; clearly a well-placed ambush as at Bafwasende could play havoc with a mercenary column. Two Ferret scout cars of Five Commando were destroyed by falling into a sort of elephant pit dug into the road. Hoare's advance on Stan on the night of November 23/24 was held up by a series of ambushes; Wicks described that night to me as the most nerve-racking experience he had ever had, and it went against Hoare's rule, which was never to move by night. On one occasion a mercenary commando in a group of jeeps came speeding round a corner and almost crashed into a group of Simba lorries heading in the opposite direction. These tactics were the reverse of conventional European tactics, for, according to the rule book, advances along a road into enemy territory must be made by 'bounds'—one vehicle advances while the other covers it—and in no circumstances must a column go speeding down a road.

The unorthodox tactics of the mercenaries paid off, however, though the Congo with its dense bush and jungle was an ideal terrain for ambushes. The mercenaries stuck to the roads and to their jeeps; they never ventured into the bush or put in the traditional sort of attack on foot, with extended lines of infantry. These tactics, though limited, succeeded and kept succeeding, first because of the speed of their attacks, which almost always gave them the advantage of surprise, and secondly because of their firepower—not so much of the firepower directly as of the enormous noise which the weapons of even a handful of mercenaries could create and which demoralized and panicked their opponents.

Admittedly the mass of the Simbas were not formidable opponents; their leaders and their commander General Olenga genuinely believed that the discovery of the *dawa* had given them a weapon as important as the atomic bomb. The *dawa*, the *Mai Mulele*, would protect the lives of the Simbas and make bullets harmless provided the Simbas observed certain rules—for instance, never to look backwards when going into battle. The failure of the *dawa* could therefore in any given case be explained away logically, and certainly belief in it, combined with the *chanvre*, the drug with which almost all Congolese—Simbas, ANC, Katangese—primed themselves for battle, gave the Simbas extraordinary powers and the ability to go on living and fighting for minutes even when riddled with machine-gun bullets and technically dead.

But the Simbas were fanatically brave, often armed with automatic weapons, and there were hordes of them. They were not negligible as enemies, and though there are stories, horrifying enough, of mercenaries mowing down with their machine guns hundreds of spear-carrying Simbas pressing around the slowly moving jeeps, many mercenaries of Five Commando were killed. They did, however, have air support—an almost decisive factor in warfare along the Congo roads and indeed in general. When the mercenaries controlled the air in Katanga, even though with only two old Fougas, a Dornier of First World War vintage, and a helicopter from which the pilot tossed hand grenades, they managed to defeat the United Nations. When the United Nations created their own air force after the first battle of Katanga, they eventually by bombing and strafing won the second battle. Five Commando whenever it met particularly fierce resistance would call for air support from the Cuban pilots. Not that this support was invulnerable—the most famous of the pilots, 'El Toro,' was shot down and his mutilated body found by a group of Five Commando (which led to reprisals on their part). The Congolese air force continually strafed Schramme at Bukavu; it seems that, to start with, the pilots were Congolese and Schramme's men shot down at least three T-28's. However, in the last attacks the foreign mercenary pilots took over once again; possibly Mobutu did not entirely trust them in an attack against their former comrades and, if so, he was justified. Schramme's men on the day of the final attack tuned in to the attacking pilots' wavelength and were warned a few minutes in advance which of the various targets was due to be rocketed. The almost daily strafing by T-28's appears to have had the most demoralizing effect on Schramme's mercenaries during the long weeks of the siege of Bukavu.

The mercenaries, of whatever sort, tended to use the type of military methods which were used in the army of origin of their officers. This was particularly true with Hoare, who attempted to re-create in Five Commando a British regiment.[1] This had its advantages and its disadvantages: Five Commando was probably more successful against the Simbas than an actual British regiment would have been, for regular armies are tied down by rules,

---

[1] And largely succeeded. A 1966 charge sheet against a nineteen-year-old mercenary lieutenant was headed '1) Conduct unbecoming an officer and gentleman.' In the summer of 1967 in South Africa I met former mercenaries whose major preoccupation appeared to be the organization of the annual dinner of ex-Five Commando officers. In 1964 in the Congo Hoare even went to the extent, I was told, of holding Church parades on Sunday mornings. Whether this is true or not, 'that mad bloodhound Hoare' (as the East Berlin radio dubbed him) certainly had a puritanical side to his character. Did he genuinely feel himself to be leading a sort of crusade? Extremely difficult to say.

traditions, and handbooks, and the mercenaries were free to experiment with new tactics and variations of method. Schramme's advance into Bukavu was led by a bulldozer; one unit of Five Commando used a repentant Simba who would dress up as a woman and scout forward whenever they suspected an ambush. Part of the mercenaries' superiority was due to this sort of ability to improvise.

The ANC by the time of the mercenaries' revolt were a far more formidable force than they had been in the early years of independence, and one of Schramme's mistakes appears to have been that he underestimated them. At the siege of Bukavu, the élite of the ANC, the 2nd and 3rd Paras, who had been trained by Israeli officers, were well organized and disciplined troops with the will to attack. Nevertheless, Schramme for months succeeded in defending Bukavu against a besieging force fifteen times as strong as his; he established six strongpoints on the outskirts of Bukavu covering a perimeter of 25 kilometres, and the military story of the siege is that of a Dien Bien Phu in miniature. Lack of ammunition, and in particular of mortar shells, finally caused Schramme to retreat. In all their campaigns the mercenaries depended heavily on mortars which they used as a regular army would use its heavy artillery. The mortar and the jeep-mounted heavy machine gun were their main tactical weapons.

If the success of Schramme in holding Bukavu for so long was extraordinary, it was less extraordinary than the success of the mercenaries in Katanga against the United Nations. The United Nations troops were drawn from modern, well-equipped, highly disciplined armies, and the Indian brigade which fought in the second battle of Katanga consisted of a Gurkha, a Jat, and a Dogra battalion commanded by Sandhurst-trained officers—a highly professional force, opposed only by a few score mercenaries and perhaps three thousand Katangese of very doubtful value. Admittedly these mercenaries were led by Faulques and other Frenchmen experienced in street fighting and supported by the local population, black and white. But even allowing for the Belgian wives who would telephone the exact position of the

United Nations troops occupying their streets or gardens, it seems incredible that so small a group could have resisted so successfully for so long.

It appears that the real basis of the mercenaries' military success was always a question of morale; and yet this conclusion is paradoxical, for the mercenaries were fighting neither for their country nor for any real cause, and therefore those feelings of patriotism or idealism which can make the worst soldiers formidable were logically more likely to inspire their enemies. Yet it is hard to see what other explanation there can be. The Irish garrison, nearly two hundred strong, surrendered at Jadotville because they were surrounded by Katangese and their water supply had been cut off. But their position although unpleasant was not desperate; if their morale had been high, they could have fought their way out and inflicted a crushing defeat on the Katangese and the mercenaries. The least that can be said is that this surrender was hardly in the spirit of Irish history. The Swedes, the other European contingent in Katanga, won the reputation of never daring to set foot outside their armoured cars. Perhaps the morale of both Swedes and Irish was low because they had volunteered to come to the Congo and had expected to find a friendly population and be involved only in police operations; even so, this is hardly an excuse for their dismal performances. The Indians at least performed respectably if cautiously, and the Ethiopians, though guilty of atrocities could not be accused of cowardice. Yet, even so, the mercenaries, man for man, were far superior to these well-equipped regular soldiers fighting for a just cause under the auspices of a world organization. In the street fighting Faulques and his men gave the impression of being everywhere at once, always shifting and firing their mortars, knocking down walls between houses and rivalling each other in rashness. It seemed, after this, to be a rule in the Congo that whenever the mercenaries had a personally courageous leader, they fought well and their morale, their *esprit de corps*, consisted in a sort of rivalry in rashness. A Congolese described to me with a sort of awe how Schramme's men drove into Bukavu standing upright in their jeeps and disdaining, unlike the ANC, to take cover. Perhaps the fundamental explanation is that the mercenaries, unlike the regular soldiers who opposed them, expected to be killed or at any rate knew that mercenaries are only hired when there is fighting, whereas regular soldiers can expect a lifetime of peace occasionally interrupted. In this sense the mercenary has inevitably adapted himself to the idea of his own death, and soldiers who are prepared to die are better fighters than those who desperately want to live.

THE MERCENARIES' REVOLT

So much for the military side. Denard's attempted invasion of Katanga showed the mercenaries' military weaknesses; but this was only one aspect of the political weakness of the whole final episode, the mercenaries' revolt. This revolt might have succeeded; Schramme might have become the Braccio of Central Africa. As it was he very nearly became the Carmagnola. The consequences of success would have been incalculable and no commentator at the time dared to forecast them. I do not intend here to examine the whole story in detail, for the blow-by-blow account has been given at least in summary in the preceding chapter. Politically, however, the revolt shows both the mercenaries' initial position of strength, almost of predominance, and exposes finally their underlying weaknesses. In the rest of this chapter I will try to analyze the causes of the revolt, the plans made, and the reasons, both political and military, for its failure.

In certain conditions it is almost inevitable that mercenaries will revolt against their employer; the moment of danger for both sides comes when the employer decides that he no longer needs the services of these always dangerous troops. In rare cases both sides will trust each other, and, as happened with Five Commando, the mercenaries will be demobilized without incident. But when an atmosphere of suspicion already exists, it is only natural for mercenaries to fear that, once disarmed, they will be killed rather than paid off and dismissed with honour; and on the other side the employer will see in every reluctance or tergiversation of the mercenaries the first signs of a revolt. In the Congo in 1968 an atmosphere of suspicion already existed: the mercenaries had seen and noted how the disarmed Katangese of the previous summer's revolt had been massacred despite promises of pardon and safety; on his side Mobutu knew that the whole country was seething with plots and acts of sabotage. He was particularly suspicious of Schramme and Ten Commando (the former 'Leopard Group'—Kansimbas from north Katanga).

Schramme in Maniema had succeeded in forming almost a state within a state; he had, with the other Belgian planters of the area, rebuilt roads and bridges, reorganized trade and education, sent on his own initiative for European technicians and missionaries, and used captured gangs of Simbas as forced labour. It was a great achievement but directly in the old colonial pattern. Schramme's base was his own plantation, complete with airstrip, at Yumbi in the heart of Maniema; his reputation and his power were spreading rapidly, and ever since the massacre of the Katangese the summer before he had been discreetly preparing the defence of Maniema against a possible attack by the central government. However discreet his preparations were, no doubt reports of them had come to the ears of Mobutu.

The second general situation in which mercenaries are likely to revolt arises when they calculate that they have a good chance of being taken on the payroll of a rival to their employer. When the rival has a more attractive personality and a reputation for being loyal to his mercenaries, a sudden change of loyalty and an armed revolt is even more likely to occur.

The third situation arises when a mercenary leader sees an opportunity to seize power himself and to take his employer's place.

None of these situations, none of the three guiding motives—fear, avarice, and ambition—are mutually exclusive. When all three conditions and all three motives exist, a revolt is inevitable. Objectively, they existed in the Congo in 1968.

It would be hard to say how and when Schramme's ambition grew. Probably he acted at first out of a mere instinct of self-preservation, though no doubt he had always felt that the way to solve the Congo's problems was to apply everywhere the methods he had used so successfully in Maniema.

It appears that the actual thought of revolt rather than defensive action did not enter Schramme's head till December, 1966. In that month he was summoned to Leo for an interview with Mobutu. There Mobutu told him of his intention to disarm the Kansimbas of Ten Commando and to replace them with ANC recruits raised elsewhere who would still, however, remain under the command of Schramme and the other white Belgian officers. Schramme replied that he was willing for both himself and his men to be demobilized—he and his officers to be sent back to Belgium and the Kansimbas to be returned to north Katanga—but that he would resist any attempt at 'disarming' his men. The tone of the conversation must have been remarkably like that of a feudal overlord confronting a powerful and semi-independent vassal. During the interview another powerful vassal, on whose loyalty the overlord counted, sat silently by without saying a word—Denard.

From Schramme's point of view Denard was a mere mercenary and adventurer while he himself was a planter and an administrator, in uniform only through force of circumstances. There was never any love lost between the French and the Belgians in the Congo. The Belgians considered that they had a prescriptive right to manage or to attempt to manage the affairs of their ancient colony in which many of them had settled; from the days of Katanga any intruding Frenchmen were looked upon with suspicion. Furthermore, Schramme suspected Denard of aiming at official military control of Maniema and at a general's baton.

Mobutu's intention was clearly to undermine the military basis of Schramme's power in general and in particular to disband the remaining Katangese still officially forming part of the ANC but potentially the inevitable supporters of any active pro-Tshombe revolt. Of the six other remaining Katangese battalions he felt fairly sure; two of them, the 7th and 9th Commandos, were commanded by Katangese officers who had been loyal the year before, and the remaining four which he intended, it seems, to disband gradually were officered by members of Six Commando. Denard had proved his loyalty the year before; he had taken an active part in halting and disarming the mutinous Katangese and perhaps even in the sinister business of their disappearance. His silent presence at the interview in December was an implied threat to Schramme.

The interview ended in a friendly atmosphere with Mobutu protesting his sincere affection and admiration for Schramme and letting the talk of disarmament drop. Schramme flew back to Yumbi apparently reassured and several months passed. Late in April, Denard paid a visit to Yumbi; he told Schramme that he had received orders from Mobutu to disarm him but that, taught by the lesson of the previous year, he did not intend to obey these orders. From this visit dates the alliance of the two mercenary leaders and the preparation of the revolt.

What was Denard's position and what were his motives? This is much more difficult to say. There were many who had said and who continued to say that Denard was an agent of the French government and in particular of the SDECE.[1] These stories appear to have been mainly Belgian-inspired and therefore suspect. Yet on the other hand there is no doubt that the mercenary leaders in general did maintain contacts with governments other than that of the Congo: Hoare was certainly hand-in-glove with the South African government and Peters tried to be, though he failed. But both the mercenary leaders and the governments seem to have preferred a sort of loose alliance to close and definite links. Official French diplomats were very scathing in private about Denard's character, activities, and attempted political intrigues. And yet of all the mercenary leaders, Denard's history is the most controversial and his motives the most suspect. He may simply have been placed in a dilemma where he either had to take up arms against a fellow European (and perhaps face a mutiny among his own mercenaries) or else join in organizing a revolt. He may have known or suspected that Mobutu had Six Commando next on the list for disarmament. He may have just

---

[1] Service de Documentation Extérieure et de Contre-Espionnage, the French Secret Service.

been preparing plans for every eventuality, including double and triple crosses. Or he may have been part of a vast conspiracy for Tshombe's return.

There were, of course, plots still being hatched in Tshombe's name, but plots had been, since independence, a commonplace in the Congo and part of everyday life or at least of everyday dreams. There was certainly something in the wind—the 'Kyrellis Plan' (the origin of the name is obscure) which aimed at the overthrow of Mobutu. But whether it was organized by Tshombe or whether the conspirators merely used his name; who these conspirators were and what were their motives; whether the plan was just a grandiose conspiracy on paper or an active plot; whether, as Schramme has unconvincingly claimed it was an ingenious smokescreen personally thought up by him in order to mislead Mobutu; what governments or vast capitalist groups may or may not have been behind it—all these are questions that are wrapped in obscurity and may never be exposed to light. In any case, 'certain circles' in Belgium had been once bitten the year before, and it seems reasonable to suppose that they would be twice shy. Admittedly, official relations between Brussels and Leo were at a particularly low point; admittedly, too, the continual squabble between the Union Minière and the Congolese government had once again touched off a crisis. But even Tshombe had attempted to nationalize the Union Minière in his time, and Belgian-Congolese relations had for eight years nearly always been sinking from depth to depth.

However, there certainly was one long-prepared and carefully executed plot—the plot that resulted in the kidnapping of Tshombe on June 30. It was not organized by Mobutu; that at least is certain. Had it been, Tshombe would have been flown directly to Leo and hanged, for he had already been condemned to death *in absentia* with the 'Pentecost conspirators.' It is unlikely that it was organized by the Algerians, who appear to have been taken by surprise and to have had no advantage to gain. The most probable explanation is that it was organized by the CIA; the CIA's duty and policy as an organ of the American government was to keep Mobutu in power. The Kyrellis Plan may or may not have existed; if it existed, it may or may not have been about to be put into execution. But in any case any plot, potential or actual, to restore Tshombe would be foiled by Tshombe's imprisonment in Algiers, and this imprisonment would not leave bloodstained consciences behind it.

But there is another explanation. François Bodenan who held up the five passengers at pistol point and forced the two pilots to land at Algiers was a Frenchman with a semi-criminal past, disposing at the time of plenty of money. If Tshombe's kidnapping was organized by the French SDECE, could Denard's actions be explained as part of the same vast and labyrinthine conspiracy aiming perhaps at the elimination of the pro-Belgian Tshombe and the pro-American Mobutu? It is a possible hypothesis.[1] Denard was wounded in the fighting at Stanleyville shortly after the revolt broke out, and this mischance may have ruined the *mise en scène* of some unknown conspiracy. Besides, it is none too certain that the bullet which wounded Denard was fired by a black soldier.

Nothing is too farfetched for the Congo, but attempts to unravel plots that fail are even more mystifying and far more unrewarding than attempts to unravel plots that succeed.

In any case, on June 22, 1967, Schramme and Denard met once more at Yumbi and agreed on a coordinated revolt in which Schramme was to arrange the initial assault. It was two months earlier that Schramme had killed the planter Quintin who had, according to Schramme's story, come to suggest precisely such a revolt. Quintin may have been an *agent provocateur* or an emissary of Kyrellis or merely yet another intriguer trying to poke his

---

[1] It may seem an impossible hypothesis. But no plot involving, whether directly or indirectly, Jacques Foccart, de Gaulle's *eminence grise* for African affairs, can be dismissed as inexistent or improbable simply on the grounds of complexity. There can be little doubt that most of the French mercenaries, from Trinquier onwards, took their orders from Foccart—or if not their orders, at least their orientation. Minor incidents and private conversations have confirmed this; but the surest evidence is France's obvious interest in the Congo, by far the largest and the richest of Africa's francophone states' and France's open support for Biafra. '*Brave petit peuple,*' de Gaulle is reported to have said. '*Foccart, il faudrait faire quelque chose pour eux.*'

finger into the Congolese pie. This killing adds another question mark which may never be fully answered.

The plan agreed on by Schramme and Denard consisted of three phases:

Phase A

Schramme to take Stan. Denard to join him there with his hundred-odd whites and eight hundred Katangese.

At the same time Noel, Schramme's officer, to take Bukavu with a detachment of Ten Commando, and Michel, another of Schramme's officers, to take Kindu.

Denard's men to relieve Schramme's men after the initial assault and to occupy and hold Stan, Bukavu and Kindu. Denard to give the order for revolt to the (entirely Katangese) 7th and 9th Commandos. 7th Commando to seize Uvira, which it was garrisoning. Noel, after taking Bukavu, to lead 9th Commando in an attack on Goma, which it would hold. Noel and Schramme to regroup at Yumbi.

Phase B

From Yumbi, Schramme (and Noel) to reinforce Michel at Kindu—which would then be the base of a reassembled Ten Commando.

Phase C

Schramme to advance (by train) from Kindu into Katanga. Rendezvous at Kongola with two thousand Katangese, already warned. Attack on Kamina. Conquest of Katanga and Kasai. Pause and ultimatum to Mobutu demanding his abdication.

Evidently Phase C of this grandiose plan was more an aspiration than a detailed scheme of operations. But Phases A and B were prepared in detail and could have succeeded.

All was fixed except the date. On July 3, three days after the kidnapping of Tshombe, Denard notified Schramme by radio and they met halfway between Yumbi and Lubutu. Denard told Schramme that his men were ready and that it was necessary to act quickly, for Mobutu had sent his 3rd Para regiment from Leo

STRENGTH AND WEAKNESSES OF THE MERCENARIES | 211

toward Stan to help Denard to disarm Schramme's men. The 3rd Para was coming along the River Congo by boat and was due to arrive in Stan on the morning of the fifth, two days later.

For what happened next, the only full account is Schramme's and in those points that can be checked it is not particularly reliable. For instance, a small group (less than ten) South African mercenaries had been hired two or three weeks earlier, held almost under house arrest in Angola, and then flown from Angola directly to Schramme's base at Yumbi on the fourth, fitted out with jeeps and guns and dispatched under Michel to attack Kindu without having the slightest idea whom they were meant to be attacking or why. That, at least, was their own account; but Schramme tells a far more complicated and less convincing story. According to this, Jeremiah Puren dropped down from the skies in March and told Schramme that 300 paratroops plus 50 fighter-bombers were standing by ready to fly in and support him in the event of a clash with the ANC. Then, the day after Denard's completely unconnected visit on June 22, a DC4 loaded with arms, ammunition and Colonel Puren landed unexpectedly at Yumbi; Puren brought with him the nine or ten South African mercenaries and left them there as guarantees of his good faith and indication of greater reinforcements before departing. Dates apart, these two stories are irreconcilable. Schramme's motives for inventing tales of intrigues and false promises are clear: they help to explain away his failure.

Not, on the other hand, that it was unlikely that Puren should visit Schramme at Yumbi, nor that Tshombe should be keeping in contact with his possible supporters. But it seems highly improbable that Schramme, whose attitude the year before had been characterized by excessive caution, should not in this period at least have sounded out the Belgian government. There are strong rumours that he was being 'covered' by the Belgian Foreign Minister, M. Harmel; and what has so far come out is certainly not the whole story. If in fact there was a Kyrellis Plan and both the mercenary leaders were consciously involved in it, they must have been hesitating and confused in the days following

Tshombe's capture, and this episode of the South Africans in Angola seems evidence of plotting, confusion, hesitation, and a last-minute decision to go ahead even after the loss of the rival pretender, the figurehead. Tshombe's name was often used by

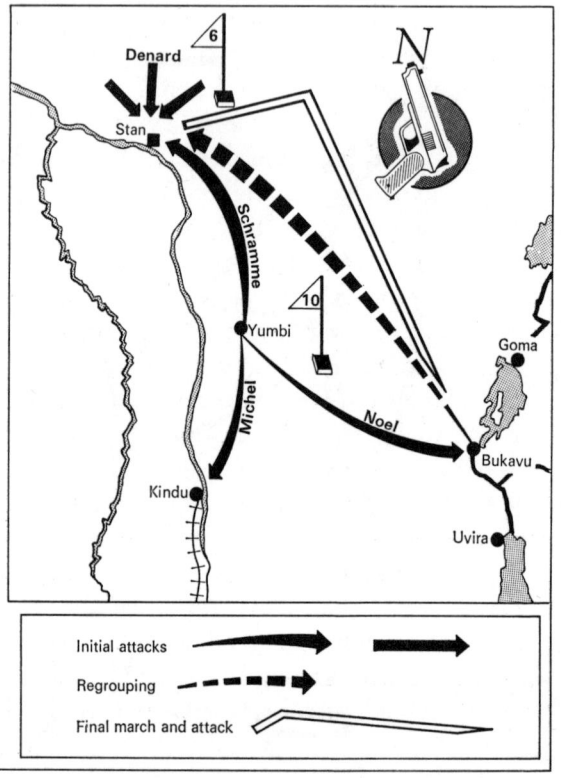

The Mercenaries' Revolt: In Practice.

mercenaries during the revolt—the journalists arrested at Stan airport on the morning of the fifth were told that they would be held hostages 'for the life of Tshombe'—but the use of a name, particularly so obvious and symbolic a name, does not prove the existence of a plot.

At any rate on the morning of the fifth Schramme went into

action. At dawn his three detachments made surprise attacks on Stan, Bukavu, and Kindu. Schramme himself occupied Stan almost without difficulty, and the ANC fled before Noel at Bukavu. But at Kindu the tiny detachment under Michel soon

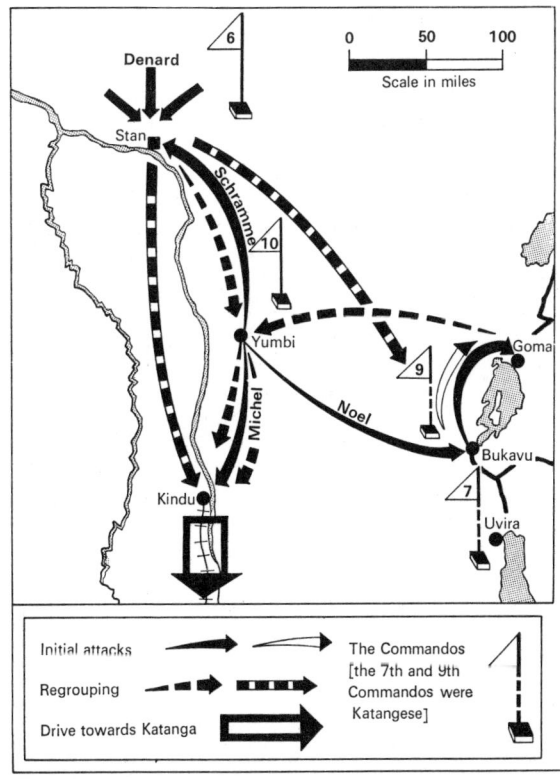

The Mercenaries' Revolt: In Theory.

found themselves defending the airport against a counterattack of two or three ANC battalions. This was the first disaster: most of the mercenaries in this group, including their leader Michel, were killed, and three or four of the South Africans escaped into the bush and eventually made their way back to Yumbi on foot, an extraordinary achievement.

At Bukavu only the initial capture went according to plan. Neither Denard's relieving column under one of his officers, Nodyn, nor the 7th or 9th (Katangese) Commandos appeared. That day Noel got a radio message, either sent or received—stories differ—by a drunken radio operator which he interpreted as an order to leave Bukavu and fall back on Stan. Less than twenty-four hours after its capture, therefore, the mercenaries pulled out of Bukavu, a retreat which left the white population of Bukavu at the mercy of a returning and vindictive ANC; many were killed or tortured as a punishment for 'collaboration.'

Schramme later blamed the failure of Phase A on Denard. Denard, according to him, had not warned the outlying patrols of Six Commando, and it took these men a week to assemble at Stan. Therefore Schramme, having to defend Stan against the fierce attacks of the 3rd Para, had not been able to relieve Kindu quickly or regroup at Yumbi. However, this does not square with other accounts, according to which on the evening of the fourth Denard's remote garrisons and patrols received orders, with no explanation, to fall back quickly on Stan. In any case the failure at Kindu, the unnecessary retreat from Bukavu, and the wounding and evacuation of Denard ruined the whole military plan of action.

The cause of this failure was probably muddle, confusion, and ill luck rather than the sinister motives which Schramme later insinuated were behind Denard's actions. Where Denard can be blamed was for his failure to warn the thirty-odd mercenaries of Six Commando at Leo; possibly he thought that these men, mainly occupied in liaison and administrative work, would not be harmed; possibly he feared that to warn them would be to risk leaking information; possibly he attempted to warn them but failed. One of them, an Algerian who had taken French nationality, had been enlisted by Denard in Paris, and was employed by Mobutu as a personal bodyguard, eventually managed to escape; he was probably the only survivor, and his account (published in *Le Figaro*) of how these unsuspecting mercenaries in the capital were rounded up during the fifth and led like sheep to the slaughter is horrifying and vivid enough. This was the first group of Congolese mercenaries to suffer the traditional fate of being massacred treacherously by their employer. For this Denard bears responsibility.

Meanwhile the mercenaries at Stan were left in much the same sort of position as Xenophon's Greeks after the loss of Cyrus and the generals. Their hopes of surprise and a quick success were gone, the enemy was assembling large forces, their position was untenable, one of their two leaders had been lost, the native 'pretender' in whose name they were fighting had been exterminated, their escape looked difficult and their future uncertain. In addition, Schramme had on his hands large numbers of local whites who feared reprisals from the ANC if they stayed where they were.

After a week at Stan, Schramme moved out. To have stayed would have been purposeless; the surrounding population, still largely Simba, was hostile and Stan was therefore neither a possible centre for a spreading revolt nor near enough to a frontier to offer a way of escape. There were several alternatives open to Schramme. The first was to fall back defensively onto his own fortified region of Maniema, but this would have been almost pointless, both tactically and strategically. The second was to go ahead with the revolt despite the failures and loss of surprise and to attempt to raise Katanga. The third was to give up and try to save the lives of the white refugees and his own men by heading toward the border.

In the end Schramme compromised, and the three-week-long anabasis of the mercenary column, only once seriously held up by an ambush at Itibero, ended in the capture, or rather the recapture, of Bukavu.

Schramme has been criticized both for choosing Bukavu as his objective and for staying there. His critics blame him for having chosen almost the only city of any size in the Congo which did not have an airstrip and where, therefore, reinforcements could not be sent. Schramme's defence was threefold: first, it was his responsibility to escort the white refugees to safety and therefore he was forced to march to a border city; secondly, Bukavu was stocked with large supplies of food, drink, and ammunition; and thirdly, it was tactically defensible by his small army. Goma, a little to the north, was the obvious alternative and Goma had an airstrip, but Schramme argued that the third criterion ruled out Goma: unlike Bukavu, it lay on a flat plain. Furthermore, Bukavu had a radio station, and Radio Bukavu beamed insults against Mobutu, appeals to the besieging ANC, and false news of the success of the rebellion all over the east of the Congo.

The question of the airstrip was obviously important only if Schramme would expect aid from outside. In fact three planes landed or attempted to land at Bukavu. The first was a twin-engine Piper, flown by a Belgian pilot, a former Katanga mercenary, Bracco; he crash-landed it on the lake where it sank but not before the two passengers had had time to inflate a canoe. One was Captain Nawej, a Katangese who had been Tshombe's head of security; the other, almost inevitably, was Colonel Jeremiah Puren.

The second plane to arrive was a DC3; for it Schramme had built an airstrip, but a hundred yards too short. The plane, though loaded with arms and ammunition, did not explode. The third, which circled overhead and in the end parachuted its supplies rather than attempting a landing, was a DC4.

These planes obviously came from the south, but whether they came from Angola, Rhodesia, or South Africa is uncertain. Their arrival proves that even if no plot had existed before, there were now outside support and outside finance for the mercenaries. Schramme was in radio contact daily with Denard in Angola and possibly with other more mysterious allies elsewhere. He remained in contact right up to the end, and he alleged that the reason he did not leave Bukavu and move on to Katanga was that Denard kept reassuring him that the second front would open, and (at the end) that a flying boat full of arms and ammunition would land on the lake. Just before retreating finally into Rwanda, Schramme sent a last message over the radio to Denard: 'ICI SCHRAMME EN PERSONNE—STOP—SITUATION SANS ISSUE—STOP—N'AVONS PLUS

DE MUNITIONS—STOP—NE SAVONS PAS ENCORE COMMENT CELA VA FINIR—STOP—RÉGLERONS COMPTES PLUS TARD—STOP—VOUS ETES DES ASSASSINS—STOP ET FIN.'

This may have been the reason for Schramme's weeks of inactivity. On the other hand, it may be that he underestimated the value of the ANC; the 7th and 9th Commandos which had been meant to join in the revolt were among the troops besieging Bukavu, and continual appeals over Radio Bukavu to them to desert and change sides had no effect. The Belgian press, which was largely favourable to Schramme, had stories of American pressure on Lisbon and Johannesburg to prevent any possible aid reaching Schramme and reports of supplies of American arms and weapons and even American 'advisers' in person reaching the ANC besieging Bukavu. They blamed the eventual failure of the mercenaries' revolt almost entirely on the Americans.[1]

Denard, for his part, blamed the Portuguese for failing to keep their promises of support to his 'second front.'

Those who blamed Schramme for choosing Bukavu and for staying there were probably more right. Apart from the obvious disadvantages, there was the psychological effect on the mercenaries' morale of having a border and safety within sight: the temptation for deserters was great; twenty mercenaries deserted immediately after the capture of Bukavu, and many more towards the end. For Schramme and the leaders the knowledge that

---

[1] In fact even the mercenaries did not believe the current tall tales of American Negroes leading the ANC against them, though they did suspect that Israeli instructors were directing the unusually accurate mortar fire. Monga's 'Presidential Proclamation' of August 10 contained an impassioned appeal to General Moshe Dayan urging 'the conquerors of the Arab demagogues to cease their aid to the demagogues of Mobutu' and 'to recall to Israel the Israeli instructors who are in the Congo'.

In any case it seems extremely unlikely that President Johnson would have risked such an involvement. His administration's proposal to put more C130's at the disposal of Mobutu had already aroused angry reactions both among Congressmen and Senators; the plans were quietly withdrawn. An interesting sidelight: Professor Samuel Hartingdon of Harvard gave a conference in autumn 1967 at the Adlai Stevenson Institute of International Affairs in which he suggested that this furore marked the symbolic turning-point of U.S. foreign policy, which, according to the Klinsberg theory, alternates between periods of isolationism and periods of commitment. If the Professor's theory is correct, then Schramme and Denard are, if not precisely historical figures, at least historical symbols, and have certain indirect claims on the world's gratitude (or, alternatively, not—as the case may be).

retreat was possible at any moment led to wavering and hesitation. If they had been isolated in the middle of hostile territory, they would have undoubtedly struck out with more boldness.

But the fundamental reason for the failure of the revolt was neither treachery nor cowardice nor bad strategy; it was quite simply that the revolt was a revolt of mercenaries, and almost by definition mercenaries' revolts cannot succeed except by speed and surprise. However discontented the subjects of a tyrannous ruler are, they will normally prefer to be ruled by a tyrant of their own race rather than by a group of rebellious foreigners formerly in the service of the tyrant. The revolt of the mercenaries at Carthage,[1] finally so bloodily extinguished, is the perfect example of a tentative still doomed however great the initial success.

If Tshombe had been free and if Tshombe had himself appeared at Bukavu or in Katanga, then the revolt would probably have succeeded. But Schramme's political ineptitude was shown by his choice of Colonel Monga as a figurehead; possibly some black leader, almost any black leader, was better than none but Monga's 'Government of Public Safety' was a farcical failure, and the appeals of Radio Bukavu did not, as hoped, fan the sparks of popular revolt. Denard seems to have realized the importance of a black leader far better; his bizarre tentative to rescue Munongo failed, but it showed Denard's political good sense—if indeed it was he that organized the attempted rescue. Munongo was a man well known throughout Katanga and the Congo; he would have been a leader of a different calibre from the obscure Monga.

In any case the revolt failed. When it broke out there were, according to the Congolese Radio, 189 mercenaries in the Congo. Of them, 123 returned to Europe in the final evacuation. Roughly 30 were killed in Leo; there were a score or so of desertions. In the actual fighting only about 20 mercenaries were killed, 8 of them at Bukavu. In the final battles two of the officers commanding the eight defensive posts were killed—a young and courageous Belgian of twenty-five, Guy Leleup, and an older man named Vanderveuken. Schramme blamed for their cowardice in the

---

[1] Described in detail in Flaubert's novel *Salammbo*.

final attack two of the other post commanders, Laboudigue and Martinez. Both of them were Frenchmen, officers of Six Commando. If there was one subsidiary underlying reason for the failure of the revolt, it was the never-ceasing mistrust and suspicion felt by the Belgians for the French and vice versa. In just the same way the Ten Thousand Greeks had been torn by national rivalries which were only patched over in moments of great danger.

Schramme appears to have been more successful than most of the other mercenary leaders in amassing and possessing a fortune. There were confirmed reports of trunkloads of banknotes passing, in the last days, clandestinely across Lake Kivu. On the other hand, the price paid by the mercenaries for their revolt was low. Mercenaries whose revolts fail usually suffer far more violent a penalty than that of having stamped on their passports 'Not Valid for Africa.'

10 The Mercenary Life

EVERY WRITER LIKES to give his references, if only because critics, both immediate and future, demand dates, names, sources and origins. Unfortunately in this chapter, which consists largely of original documents, I cannot do so. More irritatingly still for the general reader, I have been obliged to substitute blank spaces or initials for names, and occasionally to change dates and points of reference by which ex-mercenaries now living normal (or moderately normal) lives might be embarrassed. As a general rule the only names left unchanged are those of mercenary leaders already well-publicized, or of the dead, who can no longer be harmed.

A number of documents were acquired by me from a variety of different sources, both in Europe and Africa, on the understanding, express or implied, that I would observe the rules of reticence and discretion. They are, it seems to me, worth publishing even under these somewhat irritating conditions, precisely because they were not intended for publication; they therefore give a far more genuine and vivid idea of the mercenary life than any number of carefully edited memoirs or carefully planned interviews could do.

Of the many documents which I have been able to study or to 'liberate', there is only space to publish a small selection here. The ideas which have guided my choice are: first, that the documents should have in themselves some dramatic or even melodramatic interest apart from their sociological value; and, secondly, that the complete document rather than an excerpt should be set out—a general rule not always followed when the matter is too trivial or too repetitious. The disadvantage is that fewer documents can be set out; but the corresponding advantage, which in my opinion more than balances it, is that the general reader will not have that tiresome but only too common feeling of being faced with carefully edited and balanced selections. Thirdly, I have chosen only documents which refer to Five Commando. This arbitrary rule of thumb gives this chapter at least some coherence.

What follows is an extract from the unit diary kept by Lieutenant Jeremy Spencer, one of Hoare's young officers; it begins three weeks before the capture of Stan in 1964 when all the units of Five Commando were reassembling to join the attacking column.

> *29 October*   2/Lt S—— and Vol.[1] L—— sent to Kongolo to guard supplies sent from Kamina base same day.
> *30 October*   56 Commando consisting of thirty-one all told left Kamina base for Congola.
> *31 October*   Still at Congola. Very dull day. Fired the men's rifles to check gas regulators but unfortunately not allowed to fire our 75 mm. Recoiless Rifle, which we were all very keen to see firing, because the Belgians were scared we would hit one of their planes.
> *1 November*   Left Congola for Manono and spent night there.
> *2 November*   Left Manono for Samba (194 kms from Congola). On arrival did Recce Patrol down to Lualaba River (29 kms) to discover whereabouts of ferry. Fired a few shots on way but did not kill anyone. Took Sgt R—— with me as well who, when we discovered the Barque was the other side of the River, volunteered to go over in a prow and bring it back. Would like to have let him do so, plus myself, but luckily realised it was not vital—and secondly I'm not a very good swimmer!

---
[1] Abbreviation for 'Volunteer'—official title of ordinary mercenary soldier.

3 November Left Samba 10.00 hrs and camped 3 kms other side of Lafote River. Not a very safe crossing as we also had a jeep in front of us on the pontoon containing RSM Carton-Barber—everybody egging our driver on to slip his clutch and push him in. At 07.45 hrs Sgt R——, S—— and Vol. B—— detonated 48 Energa grenades and approx. 1,000 rounds of bad ammo. Very impressive bang and also blew the building to pieces in which they had placed the charge.

4 November Left Lafote river at 11.00 hrs and arrived Kibombo at 15.30 hrs and drove straight in. Then we did a recce patrol to Lualaba river (8 kms) where everybody had a swim and fired their rifles at a sniper across the river. Left Kibombo at 20.00 hrs for Kindu. About 5 kms outside Kibombo the leading Ferret met a rebel armoured car coming towards us, which opened fire with a .50 Browning at the leading Ferret armoured car. Terrific bombardment and nobody knew what the hell was going on. Lot of tracer flying about which luckily did no damage and then eventually we managed to kill the chap on the rebel armoured car and all was peace.

5 November Arrived Kindu (2nd largest rebel-held town) where we had a terrific shooting match at nothing in particular, everybody blazing as we drove through the centre of the town. We then drove down to ferry (56) where Vol. Patience killed General Olenga.[1] We also managed to sink a barge with about 50 rebels on board. At 18.00 hrs we drove 3 kms out to the airport (3 kms) —56 only—(with myself on bonnet of leading jeep expecting to be fired on any moment by .30 Browning machine-gun and very scared too!). We met one guard at Airport who fired on us but everybody opened fire on him and he was very quickly polished off. I opened fire with my Vigneron and loosed off 25 rounds but don't think I hit him! Luckily someone else did.

6 November Left airport at 10.00 hrs and returned to Kindu. Went over to the other side of the river and spent night there preparatory to leaving for Kalina next day to rescue 70 Europeans.

7 November Left Kindu at 05.45 hrs for Kalina. Arrived Kalina 10.00 hrs and once again drove straight in to discover the rebels had left at 23.00 hrs the previous night. Rescued Europeans from

---

[1] Olenga was the commander-in-chief of the Simbas. He was continually being reported killed but always survived.

Mission where I had a very refreshing gin and drove back to Kindu (100 kms).

8 November Found ourselves a house to sleep in and managed to acquire a fridge to keep our champagne in (which we acquired at Kalina) plus a few other goodies. T.B.H.[1] jumped on 2/Lt S—— and Sgt R—— when he found them in town driving around in a V/W and as he said looking like ragamuffins. Asked them where they had been and what they were doing and they said testing the car but they were, I suspect, looking for more interesting things!!

9 November Was going to be a show-the-flag parade round Kindu but luckily it poured with rain so it was cancelled. At 9.30 we crossed over the river to hold the position the other side. Fixed up two machine-gun posts with boxes and sandbags to the accompaniment of groans from all concerned. Nothing doing late at night so most people had a good night's sleep.

10 November Reveille at 9.0, so we could get a bit of sleep in. Did nothing all day—fired at a couple of rebels and shot one in chest but he escaped; were issued with 48 Primus beers which were welcomed by all—also received a bottle of Cinzano off Ian which went down well.

11 November Left Kindu at 12.00 hrs for the Elela river to hold the bridge against rebels crossing from Stan. A nasty pile of bloated bodies greeted us when we arrived which one of our men Vol. R—— proceeded to sort through! Managed to fix our jeep up with machine-gun mounting today which gives me a bit more confidence—though not very nice for the man sitting behind it.

12 November Another quiet day at Elela. Rained all morning but stopped about 10.00 hrs. A very miserable morning which the majority spent in bed as there was nothing else to do. Tried to get P—— to fix a seat on the back of the jeep but rather like trying to get a Clydeside to pull a plough when it doesn't want to.

Friday, 13 November A nervous early morning for superstitious people like myself. Having heard 9 trucks had left Stan 3 days ago to attack us I was fully expecting some sort of attack but as usual nothing materialised.

---

[1] Hoare. T.M.B. were his initials.

The entry for the following day is written in a different hand.

> 14 November This morning at 07.00 hrs Lt Spencer killed by enemy fire which opened up on us at 05.35 hrs. Jeremy was hit in the head and died without regaining consciousness at 07.15 hrs. It is my unpleasant duty as 2 I/C of the unit to take over temporary command and continue this diary. Jeremy sadly missed, a good officer and friend. Having opened fire with mortar and .50 machine-gun contacted HQ at 07.00 hrs. 57 Commando sent to reinforce. Constant enemy fire. Air support requested. Air support arrived at 10.15 hrs and opened fire with rockets and machine-guns on the enemy. 10.15 hrs 57 Commando arrived with the Commandant[1] and after brief assessment of position and after heavy mortar support led the attack over river. 57 dug in other side. 56 left to maintain position defending bridge. The men are rather shaken up but not too bad, morale still good.

Jeremy Spencer was an old Etonian and had done his national service in a Guards regiment. He was, I think, the first mercenary officer of Five Commando to be killed. This diary—indeed the very fact of keeping a unit diary at all—shows how Hoare tried to make a typical British army unit of his men and how far he succeeded or failed. As regards discipline, it was an impossible aim; as regards training and organization, they were unimaginative but successful.

FIVE COMMANDO TRAINING PROGRAMME

> Fifth day. 06.00 reveille. 06.10 to 06.30 physical training. 07.00 to 07.30 breakfast. 08.00 muster parade and inspection. 08.15 to 09.30 foot and arms drill. 09.30 to 10.00 provisional, .30 Browning. 10.00 to 10.30 tea break. 10.30 to 11.00 introduction to mine detectors. 11.00 to 12.30 introduction to field craft, judging distances, target indications, ambush drill. 12.30 to 14.00 lunch-break. 14.00 to 18.00, double march to range, firing .30 browning and 60 mm. mortar. 18.00 guard mounting.

Not only the timetables but also the skills were modelled on standard British practice.

---

[1] Wicks. Commandant is a French military rank, above captain and below major. See end of Appendix I (Article: Promotion) for ANC ranks.

UNIT ORDERS

No-one will be favoured, I repeat no-one, only the best will be selected as R.S.M. R.S.M. Burger will then resume his duties as Captain. Two of the best Lieutenants will be selected for this training. For the purpose the training will consist of the following items:

a) Different formations of movement and their different positions.

b) Exact training on fire control. Orders from officers to sergeants, and sergeants to men.

c) If in this future operation I want a certain group of men to fire at a certain target, they must know exactly how to deliver concentrated fire on the target.

d) Men *must* be trained in the exact way of movement and fire.

e) The men must be in such a state of training that when they are being fired on they act: down, crawl, observe, fire.

f) Every man will be in such a state of training that he will inform his superiors exactly where the target is:—By reference point method; direct method; Crockery method; hand degree reference method.

g) Scouts hand signals. Further training and instructions will be given on radio. S.A.P.S.

MORE ORDERS

1) Upon receipt of tools and equipment for road and bridge building, you will start immediately with this project. Use your own men and the assistance of the civilians in that area.

2) The roads between villages will be divided in half and each respective village will be responsible for the clearing and fixing of the road in that area.

....

8) Any further orders to you will be sent by radio.

9) Keep up the good work and the good name of Five Commando.

By 1967 the mercenaries' duties had become more administrative than military.

MILITARY REPORTS

To O.C. Five Commando, Lt M. G. B——, Nakalitsa. February 19, 1967.

On my patrol to the river Simunansi, Chief Katangula of the village Katanja, respectfully requested on behalf of all the minor chiefs in that area, that the traders of Albertville should be allowed to penetrate the area in order to purchase stores of rice, mealies, groundnuts and ivory, etc., of which they claim to have large amounts accumulated over a long period. The time suitable would be any time from March onward. They request that several traders come, the reason being that should there be one trader only he would command a monopoly, thus preventing competitive prices for buying.

March, 1967. Report from Second Lt B—— on the Moya-Matana road.

2) Visibility from the road is poor. There is either buffalo grass approximately four feet; elephant grass, approximately 10 to 12 feet; or thick jungle the whole way. The grass on the road itself is in the process of being cleared by the civilians.

. . . .

4) Bridges. There are eighteen of these. All the main beams are fair to good. These are the beams from bank to bank. The cross struts or beams of these bridges have all been removed or are in bad condition. They have all been replaced with saplings. These will definitely not last. Planking and nails required for all these bridges to make them sound for heavy vehicles. It would be chancy to take heavy vehicles across, although it is possible with due care. All villages along this road appear to be pro Five Commando as of now. All information was given freely. The village of King Bosel was completely deserted, with the exception of the chief and approximately six men of the air-strike. But the chief informs me that his people are on their way back. Village Ngeti is burnt out.

. . . .

6) No school.

7) There are 24 A.N.C. at Ndala under the command of their Sergeant Major.

ANOTHER REPORT

    10.4.67. From O.C. Cheta, to O.C. Paradise, info. C.O. Five Commando, Subject, civilian report.

    Chiefs and local Chiefs from surrounding area have been informed that Five Commando is vacating this area. Big deputation has just informed me that themselves and all their people intend moving at the same time we move. They will not stay in the area, under any other command other than Five Commando. A large party of women and children on their way to this position so that they can plead with us. All villages will be vacated and will follow Five Commando.

There was another side to this favourable picture quite apart from the atrocities committed[1]. Whenever immediate danger faded, discipline became almost impossible to maintain. In a mercenary force discipline can be based only on respect for individual commanders, for their authority is not backed by the majestic force of an impersonal state. Desertion for a mercenary is no crime, merely a way of breaking a contract, and as at heart all mercenaries feel themselves to be equal and equally engaged for pay or loot, they do not feel the respect for their officers or for one another that the tradition of a regular army creates. Any acts of punishment generally have to have the agreement, at least tacit, of the majority; it would for instance have been unthinkable for an officer of Five Commando to have had one of his men shot for a major crime. In that sense the discipline was tribal, and the authority of the tribal chief imposed itself more by personality than by formal rules, even though a military police unit existed. Spencer's diary shows how Hoare managed to make his authority felt but was unable to prevent looting. His successors had perhaps more difficulty.

---

[1] Which will not be discussed at length in this book. There were so many atrocities committed on all sides in the Congo that even the most macabre enquirers must have had their fill. Apologists are reduced to explaining that the mercenaries shot rather than tortured prisoners—but for a gruesome example of particularly sub-human behaviour by a South African mercenary, see Hans Germani's *White Soldiers in Black Africa*, page 50.

COLLIERS' SIGNAL SENT TO STARLIGHT[1] FROM C.O.

My instructions to you were quite clear, that you must stay at Cheta's position and that you will, I repeat will, return to Cheta's position after receiving this message. You will get medical treatment from Starlight Minor and he will put a report in about this matter and apply plaster of paris if necessary. Furthermore my instructions were that you would clear the small-pox epidemic, and until this is done you will not leave Cheta's position. Any medical staff can be trained in the field while they are doing nothing. Why was the rebel 2 I.C. not sent here with the Kookoracha today, and why was I not informed of this capture or surrender? You are paid to do your duty in the field and not to lay about in Albertville where there is nothing to do. Now this is final. In connection with this matter I do not want to hear any more of this nonsense. If Cook's case were not so urgent you could have treated him there. You have all the necessary medical equipment and if there was anything you were short of you could have sent a message. Furthermore I do not want you to interfere with the orders of my field officers. Your orders to them will be confined to the line of medical treatment in requirement. In the future if you want to transfer yourself from one position to another, you will firstly get confirmation from me, excluding the area where you are treating small-pox. Stop this childish acting of yours. You are making a fool of yourself in front of all officers and men of Five Commando and I will not allow any officer of mine to behave like that. Furthermore I want a full statement from you regarding the sinking of the P boat, also where you obtained permission to use same. I want acknowledgement of this letter. A.S.A.P.

Brawls were always common:

A REPORT

To: C.O. Five Commando,
From: Second Lt J——
Subject: Incident in   , February 10, 1967.

On the night of January 1, 1967, approximately 9 p.m. I was playing a game of darts with Sergeant Franklin. I heard a scuffle

---

[1] Starlight is normal British army code for the medical officer. Starlight Minor would be his assistant.

and saw Captain W—— and Lt P—— in a clinch on the floor. Blows were exchanged. Lt M—— was summoned and he ordered the fighting to cease. Lt P—— complied with the command but Captain W—— endeavoured to attack again and had to be held fast. Lt M—— then ordered both parties to leave the bar and go to bed. Lt P—— obeyed. S—— and myself together with volunteer V—— H—— accompanied him to his billet. As we left Captain W—— shouted abuse at Lt P—— and myself and tried to follow us, but was held back by Lt M——. I discovered that Lt P——'s right eyebrow was badly cut. Shortly after our arrival at the billet, Captain W—— turned up and the fighting resumed. Lt P—— repeatedly requested Captain W—— to stop the fighting, several of us who were present then held Captain W——. Lt M—— then arrived on the scene and after considerable persuasion Captain W—— was taken away. After only a few minutes he came back in a jeep, threatening and shouting abuse. Lt P—— remained in the house and Lt M—— managed to persuade Captain W—— to leave off the fight.

Many of the brawls were much more serious than this, and on at least two occasions officers were killed. One RSM had a particularly vicious reputation; he killed an American at Albertville who was probably a CIA agent and therefore finished up in a military jail at Leo—where he himself was probably killed in the massacre of the mercenaries in July, 1967.

To be a mercenary soldier is, and always has been, a dangerous occupation. Five Commando had a fairly high casualty rate, and though the mercenary contract specified lump sum compensation for death or serious injury, it was rarely, if ever, paid—at least to the best of my knowledge.[1]

---

[1] But see page 223 (paragraph 7) where one of Peters' officers claims that it was paid under his command. See Appendix I (Articles 24-29) for the Utopian sums which mercenaries were led to expect. In view of the Simbas' well-known propensity for mutilation, there is a curious anatomical omission in Article 27, clause A. Prudery on the part of the lawyer who drew up the contract?

A MILITARY REPORT

> To: Commanding Officer
> 5 Commando ANC
> Fort Baraka

re Tiger Patrol of 13.3.66

Sir,

It is with regret that I must inform you of the death of six of my men who were killed instantly while on patrol some eleven kilometres from this position.

Below is a fully detailed account of the patrol's progress and actions until they returned to this position.

Leaving Baraka at 20.00 hours 13.3.66 we made the top of the escarpment in good time and reached a commanding position approximately 5–6 kilometres from this position by 00.30 hours where we rested for some 45 minutes. We were very wet and cold due to the heavy downpour of rain which lasted until approximately 14.15 hours.

Leaving our resting position we moved on in a NNW direction, skirting the highest points of the range in order to locate any smoke from enemy fires that may have been present. We however neither saw nor heard anything until nigh on 05.45 hours when Lt M—— and his group of scouts reported having seen what appeared to be two fires some 3 kilometres from the 12.7 position captured four days ago.

I briefed the men and scouts on what to do. The plan was to approach the indicated position with extreme care avoiding all tracks and paths until we were within 600 yards of the fires. I would then creep forward with the scouts, make observations and return to my patrol to formulate an attack plan. On reaching our planned position we heard a number of voices. I estimated there to be about twenty persons present in what appeared to be a small camp. Suddenly a rebel appeared, walking up a path directly towards us. He saw us and opened fire. We returned the fire, killing him. This warned the remainder of the camp-dwellers, so we rushed forward until we reached a small bivouac area consisting of some eleven huts. There was some firing from the trees and we managed to kill one more fleeing rebel. I formed a perimeter and searched the camp area but found nothing of value.

We burnt the hut and then retraced our route up the path to

the first dead rebel. Not 30 yards past him was a small well-used track running off to the right which we followed with Lt M—— and his scouts some 400 yards ahead of us. We had not gone far when one of the scouts returned saying they had found a large ammo dump, but could not tell me what was inside as there was a makeshift door on the underground dump, but they had seen boxes inside with the use of a torch whilst peering through a crack. He had not yet finished his report when there was a terrific explosion which virtually shook the ground we stood on. We rushed forward and found to our horror an enormous crater in the ground which had been created by the blast. Of the scouts there was no sign. The nearby trees had been stripped of their branches, leaves and bark. We called and searched for the scouts but did not have to look far. I found a ribcage and a tattoed left arm belonging to what was once Vol. X——. On further searching we found the grisly remains of the men. Hands, bits of body, twisted legs, etc. One man vomited and another began crying, it was a terrible scene. Myself and four others collected what we could find and buried them in a shallow grave nearby. We did not search too deep in the trees for fear of mines. The morale of the men had dropped to zero so I returned to base immediately.

    I can only assume sir, that the ammo dump judging by the size of the crater was an extremely large one and it had been booby-trapped, the trap being connected to the door for any intruders i.e. 5 Cdo. Either Lt M—— or one of his men must have been attempting to open the door when the explosion took place. Possibly the trap was badly placed or the detonation set off the whole dump. A few pieces of anti-tank mines and mortar shrapnel were found, that is judging by the colour of the metal pieces.

    The names of the dead are 2/Lt M——, Vols... [*Five names follow*]

    Sir, may I request that I take my force on another patrol ASAP for I feel that whilst they sit around and brood over this tragic occurrence, their nerves may fail them on any patrol they may be sent on at a later date. I myself feel somewhat un-nerved by this shattering experience.

Witness: Adj-chef M——   Captain P. R——
Witness: Adjudant C——   O.C. Force Tiger

At first dead mercenaries were buried where they lay and often their relatives had no news of them for months. Later, the administrative system was far better organized and letters to and from other countries usually reached Five Commando safely via their liaison officers at Leo and Stan.

The following is a letter from a mother to the CO, Five Commando:

> Dear Sir,
> I wrote some time ago about my son P—— F——'s belongings. The tape recorder has been returned to me but what has happened to the clothes, passport, Private Papers, and any letters? He had with him a black leather jacket, a pair of expensive dark glasses, a black railway fireman's cap, a light leather jacket which he wore when he left Umtali on that awful Saturday. I shall always remember him wearing it. He had on a pair of dark trousers. He took lots of hankies; they were marked with his name. He also had a very old pair of blue jeans, a pair of yellow boots. These things may not be of great value to me but they are of great sentimental value because when I lost my beloved child I lost everything—he was my life. I am so worried as I never had another letter since P—— wrote on Oct. 2. He didn't answer any of the three letters I wrote to him, if he got them. Please help me if you can. . . .

By the end Five Commando's character and style had changed considerably from what it had been at the time of Spencer's diary.

When Peters resigned, he had planned to go to South Africa but was refused the right to reside there by the South African government. One of his officers wrote from Albertville to the South African Ministry of the Interior pleading against this decision:

> February 1967.
> I would like to bring to your attention that I have already been in contact with your department as well as the S.A. police and the department of Defence in connection with the above person. I would like to reiterate the following points. More than

90% of the present members of Fifth Commando are South Africans. These men fight for the unit with the ultimate idea being the suppression of communism.

1) Under the excellent leadership of Lt Col J. Peters, a terrific amount of success has been achieved and the rebel forces have almost completely been destroyed. The remaining rebels now moving in small groups—they are, too, diminishing.

2) In the past I can assure you South Africans have at times found themselves in most undesirable circumstances. Lt Col Peters was the only man who fully assisted these men and refused to hand these men over to black authorities for trial.[1]

3) On various occasions did men of the Fifth Commando, including myself, hand rebel weapons and ammunition to the S.A. police and the Department of Defence in order to assist their study of communist weapons. This was insisted upon by Lt Col Peters.

4) Since Lt Col Peters has been appointed Commanding Officer of Fifth Commando there has been no warranted complaints of wages not being paid.

5) Under the command of Lt Col Hoare this was not the case. The men were never sure of receiving their pay.[2]

6) In excess of 90% of the Fifth Commando officers are not only South Africans but actually Afrikaans speaking, which again proves that Lt Col Peters promotes his men on merit only, regardless of the language they speak. The following are the names of some of the Afrikaans speaking officers in this Commando: Major G. Schroeder, 2 I/C, Captains B——, B., S——, A., B——, S., Lieutenants A., S——, G., L——, C., Captain Q. S——, M.B., C.H.B., University, Cape Town, served as intern at Groote Schuur Hospital, Cape Town. In the past these men were not even considered by Lt Col Hoare.

7) The relatives of all men who die in the Congo receive an amount of Rand 14,000. When Lt Col Peters took command of this unit more than 80% of these claims were outstanding, but

---

[1] Perennial problem for mercenary leaders. For the formal position see Appendix I (Article 3). A similar clause is always to be found in Italian *condattas*.
[2] True, but in Hoare's defence it can be said that Puren, not he, was responsible for this side of the administration, and that Hoare was, unlike Peters, fighting a war of movement in conditions unfavourable to efficient paper work.

have now been settled. This again proves the negligence of Lt Col Hoare, compared to the efficiency of Lt Col Peters who immediately took steps to have these claims settled.

8) As far as discipline is concerned we endeavour to uphold the good name of Five Commando, but as usual the individual can do a lot of harm; a problem also encountered by the authorities in R.S.A. The men applying in our recruiting office can be divided into the following groups:
   a) The man with domestic problems, viz. the recently divorced;
   b) The fortune-seeker;
   c) The man who wants experience;
   d) The man who wishes to dodge the law;
   e) There are also those who arrive here with disreputable pasts who wrongly imagine he can continue with his criminal career.

With the above types we have to maintain our good reputation. On the last flight, for example, a number of men were sent back after being found in possession of 'dagga'. This is the type who usually goes back to S.A. with untrue stories to blacken our name. These are normally the people who cannot submit themselves to discipline. The most prominent excuses for their sudden return are given as—
   a) Not being paid;
   b) Murder is being committed;
   c) Looting;
   d) The non-existence of apartheid.

With regards to the latter, the latest order from Lt Col Peters read in part, as follows:
   a) If found guilty imprisonment for the balance of the contract.
   b) No further wages to be paid.

This proves once again how strongly Lt Col Peters supports apartheid.

9) The authorities are aware that Lt Col Peters invested all his money in the Republic of South Africa with a view to settling there. Due to something in his past he was banned. I do believe that if a person has the desire to start anew he should be given the chance.

10) I am aware that the honourable late Dr Verwoerd was assassinated by undesired immigrants and can assure you that we

fully supported the late Dr Verwoerd, as we now do Minister Vorster. I do beg that should it meet with your approval, Lt Col Peters be permitted a reasonable period of time in order to present his case to the authorities, even if this period is for three days only. Whatever his plea is I do not know, but I am convinced that he is better equipped to present his case than any of us or even his counsel.

11) I am also aware that the S.A. Police and Department of Defence desires an interview with Lt Col Peters, even though they are not prepared to submit this request to you in writing.

12) With reference to a report in some English newspapers, I can only repeat what I always say to the officers here, that during the time of Lt Col Hoare he never had the well-being of his men at heart. He was more interested in publicity as his name did appear on the front pages of newspapers. This was mainly due to evidence of success on the side of Lt Col Peters who at that time served as a Sub Lt in command of force John John.

13) In the past we also experienced shortage of medical supplies. Thanks to the efforts of the present Commanding Officer of Five Commando, we now have sufficient. Most of the supplies, however, were bought in South Africa out of his personal funds.

14) He also supplemented all shortages of uniforms. This again was also from South Africa and paid for with his own money. Our present uniform compares favourably with that of any army in the world, unlike the past when every member wore a different style or colour of uniform.

It is most certainly not my intention to glorify this man's past but I do feel that people's newspapers are victimising him for actions he was not responsible for. It is my honest opinion that what Five Commando is doing here is also indirectly done for South Africa; perhaps not now but certainly in the future and all this is due to the Commanding Officer of Five Commando.

I have stated the above facts to impress upon you the type of person Lt Col Peters really is. I again respectfully request that you grant him the opportunity to visit South Africa and put his case personally to another departmental head. I do appreciate your co-operation and interest in this case. A reply from your department by return of post will be esteemed a favour to me and many other fine South African officers serving under a man who is respected by Great Britain.

Not everything in this extraordinary apologia need be taken *au pied de la lettre*. The word apartheid in paragraph 8 is enigmatic; it is probably a euphemism referring to sexual intercourse with black women, a crime by South Africa's apartheid laws. It seems unlikely that Peters could have controlled this; one of the pleasures of mercenary life was the solace derived from 'jungle bunnies.' As regards the reference in the next paragraph to the honourable late Dr Verwoerd, this is even more obscure. Can the writer seriously have believed that Peters was banned for fear that he might assassinate Vorster? Is there an echo here of the rumours surrounding the mysterious death of the South African mercenary officer Hugh Von Oppen?

The list of the motives which pushed men to join the mercenaries is interesting but rather too black to be convincing. That, however, is the subject of the next section, again like this one largely consisting of original documents which tell their own story and from which the reader can draw his own conclusion.

Mercenaries for Five Commando were recruited openly in South Africa, where there was a semi-permanent office, and almost as openly in Rhodesia. In Europe the system was rather that of personal contacts; the *Chat Noir* in Pigalle was the reputed recruiting ground for Six Commando, while Earls Court in London and various bars in Brussels eventually became known as meeting places. At the time of the first mercenaries in Katanga the system had been roughly the same.[1]

There was not an unlimited supply of would-be mercenaries, as the following letter from Hoare to the C. in C. of the ANC, General Bobozo, reveals. It proposes an interesting solution which was never put into practice:

---
[1] See pages 162, 163,

Sir,
   Further to my letter of July 22, 65—
1. 2/Lt Von Lieres has just returned from our office in Johannesburg. He confirms my fears that we shall be unable to raise 300 men in South Africa in the next few weeks.
2. I therefore intend sending Captain S—— B—— to Leo to await your further instructions in the event that you should instruct him to raise the men in England.
3. A third possibility has occurred to me since writing to you yesterday. It may be possible to persuade the South Africa Defence Force to let us have 200 regular serving soldiers expressly for this campaign who would be sent back immediately it was over. These men could be given special leave from their units. From our point of view this would be entirely to our benefit but I would point out that if complete secrecy were not maintained the political reaction might be disastrous. However, if so decided I feel confident that I could arrange such a force on a short term engagement.
                                                   T. M. B. Hoare

Eventually recruiting was done largely by correspondence. The following is a letter from Five Commando written in November, 1966, in reply to an application to join:

Dear Mr Y,
   Thank you for your letter dated September 12, received here today. Unfortunately Five Commando does not have a recruiting agency in England; our only office being in Johannesburg. The liaison officer there is Lt D. L. S—— at Rooms 112–3, Sheffield House, 29 Cruit Street, Johannesburg.
   Due to restrictions imposed by the Congolese government, we cannot offer you a paid passage to the Congo from England. However, if you would make your own way to Johannesburg or alternatively direct to Kinshasha, Leopoldville (carnet de route may be obtained from the Congolese Embassy in London), I would be glad to accept you at Five Commando. In view of your military experience, I am prepared to offer you the rank of sergeant which carries a basic salary of £182 per month. Half this amount may be transferred at the official rate of exchange, 504 Congolese francs to £1 sterling, to any bank in the world,

and the other half will be paid in cash in Congolese francs. In addition to this a family allowance which is transferred in its entirety in hard currency is paid: £19 16s per month for the volunteer's wife, £11 18s per month for the first child, and slightly more for each subsequent child. Marriage and birth certificates must be produced. Whilst in a danger area, although not necessarily in combat, a danger-pay premium of £144 per month is paid. Again half of this is transferred in hard currency and the other half is paid in Congolese francs. Upon completion of the six months contract, a volunteer may transfer at the official rate of exchange, one half of the cash received in the Congo. So, in fact, three quarters of the gross pay and danger pay is paid in hard currency in a foreign country.

In conclusion, I may add that there are ample opportunities for promotion, providing a recruit exhibits capability. Also in exceptional cases, upon my discretion, paid leave and free return passage to England may be granted. If there is any further information that you may require, do not hesitate to write.

The letter which drew this reply had come from Buckinghamshire:

Sir,

I would be most grateful if you could tell me how to become a member of your Commando, together with details of pay, etc. I am at present serving in the X—— Regiment and have been in England for almost two years on an E.R.E. job, and have now decided to purchase my discharge, as an alternative to wasting my time in B.A.O.R. My present rank is Sergeant; age 26 years; seven years service. Active service Brunei revolt, Sarawak. I am married, luckily to a woman who understands that I am not a nine to five man. It is very difficult to find out anything about your Commando here in England, but I would like to point out that I am willing to do whatever necessary in order to enlist under you. I am not a glory hunter or an idiot; I just want more out of life than I can get at present. I hope that you can find time to give this letter your consideration and let me know one way or the other as soon as it's convenient to you.

Yours sincerely,

X—— Y——

It was not the only one of its sort:

> Dear Col Peters,
> It was with great interest that I read an article in the *Sunday Telegraph* concerning the mercenary force in the Congo. A group of friends and myself are due to be demobbed from the S.A.S. next year. Consequently we would be interested to know if there are any opportunities in your command. I have served in operational theatres both in the Middle and Far East. I would be grateful if you would send me detailed information on current recruitment training, the political and military situation and pay.
>
> Yours faithfully,
G—— H——

Five Commando replied promptly, offering indeed slightly more favourable terms for travelling:

> Dear Sir,
> I acknowledge receipt of your letter dated October 15, 1966. You will, upon deciding to join Five Commando, have to pay your own fare from England to Brussels, where the necessary papers and tickets will be available for you to fly to Leopoldville. Before this can be done you must furnish me with a list of names of those wishing to join Five Commando, so that these papers and tickets can be forwarded from Leopoldville to the Congolese Embassy in Brussels. It would be to your advantage to attend to this matter as soon as possible.
>
> Yours sincerely,
Lt Col Peters.
>
> General information:
> 1) Basic training is for a period of two weeks, as recruits are accepted only if they have had previous military training. This period of training is a refresher course.
> 2) The enlistment period is initially for a period of six months. However, service can be continued provided the commanding officer is satisfied with your service and conduct.

3) A volunteer's basic salary is £150 per month [etc., as before].

4) There are ample opportunities for promotion providing a recruit exhibits capability.

From Yorkshire another professional soldier wrote:

Sir,

As I have been in the army for five years in which I served in Korea, Hong Kong and also in East Africa, now I have finished my time with the . . . regiment and the reserve, I would like to serve once again in a battalion that serves overseas. Could it be possible to join your battalion.? I would very much like to be of some service and doing a worthwhile job abroad, as I have always been wanting to serve and do a duty to others abroad. If I can be of service to your regiment, could you please put me in touch. If I cannot be of service to your regiment, could you please put me in touch with any other foreign regiment which I could write to.

Yours faithfully,
A—— B——

And from Rhodesia:

Sir,

Subject: Recruitment of medical orderlies.

Have you any vacancies for medical orderlies in the mercenaries? I am a fully qualified male nurse, qualified in 1960. I am fully conversant with all forms of casualty work, having been in charge of an acute surgical and orthopaedic ward for three years. My qualifications are . . . I know how to apply all kinds of splints and plasters; casualty evacuation, microscope work, X-ray technique, medical administration. I am aged 29, married with two children. I am at present serving as a sergeant in the Rhodesian army, and due for discharge soon. I will be pleased to send you any further particulars necessary.

Your obedient servant,
L—— M——

Apart from professional soldiers, former mercenaries were another source of supply, either voluntarily:

> Col Sir,
> How is things still up there. I hope you are still having a nice time up there. Sir, I would like to be with you again because you are Five Commando. Sir, if it is possible for me to come up again and if you want me back, please let me know when I can come up. I believe maybe there would be another contract. If so, do let me know please. Well, Sir, I hope I will be with you in Five Commando soon.
> Always yours faithfully,
> D—— E——

> Dear Sir,
> I acknowledge your letter of November 8, instant. You may return to the Congo and rejoin Five Commando. I suggest that you report to the liaison officer, whose address appears below with this letter at the earliest opportunity.

Or, perhaps, involuntarily:

> Dear Sir,
> My husband, X—— Y—— Z——, was a mercenary in the Congo from September 1965 to January 1966. For personal reasons I would like to know if it is possible for him to return to the Congo to be a mercenary again. Would you please let me know if he has re-applied for this position? Looking forward to your reply. Thank you.
> Yours faithfully,
> Mrs X—— Y—— Z——

Not all, however, were acceptable:

> Dear Sir,
> With reference to your need for miners and tradesmen, I wish to bring to your notice that I have the qualifications.... Although aware of the fact that I am on the not-wanted list, I would

appreciate it very much if you can reconsider my request to return to the Congo in the capacity as mentioned above. I will conduct my duties to the best of my abilities and to your satisfaction. Hoping for an early reply,

Yours faithfully,
B—— C——

Dear Sir,
. . . We must inform you, however, that once your name appears on the not-wanted list for returning to the Congo, we cannot change it. It will, therefore, be impossible for you to enrol for service in the Congo.

Many youths in Rhodesia and South Africa joined or attempted to join Five Commando because it had become almost normal to spend six months as a mercenary in the Congo:

Dear Sir,
I should be grateful if you would accept me as a volunteer mercenary in your Commando unit. I am at present 18 years of age, and have no physical defects, my eyesight being normal. I have my parents' consent and I am available for service at any time.

Yours faithfully,
A—— D——

Dear Sir,
Re *Application for enrolment.*
We are in receipt of your letter dated 2nd instant, and have noted contents thereof for which we thank you. We must bring the following to your attention:

1) It appears from your letter that you have had no previous military experience.

2) You will need, if you are under the age of 21, a proper document signed by your parent in front of a magistrate in a juvenile court, granting you permission to join up for service in this Commando.

3) In the absence of any of these two points you would not be allowed to join our forces at all, etc.

Nonetheless there were, at most stages, plenty of young and inexperienced mercenaries in the Congo. Strict selection was not the mark of the more active periods. The typical young South African or Rhodesian 'volunteer', none too intelligent or well-educated, would have been hard put to explain why he had come to the Congo. His motives were, as in the case of many of his seniors, a curious mixture. For a certain class it became almost fashionable to enlist as a mercenary: the Congo was looked upon as a sort of test of toughness and virility, suitably undertaken before settling down to a job. Hopes of quick earnings and loot were probably less important than the thought of impressive tales to tell friends, and particularly girl-friends, on return. There was just enough danger to add glamour but not so much that the chances of getting killed were really serious. Above all, it was not a question of signing away five long years of life as with the Legion; the contract ran only for six months, so that even if things should go wrong escape would always be within sight.

In certain cases the threat of running away to join the mercenaries seems to have been just the updated version of a very old tactic endemic in the conflict of generations:

Dear Sir,
    This is to notify that my young son, R—— B—— D——, intends to apply to join the Congolese Army, as he is only seventeen years of age and said he would get someone else to sign the necessary. I am writing to you to please look into the matter, as I have forbidden him to do so. He would most likely put his age as more than seventeen years. He was born November 4, 1949. I have written this so that if he does apply you will know that it is not me who has signed his paper. I would therefore estimate it as a favour if you would put this on record for future reference, as I have no intentions whatsoever of ever allowing him to go. Hoping this will be kept in mind.
    Thanking you,

Yours faithfully,
P—— D——, Mrs

Would-be recruits who were not accepted did not only fall into the not-wanted or too-young categories. One hopeful volunteer wrote directly from Shaftsville in South Africa, of all places, only to receive a distinctly bureaucratic reply:

Dear Sir,
   Please may I hereby apply to join the Congolese Army Force. I am 25 years of age and have had no previous training.
   I can speak English, Afrikaans, Zulu, Northern and Southern Soto (mother's tongue). I have applied on many occasions at our local office dealing with mercenary recruits for the Congo. My application was turned down because of my being a non-white.
   No wonder I am writing you this letter directly to the Congo Army Force. I am six foot high, and the weight of 180 lbs, with a strong eyesight. I am a hundred per cent fit and also courageous.
   Kindly know that I have had no previous training in army and am not a white man. I am an African (Southern Soto exactly in nationality). Will you kindly let me know, when my application is accepted, how much shall I be paid monthly? I am ready and prepared to leave for the Congo and offer my services to your army force as soon as I can receive your military call-up. I am prepared to leave on exit permit if necessary. Hoping that you will not turn a deaf ear, nor a blind eye on my request, I am waiting anxiously to hear from you soon.
                              I am,
                                    Yours faithfully,
                                          Z——

Dear Sir,
         Re *Application to join this Commando*
   We are in receipt of your letter to enrol with this unit, for which I thank you. We must point out, however, that it is impossible to accept your application as we only engage white mercenaries to serve in this force.

Five Commando had from its formation always been an exclusively white unit; its relations with the black allies, the ANC, were extraordinarily limited, and even at the officer level there was little pretence that the senior black officers were seriously in charge, however punctiliously they might be saluted. There was on the other hand a nauseating amount of proclaimed devotion to Tshombe in person, though not among the 'other ranks'. In general the English-speaking mercenaries lived an isolated life; even the batmen and the barmen were white, though a few natives might be employed here and there, for instance as laundrymen. This openly racist attitude was, in a way, preferable to the hypocrisy of the French-speaking mercenaries. Schramme made great play of his devotion to his 'Leopards'. But it was noticeable at Bukavu that the mercenary officers lived a strictly segregated life; even 'President' Monga was only rarely admitted to the white officers' mess. On the other hand the ordinary French mercenaries lived openly with black women, and several mixed 'families' disembarked from the Red Cross aircraft which eventually brought the Bukavu survivors back to Europe. Five Commando mercenaries were far more affected by apartheid feeling, and few if any kept Congolese 'wives'.

Nationality, in at least one set of cases, was as great a bar as colour. To a certain New York doctor who wanted to join Five Commando as an orthopedic physician Peters wrote:

> ... Unfortunately Five Commando has an agreement with the United States Embassy not to accept American citizens. It is the law of your country that upon enlistment in a foreign army you will lose your American citizenship. We thank you for your application and regret that we cannot assist you. ...

Some American citizens, however, were not to be put off so easily; in early 1967, P—— R—— wrote:

> Sir,
> I make application to join your unit in the capacity of private mercenary soldier. In support of my application I submit the following particulars: I am 22 years of age, born November –, 1944 in Dakota, and I am a United States citizen by birth. I am

white. I am in good health and have not had any serious illness since I was a child. I stand six foot tall and weigh 13 stone. This I know is overweight by about 10 lbs but it can be easily corrected. I have completed 2½ of the required 4 years of the A.B. course at the X—— University. I am presently employed as a debt-collector in the credit department of the Y—— Co. in Cleveland. I lack prior military experience but I submit that this is an asset since I would adapt more readily to your training in irregular warfare. My savings are about 200 dollars and will no doubt increase. Also I own moderately valuable items of personal property which I can sell in aid of raising passage over, if need be. My salary is 68 dollars a week—after taxes, 55 dollars. I am free of debt. However, I would like to discuss by subsequent correspondence borrowing passage money from the unit and repaying it by payroll deduction from my first contract, unless you provide passage to the Congo as a condition of service. If formal amplification of this application is necessary, I request you send the relevant forms to me at your earliest convenience. I will answer such questions as you think necessary in further support of this application. If transportation to the theater of operations is your unit's policy and in pursuit of this you send me an airline ticket, I will give security to the limit of my ability to do so, to any agents in the United States you specify, that I will use the tickets only for passage over and will not convert it to other use. The same for passage assistance loan or any other aid.

I have a legally clear background and have never been arrested nor cited for anything more serious than a parking violation. I hold a valid United States passport and driving license. I request you instruct me as to the type of visa I should secure when you answer this application and also about import licensing requirements for my weapons. I am going into this with my eyes open. A year ago I researched the Congo mercenaries to the limit of the Cleveland Public Library, and I will review and update my research while awaiting your reply. I realize the possibility that I may be killed in action and I accept it. I also realize the sureity that I will forfeit United States citizenship by taking service with you. This also I accept. I can in good conscience give a note of loyalty and obedience to the mercenary commander, and determined upon this I will whole-heartedly commit myself to this course of action, with your help and participation in this.

> I am,
> Faithfully yours,
> P—— R——

Five Commando replied:

> Dear Sir,
> In reply to your letter of 25th instant, we regret to advise you that we do not take persons of American nationality. This is in accordance with the wishes of the American Government, who have requested that we employ no American citizens.
> Yours faithfully, etc.

But P—— R—— was persistent:

> Sir,
> The United States Department of State has reiterated this advice to me, to the effect that enlistment in a foreign military force operates as an immediate and automatic revocation of United States citizenship and nationality. It would seem, therefore, that if I did join Five Commando, as I fully intend to do so if given permission to do so, the automatic loss of United States citizenship and nationality that I would thereby incur, would render the State Department's objection to American mercenaries irrelevant to me. I would no longer be American, etc. etc.

His logic, though unanswerable, was unavailing. Five Commando replied:

> I would like to bring to your attention again that we are *not* taking persons of American nationality. Secondly, Five Commando will cease to exist as from between June and July. . . .

These letters of application[1] are obviously not conclusive evidence in any sense, except to show that extraordinarily different types of people considered at one stage or other becoming mercenaries and that talk of pathological derangement is

---
[1] The ones quoted are a cross-section of the more interesting letters, in which at least a hint of motive appears.

exaggerated. Those who made the best soldiers from the employer's point of view and whose motives are least suspect were the professional soldiers of regular armies who appear to have been bored with the lack of an opportunity to put their training and their acquired skills into use. This is not a class with which there is much general sympathy, in principle; yet it is not a class where motives and attitudes can be particularly despised or condemned as a matter of practice.

Even if the motives of would-be mercenaries were extraordinarily mixed and by no means as simple as it is at first tempting to lay down, money was obviously important and hopes of money even more so. Were these hopes satisfied? Whether the rewards of mercenaries are viewed as ill-gotten blood-money or as justifiable pickings, this is a question that rarely fails to excite interest.

The short answer is: probably not. Xenophon at the end of the march of the Ten Thousand was reduced to trying to wheedle back pay from an evasive Thracian prince and to borrow a little ready money from unsympathetic Spartan officials. Eventually he had to put his favourite and sole remaining horse up for sale; and only a successful last-minute raid on a Persian nobleman's estate left him comfortably off. And this περιπατεια was due, quite simply, to the assistance of the Gods: the favourable omens which prompted his decision and led him to restrict the numbers of equally impoverished mercenaries eager to take part in the raid were, in Xenophon's opinion, merely the long-delayed reward justified by his own exceedingly careful attention to his religious duties. It is not every mercenary leader who has deserved, or would be wise to rely on, celestial approval of this sort. As a general historical rule, the blissful state represented by riches and continuing prosperity is one to which few mercenaries have ever attained; and there is no reason why this rule should have been modified for the benefit of the twentieth century.

From the general to the particular, though with a note of caution—this is the most difficult of all the facets of mercenary activities in which to get at the truth. Rumours of riches, such as those of Schramme's treasure-chest saved from Bukavu, may well be simple rumours; on the other hand they may not. In any case such stories pale into financial insignificance by the side of the legends that float around the gold of Kilo-Moto. These gold mines are to be found near Watsa north of Stan in the area liberated by Five Commando in March 1965, and there are tales of gold bars (and ivory) being smuggled out through Uganda with the complicity of a senior Ugandan army officer who subsequently lost his post.

Hoare in any case is recognized as being very comfortably off. On the other hand he probably made a considerable part of his money from the serial rights of his story, which were sold to various newspapers. These certainly brought him in a small fortune, which his book did not.

Of course loot (and pay—see Appendix I, Article 35) had the added advantage of being tax-free. But pay was not to be relied upon. Six months after the disbanding of Five Commando Schroeder had finally managed to obtain a lump sum from the Congolese government, and was advertising in the South African newspapers for ex-mercenaries to submit applications for back-pay still owing to them. This admirably honest attempt only involved him in accusations of embezzlement and of retaining percentages—exactly the sort of accusation which Xenophon had to face from the ungrateful Greeks when he was doing all he could to obtain their promised pay from Seuthes. Schroeder, incidentally, was at the time running a travel agency in South Africa in partnership with several other ex-mercenaries; and there were no external signs of wealth, or even great prosperity, to be seen. On the other hand a travel business is an ideal cover, actual or potential, for mercenary activities, and quite possibly these mercenaries were, like many other ex-mercenary leaders throughout history, wasting the fortunes they had made in unprofitable attempts to set up another mercenary venture. The temptation for any former mercenary leader to keep an organization going at his own expense in the hopes that opportunity will knock once more is strong; but if the knocking is delayed the expenses become ruinous. It is my impression that Peters at any rate yielded to this temptation, and probably lost a considerable amount of his accumulated fortune thereby.

Puren on the other hand was universally known as a '10 per cent man'; his position as administrative officer at Leo was not unrewarding; he is reliably estimated to have made nearly £100,000 during his time there. Inevitably there were bitter recriminations from the mercenaries in the field against all the administative officers, Belgian or otherwise, who were accused of embezzling pay and equipment. More than one Five Commando paymaster disappeared, unwisely, I would think, in view of the far from empty threats that such behaviour evoked.

One actual example of the sort of situation that occurred: on January 1, 1965 three-and-a-half months' long-awaited mail finally reached the nine mercenaries of 53 Commando then in Stan, all of whom had arranged for that part of their pay which could be paid in hard currency (see Appendix I, Article 32, clause A) to be transferred to South Africa. B—— had a letter from his bank posted on December 7 informing him that fifty pounds ten shillings had been paid into his account. V—— had a letter dated December 24 from his Johannesburg branch to say that no money at all had been received. The other seven had no news. These men promptly wrote nine letters of resignation to Hoare—which were not accepted but treated as a tentative of mutiny. For ready cash they were occasionally paid Congolese francs (almost worthless even on the black market); but not too regularly to judge by their account of how they made a little cash on the side: when given bottles of whisky by rescued and grateful missionaries, they would open a bar and sell it off by tots to the Belgian technical assistance officers, and thereby make a little profit.

Any mercenary, therefore, who joined for the pay was woefully naïve. But the heartbreaking tales of poverty were not, of course, the full side of the picture. The same group at Stan had at one time taken half a million Congolese francs off a rebel paymaster's truck and also blown up the Governor's safe at Balembu when they had liberated that town. The blowing up of safes was a primary mercenary distraction, and there is much controversy (among the fairly limited circles in which such topics are heatedly debated) as to Schramme's behaviour at Bukavu: were the guards which he ostentatiously placed outside the banks really placed there to protect the deposits of this rich trading city or to deceive observers? Had the safes already been blown by the ANC or by the first group of mercenaries who captured the city so briefly? And, if not, did he really manage to get the millions involved across to Rwanda before the fall of Bukavu, and if so where are they now?

Not only banks but also safes in business premises and private houses would be toured by small groups of determined and dynamite-carrying mercenaries as soon as a town was 'liberated'; the looting was therefore much more resented by the Belgian settlers and businessmen, who had unwisely imagined that, thanks to the admirably brave and devoted mercenaries, they would recover their homes and offices intact, than by the Congolese whose premises for obvious reasons attracted far less mercenary attention. 'Ah, if only it was the rebels who held this town!' said one Rumanian officer longingly as he drove slowly through Leo at about this time, gazing at the pavement cafés on the main avenue which were crowded with prosperous businessmen and well-paid U.N. officials. Years later in Johannesburg an ex-NCO of Five Commando described with glee and, I would say, almost without exaggeration how he had commandeered a C130 to transport all his personal loot from Stan to Leo to be sold there to Indian traders—refrigerators, prams, cameras, furniture, and several cars. Two South Africans are said to have found $65,000 in the safe of a private house, whereupon they bribed a medical orderly to certify that they were ill, and disappeared for good. Of course each individual story of this sort needs to be treated with scepticism; but though every symptom is suspect, their accumulation indicates a disease.

Certain officers attempted to repress this looting; but most, for reasons that are only too clear, turned a blind eye. Protin once ordered a group of his mercenaries, who had captured a rebel paymaster's suitcase holding a million francs, to hand it over intact to the local Congolese police commissioner; the police commissioner and the suitcase disappeared without trace. What the mercenaries left, the ANC looted. The only armed bands that showed any restraint seem, surprisingly enough, to have been the Simbas; there are well-attested and convincing stories of systematic plundering even by the U.N. troops in Katanga. Morally, therefore, it seems difficult to adopt too rigid an attitude. And in any case all this money gained by looting seems to have gone very quickly. Siegfried Mueller, for instance, is now apparently back where he started, as a barman in South West Africa. Few of the mercenaries had the strength of character of that South African who came to the Congo for six months determined to take back with him enough money to satisfy his life-long ambition to open a garage; and then did so. Proudhon at any rate would have approved—particularly given the victims.

Rather more intriguing is the question of the financial relationship between the mercenary leaders and the large capitalist groups with African interests to defend. The motives of the senior mercenary officers were in any case far more difficult to disentangle than the comparatively simple explanations for the enrolment of the ordinary 'volunteers' or NCOs. 'We shall show them,' Hoare is reported as having said, 'what a small group of determined white men can do.' No doubt this was a partial explanation for his presence in the Congo; but he and others such as Wicks were skilled in proffering with every appearance of total sincerity what can have been at best only half-truths. There can be no serious dispute over the existence of links between the mercenary leaders and foreign governments, particularly the French, which one may fairly assume were profitable (in the strict sense of the word) at least to the former. But the precise relationship between the Katanga mercenaries and the Union Minière, to take the *locus classicus*, is obscure; if there were any formal links, they have not yet been established.

A priori there does seem to be a case for asserting that there must have been a close working arrangement: Union Minière supported Katanga's secession, Katanga's secession depended largely on the mercenaries, therefore Union Minière supported the mercenaries. Even Denard's threat to blow up the hydroelectric installations could be taken as the threat of a minor employee in the happy position of being able to blackmail his undeservingly rich employer. But for the moment all is conjecture, and the case must be regarded as non-proven: there is no evidence to prove that the Union Minière hired, approached, or paid money to mercenary leaders—except in the indirect sense that the bulk of Katanga's financial resources, from which the mercenaries were paid and armed, came from the taxes and contributions of Union Minière. My personal impression is that, at any rate once the euphoric initial period of Katangese independence was over, the Union Minière was continuously torn by internal dissensions; different policies were being canvassed by different officials and different internal pressure groups, as is bound to happen in an amorphous, overgrown and multinational organization, further complicated by the need to reconcile the interests of all its disparate shareholders or shareholding groups; and the result was a hesitancy and confusion which made the Company taken as a whole the most unreliable of allies and the feeblest of enemies.

But this, let it be stressed, is merely a personal opinion; the only thing certain is that from Union Minière's point of view the mercenaries were not an unmixed blessing. But whether their leaders managed successfully to bleed Union Minière's coffers, an almost pious temptation which surely must have been often present in their thoughts, and, if so, precisely to what extent, are questions to which, unfortunately, the answers are likely to remain wrapped in indecent obscurity.

11 The Yemen and Biafra

VARIOUS MERCENARIES HAVE BOASTED from time to time that there would always be a job for them somewhere or other in the world; one with whom I talked claimed to have had offers from fourteen different countries or groups. This, in a sense, may be true: in the nuclear age the conflict between East and West is marked by a series of minor, local wars in which the professional soldier can always find a role. It seems likely, for instance, that the Portuguese would be ready to employ in Angola or Mozambique former mercenaries of the Congo. But the rôle the former mercenary could play there would be comparatively unimportant: he would be just another white soldier fighting under Portuguese colours. There has been talk of mercenaries in Vietnam; if there is any truth in this talk, their rôle in a conflict between two large and highly professional armies must be even more marginal. It appears that only in the Congo have present-day mercenaries dominated as a group the military and, indirectly, the political history of a country, and that with Schramme's defeat there (Denard's even more) their importance has faded.

Yet even though the mercenaries are inextricably linked with the Congo, they have played a noticeable though comparatively minor part in two other wars, in the Yemen and Biafra. Though there is far less documentary evidence available, it is now clear that the Royalists in the Yemen and both sides in the Nigeria-Biafra war made at least some use of white mercenaries.

The beginning of the Yemeni civil war, sparked off by the death of the aged Imam, overlapped with the end of the Katanga secession. The Royalist guerillas under the Imam's successor, El Badr, were indirectly supported by King Feisal of Saudi Arabia; and the Republicans, who held the capital, Sanaa, were directly helped by up to 50,000 of Nasser's Egyptian troops. There was, therefore, a clear enough conflict of ideologies for the West to support, at least tacitly, the Royalists; there was, on the Royalist side, plenty of money but a lack of troops. Given these conditions, a number of the Katangese mercenaries went out to the Yemen to help the Royalists train their army.

Faulques was the first to join El Badr; Denard certainly followed—there is a story that he can no longer set foot there. Laboudigue of Six Commando, who defended Bukavu under Schramme, and Goosens, who was to die in Biafra, were there too. But it appears that none of the English-speaking former Congo mercenaries went there, though from time to time there were rumours that the whole of Five Commando was about to go out; certainly Schroeder had had the idea of leading a group from South Africa out to the Yemen. But it was a far-fetched scheme that was never really taken seriously.[1]

Though all the mercenaries in the Yemen seem to have been French it is hard to see what French interests, actual or potential, were at stake there, and it seems that for once the French government had nothing to do with what was purely private initiative.

---

[1] Far less nebulous is Hoare's intention to raise a mercenary force to replace the British troops due to be withdrawn from the Persian Gulf. Hoare is at the moment living in Durban, apparently in 'retirement', but he has certainly been in contact quite recently with British regular army officers eager to serve in such a force. Such officers may of course be able to bypass Hoare; Major David Neal, a regular British army officer serving with the Trucial Oman Scouts, left the British Army in the autumn of 1969 and entered the service of Shaikh Saqr Bin Mohammed al-Quassini, ruler of the Gulf state of Ras al-Khainah, as head of his 300-man 'mobile striking force'. This could well be the next part of the world to see a pullulation of mercenaries.

In any case there were never more than 45 mercenaries there at any given time, and all were officers or NCO's. That is to say, the mercenaries in the Yemen never exercised the sort of influence that they did in the Congo; they were specialists whose job it was to train the Royalist forces in the use of modern weapons, much in the way of an ordinary military mission such as any major military power might send to help train the army of an underdeveloped country—though indeed such military missions do not usually make their appearance at the height of a civil war.

The system used was one of rotation: a mercenary would serve for six months, and then be recalled and replaced by another. From the point of view of the mercenaries it was a very different sort of war from that which most of them had been used to in the Congo. The main advantage was the lack of danger; it was a roving, mountainous guerilla-type life, and during the four-odd years that the 'operation' lasted only one mercenary was killed—Tony de Saint Paul, hit by the shrapnel from an Egyptian bomb at Christmas 1963. On the other hand drink, women, glory and loot were unobtainable; there were dangerous moments when various of the mercenaries were held to ransom by the rival Princes of the royal house; and the whole affair finally fizzled out when the pay began to become irregular.

Politically the presence of this small group of mercenaries had no direct effect. Militarily they were probably fairly successful in training the tribesmen. But had they not been there, the war would still have gone on—neither motive nor the sinews of war were lacking. No great military success marked their efforts.

The rôle of the mercenaries in Biafra merits a more detailed account. Though their importance was limited, their presence aroused great curiosity and many wild rumours; no full account of this aspect of the Biafra war has yet appeared. Secondly, from the mercenary point of view Biafra was an opportunity, a postscript and, in many cases, a swansong. And, thirdly, it is a matter of considerable psychological interest. For once, the mercenaries were fighting on what was almost indisputably the right and in any case invariably the weaker side; in such a situation their inherent weaknesses and the importance of their motives stand out all the more clearly.

Biafra seceded from the Federation of Nigeria on May 30, 1967. Fighting did not start till five weeks later, coinciding almost exactly with the outbreak of the mercenary revolt in the Congo. The initial Nigerian successes were countered by the sudden Biafran invasion of the Mid-West; it looked, in early August, as if the Biafrans might even capture the Federal capital, Lagos. By the third week in September, however, the balance had once again swung back in favour of the far superior Federal army; the invasion of Biafra had begun in earnest; and the first names had been inscribed on that long list of towns which one after the other were in the course of the next twenty-eight months of of the war to fall to the advancing Nigerians as 'Biafra' shrank to less than a third of its original size.

Tall tales of mercenaries immediately began to circulate; and with a certain justification, for a Congo-type situation was developing in an area not far from the Congo. At first there were rumours that Faulques, who had been lost sight of, though believed still to be in the Yemen, was leading the Biafran forces—when this rumour was at its height he was discovered by a correspondent of *The Times* in a Paris hotel. Denard had disappeared after the Katanga fiasco of November, and inevitably rumours started that he had made off to Biafra, with the rider that he had treacherously been selling arms and ammunition meant for the Katanga invasion to the Biafrans. Hoare claimed to have visited (by invitation) both sides before deciding that for the sake of the Commonwealth all decent mercenary leaders should keep out of the conflict. 'Mercenaries quarrel over £1,000-a-month civil war jobs' ran the headline on the front page of *The Observer* on a Sunday in December—so important had even potential mercenary activities become. According to this article Wicks was using the Officers' Association in London as a recruiting base, Hoare was deliberately avoiding Wicks, and Peters was 'morally committed' to the Federal government. There was a spate of similar stories in other serious newspapers.

There did not appear to be very much behind all this whirligig. What is true is that there was certainly effervescence in mercenary circles. In Johannesburg Schroeder had a list of 2,000 ex-members of Five Commando, and appeared to be waiting for a summons that never came. In London Peters had another list, and claimed to have supplied pilots to the Federal government. Pilots there certainly were, both Egyptian and English-speaking, hired by the Federal government to fly the planes which they gradually accumulated; and the Nigerians claimed at this stage in the war to have found several white bodies in a Biafran bomber which they had shot down—an unlikely story in view of the uniqueness of the Biafran bomber then available. But of the rival airforces more later.

In any case a very particular phenomenon appeared which rather tended to prevent the use of mercenaries. At this early stage both Biafrans and Nigerians added to the general furore by accusing each other violently and often of employing white mercenaries, while denying that their own side was doing so. The result was that any white man on either side was in a dangerous position. There were numerous accounts of journalists, businessmen and even missionaries being arrested, particularly in Biafra, on suspicion of being an enemy 'mercenary', and one or two stories, less substantiated, of summary executions.[1] Neither side had much control over its junior officers, who tended to take their own official propaganda literally; and it was therefore a dangerous business for a would-be mercenary to arrive in Nigeria or Biafra hoping to enlist on the spot. It was also difficult for either side to admit openly after this initial stand that they

---

[1] Walter Schwarz, the *Guardian* correspondent, though well-known personally to Biafran leaders, was kept *incommunicado* for several weeks in a remote Biafran jail and appears lucky to have escaped with his life.

were recruiting white 'volunteers' in the Tshombe manner. There was therefore no open or widespread recruitment at any period.

Blockaded by the Nigerian navy, Biafra was even at this stage forced to rely for its supplies of arms and ammunition on the air route. A freelance American gun-runner, by the name of Hank Wharton, flew direct flights from Lisbon into Biafra with his three Super Constellations; he was later hired by the charitable organizations and the Red Cross to ferry food and relief supplies into Biafra, until they managed to discover the landing-codes which his pilots had been attempting to keep secret, break his monopoly, and organize their own flights. This air bridge and arms supply interested various former Congo mercenaries, who took part or attempted to take part in this comparatively riskless activity.

The Biafrans, however, were faced not merely with the problems of getting arms in but also with the difficulty of getting out the money to pay for them; and it was in this field that the first curious but authenticated episode involving a well-known mercenary leader occurred.

In the early stages of the war the currency—the Nigerian pound—remained valid both in Nigeria and in Biafra. The Biafrans' aim, therefore, was to unload their banknotes on the European market before the Federal government should decide to change the notes and declare the old currency null and void—which effectively occurred in January 1968, that is to say just over six months after Biafra's secession. In their financial negotiations, however, the Biafrans were too avaricious; they were offered twelve shillings and sixpence in British currency per Nigerian pound, and the Banque Rothschild (of which, possibly *à propos*, Georges Pompidou had at one stage been a leading light) was ready to open a credit of £5 million a week for them. But the Biafrans turned the offer down and held out for a higher price; eventually the Federal authorities announced their decision to change the currency, a move which of course would reduce the Biafran reserves to so much worthless paper; and in a last-minute panic-stricken effort the Biafrans loaded planes with millions of pounds worth of banknotes to be flown out of the country. In charge of one part of this operation was Alastair Wicks; however, his plane landed (possibly to refuel?) in Togoland where the local authorities confiscated the money. There Wicks was detained in jail for three months before being released.

Another former Congo mercenary was, if less deserving, more fortunate. He was due to land one December night at Geneva airport with eleven tons of Biafran banknotes; there waiting to meet him on the tarmac were the Biafran representative, a bank official, a former French mercenary, and, interestingly enough, a member of the French consular staff. They waited for a considerable period. Meanwhile the mercenary in question had landed at Lausanne, unloaded his cargo, visited a number of banks, and disappeared to take refuge in South Africa—where presumably the interest alone on his various investments must be providing him with a none-too-low standard of living. This should, no doubt, be a cautionary tale but it is difficult to point the moral.

The Officers' Association proffered a strenuous denial of any participation in Wicks' activities; and indeed there were no reports of others of its members languishing in tropical jails.

Denard was, in fact, in this autumn of 1967 still in Angola, though not with the large number of mercenaries alleged; it was after the failure of his Katanga invasion, and his reputation as a mercenary leader was very low indeed. He got wind from Paris that there would be clandestine but official support for a mercenary venture in Biafra, but despite his intrigues he was rejected as its potential leader. However close his links with the French 'services' may have been, it was improbable that they would choose to use once again such a dubious tool. Reputation—a reputation at least for efficiency and bravery—is absolutely necessary for mercenary leaders. Reputation once lost, they can find neither employers nor followers; and the Dilolo affair ruined Denard's reputation.

The choice in Paris, therefore, fell upon Faulques. His task was to be 'to form a black army equipped and encadred by Europeans'; and a contract was signed with Ojukwu (apparently against his better judgment—his encounter with Hoare had been fruitless) which stipulated that 100 mercenaries would be recruited, that they would be paid six months' wages in advance, and that they would be provided with modern weapons and equipment.

Faulques had been in Angola, at the Hotel Katekero in Luanda, at the time when Denard retreated from Katanga; it is probable therefore, that he was already in charge of the Biafra operation. He himself, however, much to the disgust of his subordinates, spent only a week in Biafra—just time enough to set up a mercenary camp near Port Harcourt in late November—before flying back to Paris. The conflicting reports of his whereabouts are therefore understandable. He left in charge of the camp a former colleague, an ex-Legion officer named Picot, and in charge of operations a paratroop lieutenant, B——. Both these officers were bitterly criticised afterwards by the men under their command for their regular-army approach and their addiction to the bottle, two factors which were viewed as being equally responsible for the events which followed.

For the venture ended in yet another mercenary disaster. It got off to a bad start, with only 53 mercenaries (of whom 47 were combatants) arriving instead of the 100 stipulated. The Nigerians meanwhile had made a sea-borne landing at Calabar near Port Harcourt, and the French decided to 'clean up' this incursion rather than to train Biafran units, the task for which Ojukwu had originally hired them. Nine however preferred to fulfil their original rôle, and Picot gave them permission to go off and form their own units in various parts of Biafra; the remainder made a frontal attack against Calabar, found Nigerian fire-control to be extremely different from Congolese, fell back, formed an unprotected front, were outflanked by Colonel Adekunle, the so-called Black Scorpion, and suffered a stinging defeat. Five mercenaries were killed in one day; this is the sort of loss that inevitably demoralizes a small mercenary force. Faulques was informed, flew out from Paris, and decided to wind up the operation. His critics have said that though in his day he had been an efficient officer and inspiring leader, his day was over and his one intention was to risk as little and to gain as much as he could. This he apparently did, having collected six months' advance pay for 47 non-existent mercenaries, a total (according to a not-too-reliable source) of 110 million *anciens francs*, or close on £90,000. What the French government thought of this it is hard to say; what Ojukwu thought it is easy to imagine. As a pretext for their withdrawal after roughly two months—they flew out on February 2—the mercenaries alleged that they had never received the modern armament stipulated in the contract. Though disarmed and therefore justifiably apprehensive, they were allowed to depart without difficulty. It seems likely that the last has now been heard of Faulques as a mercenary leader.

However, of the nine mercenaries scattered over the bush four decided to stay on;[1] these were Rolf Steiner, a German and former NCO in the Legion, the 1er REP; Giorgio Norbiatto, an Italian frogman who had taken part in the unsuccessful raid on the island of Bula Bemba; 'Taffy' Williams, a South African of Welsh origin who had been under Peters in Five Commando; and an Englishman, who left shortly afterwards.

1968 saw the war take a turn for the worse from the Biafran point of view. One after another towns and provisional capitals fell to the advancing Nigerian forces: Awka, Onitsha, Abaliki, Afikpa, and finally, at the end of April, Port Harcourt. Nearby, Norbiatto was killed, in the first week of May. It was at this stage, with only two mercenaries left, that Ojukwu decided to form the Fourth Commando Brigade, a unit of mercenary-led raiders with Steiner in command. A camp was set up near Umuahia and training began, even though Williams left on May 12 after the expiration of his contract.

It was during the summer of this year that rumours of starvation

---

[1] Two of the French had also wanted to stay on, but were overheard being told that if they disobeyed orders there would be no more contracts—another indication of official control of the operation.

and mass killings in Biafra began to arouse world-wide alarm and the war world-wide interest. Many of the journalists who went out there made incidental enquiries into the question of mercenaries, and in particular the French. From their accounts it becomes clear that once again Legion mythology ruled; Steiner had decided to form the Fourth Commando on the lines of the only model he knew. The Commandos wore the green beret,

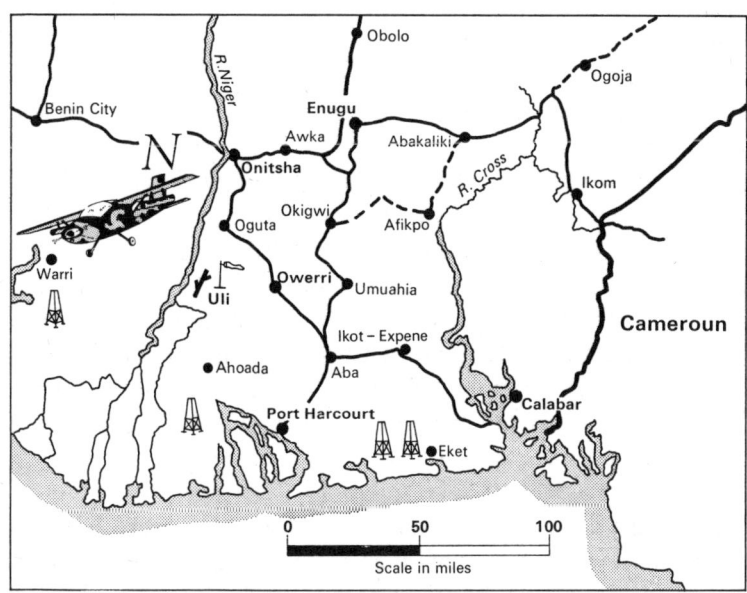

Biafra.

had as their colours the green and red of the Legion, and as their device 'Honour and Fidelity'—the Legion's first standard, presented by Louis Philippe, had borne the legend 'Honneur et Fidelité'.

By the end, intoxicated at his promotion to Colonel, Steiner was being driven around in a white Mercedes decorated with Legion colours and, as a personal pennant, the death's head which he chose as the emblem of the brigade. The Marseillaise alternated with the Biafran national anthem; and the whole affair had a touch of Grand Guignol suitably expressed in its tragi-comic ending.

In early July Williams had returned from London for another contract, bringing with him a Rhodesian, and a British mercenary who had been at Bukavu.[1] They were joined in August by Armand Ianarelli, an Italian who appears to have known Steiner in the Legion and to have been involved in Algerian affairs. The Fourth Commando Brigade was divided into three battalions, each roughly a thousand strong: 'The Guards' led by Williams, Ahoada Strike Force under Ianarelli, and Abaliki Strike Force under the Rhodesian. Their training was rudimentary, their equipment minimal, but their morale was apparently good.

Talking (at a somewhat later date) to Christian Brincourt of *Le Nouvel Observateur* Steiner said: 'I command 8,500 men that I have formed into commandoes: the youngest are fourteen years old. We only have 1,000 rifles for 10,000 men, so we can only attack the enemy when they are on the roads. The plan is to kill the maximum number of Nigerians in order to get hold of their arms . . . The Egyptian pilots in their MIG 17s drop their bombs from 1,000 metres up, so we have no chance of getting them . . . On the other side there are also mercenaries; last week we killed seven. They had no papers on them but they looked like Englishmen . . . I came here with some Frenchmen, ex-Congo types. They left, I stayed. The Nigerians are advancing every day but I will not leave my men. Here we have only one choice, to defend ourselves or to die; they don't take prisoners, nor do we.'

This raises the interesting but obscure question of mercenaries fighting with the Nigerian forces. Ianarelli's unit diary notes, at a later date: 'Strike Force Ahoada killed 4 mercenaries and 6 were seriously wounded. These dead and these wounded are enemies.' Here, as in Steiner's remarks, the figures appear to be exaggerated. Certainly there were a few whites with the Nigerians who defeated the French at Calabar, and one at least was killed there.

---

[1] So much for passports stamped 'Not Valid in Africa'. Several of the French had also been at Bukavu.

Probably these were British or South African mercenaries of the somewhat nebulous 'Peters Commando'; in any case their numbers never amounted to much more than a dozen, most of whom were training officers kept in the background. At an early stage of the war Peters was present at Lagos in the ill-defined rôle of 'military adviser', accompanied by a former bodyguard of Tshombe, by name Schrot. He was also in contact with a Frenchman, Michel de Clary, a former officer who had been in Katanga. It appears that his attempts to achieve a position of influence were unsuccessful, even though he did become involved with 'military security' in the Federal capital. What is more significant than the question of numbers is that such mercenaries as these were prepared to fight and kill each other, thus reviving an old mercenary tradition which had never quite made its appearance in the Congo where the mercenaries remained emotionally linked by memories of the old Katanga days.

In the autumn of 1968 the fighting centred around Aba, the one large city remaining in Biafran hands. At this stage a further complication occurred on the mercenary front. It seems that the French felt that the situation was slipping out of their control—Steiner was in contact with West German reporters and relief groups, and the presence of South Africans was not found reassuring in Paris. Libreville in Gabon[1] had a French military base and aerodrome; with the elimination of Hank Wharton's gun-running activities (suspicions of treachery led to this), Libreville became the main link between Biafra and the outer world. From it supplies, arms, ammunition and mercenaries were flown in, largely under French control or at least under French surveillance. In any case another former mercenary now made his reappearance, an ex-cavalry officer, Maurice Lucien-Brun, who had taken part in the Simba war and had at the time of the 1966 Katangese revolt played a role as a would-be intermediary which aroused the suspicions of Five Commando.

In July Lucien-Brun (under the alias of Paul Leroy) arrived in

---
[1] Ruled by President Bongo, who had Jacques Foccart to thank for suppressing a military *coup* in February, 1964.

Biafra; he left for France in mid-August and returned to Africa on September 1 with a group of fifteen French mercenaries. Rivalry between himself and Steiner's group was inevitable; but in any case this second French tentative ended in an even greater fiasco than the first. The military situation appeared desperate, a dispute about money arose, and Lucien-Brun's group decamped on October 2 with two months' pay—which they had earned for three weeks sitting at Libreville and one week inactive in Biafra.

This was after the fall of Aba on September 4, which heralded in the eyes of the world the final collapse of Biafra. Fourth Commando Brigade was blooded in the fighting around the city and suffered the first of its defeats. Of its 3,742 men, only 922 remained alive and unwounded by the time it was pulled back from the lost battle.

There is a curious story of Steiner's behaviour after the fall of Aba: he apparently persuaded some charitable West German groups to support a project for a sea-borne commando raid on Nigeria. This involved the purchase of expensive Zodiac canoes. At the end of September Steiner flew out to Libreville, banked the $25,000-odd he had received for the financing of this venture, announced that it was impossible, recruited a few whites from the bars of Libreville, and reappeared as commander of the Fourth Commando Brigade, which had been raised to the dignity (and nominal strength) of a division in early October and of which great things were now hoped.

For September had seen the fall of Oguta, Obinza, Okikwi and finally of Owerri. November was marked by the signing of the Soviet-Nigerian pact, the massive appearance of Ilyushins and Migs in the sky, and the Biafran counter-attack on Onitsha.

Steiner by this time appears to have been suffering from Napoleonic illusions. He planned not only to recapture Onitsha (in two hours) but by an outflanking movement to seize the Nigerian base of Asaba on the other side of the River Niger and then, amidst the total Federal confusion, to lead a mobile column in a swift dash upon Lagos. Had the attempt succeeded it would no doubt have been hailed as a feat worthy indeed of a Bonaparte.

As it was, disorganization reigned, and the Fourth Commando Brigade was once again decimated. On November 10 Steiner, who had admittedly been longer in Biafra than any other mercenary and had been living under conditions of strain, burst into State House at Umuahia, bottle of beer in hand, and insulted Ojukwu to his face. The dramatic scene that followed ended with the arrest and expulsion of Steiner and all but six of the remaining mercenaries. Steiner arrived in Libreville still handcuffed; he was extraordinarily lucky to escape with his life.

Two days later saw yet another attempt by the remnants of Fourth Commando Division, now commanded by Williams, to recapture Onitsha. A French television camera team, there on the spot, filmed the initial attack led by the Flemish Marc Goosens and his grisly death—a sequence which must have given pause to a number of would-be mercenaries in France.[1] 'Major Marc is dead,' noted Ianarelli's unit diary, 'after having destroyed a reservoir of enemies. The fossil is being taken to his native land without delay. Captain Armand has been bitten by a snake during the attack . . . It is very pitiful, the death of the Major. His death has saddened all the commandos of the Republic of Biafra.'

Next day saw the final attack against Onitsha; and there is an extraordinarily unpleasant account of Williams shooting down at least six Biafrans who refused to go forward in this hopeless assault against fortified positions. Once again the unit diarist gives a vivid, indeed almost homeric idea of the battle: 'The Abaliki Striking Force which should be the reinforcement, they have not been able to. They withdraw backwards. So do the Guards . . . All the troops of Captain Armand, that is to say Ahoada Strike Force, are almost finished. The enemies are content to say: "Charge them, charge them! Those commandos of the red scarf of Ahoada Strike Force!" The enemies also say: "These

---

[1] An interview with one of the minor French mercenaries in Biafra gives a significant idea of the kind of reasons which induced some men to enlist. 'One day in the Ardennes a friend approached me. Proposed I come to Biafra: 1,000 dollars a month. Mind you, I think that even for half that I would have come to Africa. I like taking risks. I liked the idea. I had always dreamed of becoming a mercenary, it attracted me. Why? I don't know. It attracted me because I had seen some stuff on the mercenaries in the Congo, photos and things in *Paris Match*.' This was a 27-year-old builder.

are the ones who have killed our four mercenaries and wounded our six mercenaries the last time." The enemies also say: "These commandos of the red scarf are the most dangerous. Take them alive, these assassins, these commandos of Ahoada Strike Force!"
... Towards six o'clock in the evening nobody knows anything about the commandos of Captain Armand. We hear the enemy say: "Ahoada Strike Force is finished, they are all finished." When Captain Armand has heard this, it saddens him. He has had the wounded brought back and he has departed in misery.'

This indeed was the miserable end of the Fourth Commando Brigade. Ianarelli, Williams, and a couple of others stayed on till the first months of 1969; but when their contracts expired they were not renewed, and their last month or two were spent as training officers. From that time onwards it seems that Ojukwu for understandable reasons employed no more mercenaries on the ground. His attitude was in any case extraordinarily clement, indeed, almost unexampled in the annals of mercenary employers —pay forthcoming even when no services had been rendered, and, as reprisal for open rebellion, merely handcuffs and expulsion.

The mercenary experience cost Biafra dear both in lives and money, and was a total failure throughout. Their major mistake had been their obstinacy in attempting to fight an orthodox war on a fixed front and in launching direct attacks with inferior armament upon strongly fortified positions. The one Biafran military success of note was gained *after* the departure of the mercenaries when Owerri was recaptured in May 1969—not by a frontal assault but by the use of 'maoist' encircling tactics.

In Biafra white mercenaries were for the first time in Africa faced with an enemy whose armament was consistently not only equal but vastly superior to their own. If one single factor can account for the successive Federal military victories, it is the Saladin armoured cars and Ferret scout cars supplied by the British government. The mercenaries failed to develop any tactics capable of stopping this armour; they never ceased to complain of their lack of grenades, mortars, and bazookas, and of the World War One equipment issued to their troops—the non-automatic Mausers, and the cannon on two wheels. They seemed incapable—surprisingly, in view of their success against the United Nations eight years before—of adapting themselves to difficult circumstances and to the lack of orthodox equipment. This was not to be the case with the next mercenary to appear on the scene, who found precisely in these difficulties his opportunity.

There are those who reject out of hand the sobriquet of 'mercenary' when applied to the Swedish flyer Count von Rosen. Let them, however, consider the problems of definition posed in the first chapter of this book; by his situation von Rosen was a mercenary, even if his motives were exceptionally pure. That he was of a different class from a Steiner is only too clear—just as Federigo da Montefeltro was of a different category from a Roger von Blum. There was a difference of motive but also difference of age, experience, metier, origin, contacts and background.

More is known of this man's background than of any other contemporary mercenary; and it is interesting enough to merit recording in detail. Carl Gustaf von Rosen was born in August 1909 into a family of aristocratic adventurers. His most famous ancestor had been a distinguished officer and personal friend of the great Swedish king, Charles XII; another had fought with Byron and married a Greek princess; his father, Count Eric, a well-known explorer, had in 1911 traversed Africa from Cairo to the Cape. He himself was educated at Lundsberg, Sweden's Eton, at the same time as the then Crown Prince; expelled, he became an engineer apprentice in a naval yard. From 1928, when he bought an old Sopwith Camel, his life was devoted to flying and to teaching others to fly. Before the War, he flew for the Swedish Red Cross in Ethiopia, and later flew in supplies to the guerilla fighters in western Ethiopia. Three years later he converted a KLM DC3 into a bomber, and flew for the Finns against the invading Russians. At the outbreak of the War he was married to a Dutchwoman (one of his three wives) and working for KLM in Holland; he flew another DC3 over to Britain, only to be very nearly shot by the British as a spy. Returning to Holland, he was arrested by the Gestapo but released thanks to the personal intervention of Goering, who had married his aunt.[1] For the rest of the War he flew a courier service between Berlin and Stockholm, like his uncle-in-law before him, and at the same time aided members of the Dutch resistance. The ten years after the War he spent back in Ethiopia, helping Haile Selassie to build up the Royal Ethiopian Air Force. From 1957 to 1969 he flew for the Swedish charter company Transair, with a two-year spell (1960-1962) flying in supplies to the United Nations in the Congo.

This, complete with the castle in Sweden, is the portrait of an outdated figure and indeed of an outdated epoch. By the spring of 1969 von Rosen was a grandfather approaching sixty, the retiring age for civil airline pilots. He was a large, sympathetic, rather tired-looking man, dominated apparently by his passion for flying and either by an inherited love of adventure or by a genuine devotion to the military Davids of the century, or possibly by a combination of both. At sixty he might have seemed too old to repeat what appeared to have become the regular pattern of his life.

Biafra had begun the war with a lone B26 bomber piloted by a Pole known as Kamikaze Brown and six Alouette helicopters under the command of a young Biafran named Augustus Opke, the 'head of the Biafran air force'. These planes were destroyed on the

---

[1] Impossible to resist quoting here from the ironic, and doubly apposite, description of Goering by the French ambassador to Berlin: 'L'héritier présomptif du IIIe Reich . . . a de brillants services de guerre. Il s'est faufilé, de sa propre initiative, de l'infanterie dans l'aviation. Il y a montré un courage intrépide; il y est devenu un "as" et, à la mort de Richtofen, c'est lui qui a pris le commandement de la fameuse escadrille. Après la guerre, il a dû, pour gagner sa vie, se faire pilote de ligne. Il conduisait un appareil assurant la liaison entre l'Allemagne et la Suède, quand, un soir, une panne l'a obligé à atterrir en Suède, sur les pelouses d'un château. Accueilli par le châtelain, il voit paraître, au dîner une jeune femme d'une grande beauté. Il s'éprend d'elle, comme le héros du Vaisseau Fantôme. Elle divorce pour lui. Il l'épouse; et c'est en souvenir d'elle qu'il baptisera Karin-Hall le palais qu'il bâtira par la suite.' André François-Poncet *Ambassade à Berlin* (Flammarion, 1946).

ground at the end of the spring of 1968 when Port Harcourt fell, and the only substitute had been a lone B25 flown by a former Luftwaffe pilot, Herz—not particularly effective against the Nigerian aviation which, almost from the beginning dominated the skies.

It is said that it was Hank Wharton who first supplied the Nigerians with Ilyushin bombers and Mig fighters; at any rate the Soviet-Nigerian pact of the autumn of 1968 saw a vast increase in the number of these planes, though they were manned mainly by ineffectual Egyptian pilots who never flew low or by night.

At the beginning of 1969 the situation became more menacing for the Biafrans. The Nigerians had, reasonably enough, decided that airpower was the key to the war, had imported new and far more effective pilots (a mixture of British, East Germans and South Africans), installed radar and purchased far more sophisticated aircraft—MIG 21 night flyers, SU 7 attack planes, six Canberra bombers, a few Hawker Hunters, and at least two Hastings. This gave the Federal forces undisputed air control, the Biafran air force having long since ceased to exist.

At the end of May, however, this non-existent air force, according to a Biafran communiqué, attacked the Nigerian airbase at Port Harcourt, and in quick succession raids against Benin, Enugu and Port Harcourt again followed. The first announcement was greeted with some hilarity, which quickly dispersed as eyewitness reports of the raids came in. It appeared that at least eleven Federal planes (including two Migs, three Ilyushins, a Canberra and a Heron) had been rocketed to pieces on the ground by a group of five twin-seater light aircraft that looked more fit for World War One than for effective air attacks in the atomic age; and the Swedish magazine *Expressen* revealed that this group was led by von Rosen, a name hitherto unknown to the world at large. The romantic side of these exploits, the first touch of the heroic in this barbaric war, at once appealed to the popular and embarrassed the official mind. On May 28 the Swedish government officially informed the Federal government that they disowned Count von Rosen's actions entirely and explained apologetically that the five aircraft, bought from the firm Malmo Flygindustrie, a subsidiary of Saab, were listed as 'light sporting aircraft' for which no export licence was required. On July 24 the Swedish government held a special Cabinet meeting and decided, ridiculously and tardily, to classify these light MFI-9B's, or Minicons, as 'war material', and to instigate official enquiries into von Rosen's legal position vis-a-vis recruiting Swedish nationals for foreign service. But by this time von Rosen had left Biafra (on June 6, less than two weeks after his first raid) and had in any case become a national hero; the court of enquiry acquitted him and the MFI firm of any possible charges. 'There are no Swedish pilots there now,' he said shortly after his return. 'But we will be happy to go back if they call us. I think half Sweden would stand up and go down there.' He was probably right.

In August 1968 at the height of the famine crisis Nordchurchaid had chartered Transair to fly in food supplies from Sao Tomé. Von Rosen broke the Nigerian blockade with a hedge-hopping flight in a DC7. 'But I soon realized,' he said, 'that every priest, every doctor, every black and white man in Biafra was praying for arms and ammunition before food, because the idea of feeding children only to have them massacred later by cannon fire from Saladins or Migs doesn't make sense.' It seems that he then took the law into his own hands and flew in a cargo of arms and ammunition—exactly the crime of which the Nigerians were accusing the Church relief organizations. He was therefore allowed to 'resign', and spent the next few months preparing his ingenious scheme.

'When I thought of Biafra I realized that they would never be able to buy or fly in a jet fighter.[1] Maintenance and fuel would pose an insurmountable problem anyway. The Minicon has many advantages; it cannot easily be hit by anti-aircraft fire nor

---

[1] This idea had of course occurred to the Biafrans—and to the French. Faulques had at one stage announced that Mirage fighter-bombers were due to come in and had started the recruiting of pilots. But their thinking ran on orthodox lines, and the projects were therefore chimerical.

detected by radar because it flies too low. It's easy to fly and simple to service. It's a new weapon of war.'[1]

Von Rosen paid a visit to Biafra in December 1968 and Ojukwu eventually allowed himself to be persuaded. Plans were made, and early the following May a message reached von Rosen in Sweden. The five Minicons were assembled at Libreville and flown down to a secret landing strip in Biafra by von Rosen, two other Swedish pilots, and two Biafrans (one of whom was Opke) —two Swedish technicians accompanied them. Von Rosen's tactics proved astonishingly successful. The Nigerian air force suffered heavy and expensive losses, its supremacy in the air was challenged, the oil companies whose rigs were rocketed were made to realize that the war was not yet won nor their profits safe, and Biafran morale received an enormous boost. In the five raids von Rosen led none of his planes were damaged, though it was apparently a very close thing in the third raid on Port Harcourt. It was after this that he was reported to be ill and overwrought; his return to Sweden followed. Ill-health apart, he felt that he had given the Biafrans the necessary impetus and that he would be more useful as a propagandist for Biafra in Scandinavia than a pilot for Biafra in Africa.

---

[1] There are two accounts of the transactions which preceded the arrival of the planes in Libreville, of which the following is the more convincing. The Tanzanian embassy in Stockholm (Tanzania had been one of the four African states to recognize Biafra) approached Malmo Flygindustrie and announced that their government was interested in establishing a small flying school; to make this request more convincing, word was let out that Tanzania was looking for pilot instructors. The Tanzanian government then purchased the five Minicons for $60,000 (a very cheap price for an air force, though refitting plus the pay of the Swedish pilots and technicians cost Biafra a further $140,000). The Minicons, now the property of the Tanzanian government, were on its orders flown by MFI technicians to France and landed, somewhat to their surprise, at a military airport. There French technicians measured them for rocket fittings, switched over the electrical system, and added an extra fuel tank. This done, the aircraft were dismantled, crated, loaded into a couple of Super Constellations, and flown off to Africa, there to be reassembled under the supervision of the one remaining MFI technician who accompanied them, Per Hazelius. To his bewilderment he and the cargo were landed at Libreville where he was met by Von Rosen—who told him that the flying school had been temporarily transferred to Gabon. The Minicons were off-loaded, assembled, flown to a small airstrip in the bush where the Swedish markings were painted out, the planes were camouflaged, and twelve rockets were fitted to each plane, six to a wing. There several days were spent training the pilots and testing the rockets until Von Rosen was satisfied that the first raid could take place.

Both his propositions were probably true. Biafran pilots continued to raid sporadically; yet it was noticeable that their attacks became sharper and more virulent after mid-September, when von Rosen was certainly back in Biafra though probably only for a short visit. In November the Biafran air force were reported to have some T6 Texan Harvards. On November 9 the Biafrans for the first time lost a Minicon, shot down by a Federal Mig while on a bombing mission over Benue; on November 13 they rocketed Port Harcourt and another aerodrome and claimed eight Nigerian planes destroyed; on November 19 they strafed an American cargo boat and a Norwegian ship near Warri, 200 miles from Lagos—interspersing these with attacks on oil rigs. It is difficult not to see in bold tactics of this sort at least the masterminding of von Rosen.

His motives probably explain his success: 'I had no intention of getting mixed up with this war or the fighting in any way. I had flown for the United Nations in the Congo and after that fiasco I resolved never to get involved in the affairs of new African states again. But when I understood the Biafrans were a people, a united people headed by a legal government and a very honest and brave man whom the people could dismiss if they wanted to, then I went all out to try and stop this terrible killing of innocent women and children. The idea was not to add fuel to the war but to keep the sophisticated war machine that the Nigerians have at their command—the Saladin armoured cars, the Migs and the Ilyushins—away from the little children . . . And so in the end if you are an honest man and you have gone to fight for Finland because it was close to your own country and because they are white people, there is no excuse for backing out of a similar situation because it is further away and because the people are black.'

In any case this is one explanation for the difference between the Swedish and the French mercenaries—who could never be accused of naïvety. Admittedly they alleged that they would never have accepted a contract from Nigeria, and criticised Peters for being more 'mercenary' than they. Both French and English, however, appear to have been acting at the instigation of a government, and the conclusion must be that from the employers' viewpoint mercenaries of this sort are almost valueless. Their overall performance in this grim war must make all potential employers suspicious of even their professional capabilities.

An intriguing point is that none of the notorious mercenary leaders of the Congo distinguished themselves in the Biafran war. Some, like Schramme, never even attempted to take part. Others, Denard and Hoare, for example, offered or were asked to offer their services but did nothing. The rest, like Wicks, Faulques and Peters, played a minor or ignominious rôle. Williams, apparently the most efficient soldier of them all, was virtually unknown before; and in any case, efficient or not, defeated.

The two who became the best known were precisely the two who had taken no part in the affairs of the Congo. Yet even if for every hundred Steiners there is only one von Rosen, perhaps that hundred may be worth enduring precisely for the one that emerges. It is after all possible, and it may one day be proven, that von Rosen, by his efforts and by his efforts alone, postponed—though he failed to prevent—the eventual collapse of Biafra. If so, there will be a certain saving grace illuminating the sordid tale of treachery, intrigues and bloodshed of which most of the history of mercenaries in modern Africa has been compounded.

Not that it is certain that their history ends here. Indeed by the time this book appears the Congo may once more be in eruption and mercenaries in the headlines. Prophecy is dangerous.

12 The Future of Mercenary Soldiers

A MAN WILL NOT BECOME A MERCENARY unless the possible rewards are greater than the possible dangers. Not all danger and not all rewards are direct, but as a general rule a group of mercenaries will not band together unless there is at least a good chance of making money, either directly by pay or, more attractive, indirectly by loot. This does not mean that in a war involving a poor country—for instance, the Yemen—there will never be any mercenaries, but it does mean that the number and the style of the mercenaries involved will be different. In the Yemen the mercenaries relied on regular pay supplied from outside; the prospect of getting rich through booty did not exist. Therefore the mercenaries who came were limited in number and behaved more like military technical advisers than like mercenaries. On the other hand when a wealthy and prosperous land—Italy, the Congo—is torn by war, the hope of sudden riches through loot is high and it is more likely that bands of mercenaries will form.

Danger, however, must not outweigh the prospects of riches. The normal mercenary has always had a horror of being killed. Casualties destroy morale in a mercenary army far more quickly than in a normal army, and if the war is particularly ferocious or the enemy particularly skilled, mercenaries will take no part in it.

Danger comes, moreover, not only from the enemy. If the land of origin of the mercenary disapproves, would-be mercenaries hesitate. Because of the law by which any United States citizen enlisting in a foreign army is automatically deprived of his citizenship, few Americans seriously think of becoming mercenaries. There is a corollary to this, however: that is, if public opinion in the country of origin generally approves of the mercenaries, no number of laws can stop their enlisting, and the laws, however severe, will not normally be applied. The most striking example of this is the attempt, completely futile, of the Swiss cantonal governments to stop their citizens enlisting unofficially in the Italian wars. There are laws against the recruiting of mercenaries for a foreign government in France[1] and Belgium; after the Schramme affair, a law was proposed in Belgium making it an offence to enlist as a mercenary. In Britain during the Katanga crisis the Lord Privy Seal, Mr Heath, announced that British passports would be withdrawn from any British subject enlisting in a foreign army in the Congo. These various measures were barely applicable and hardly applied. These three governments continually disowned mercenaries originating from their three nation states, but in the last resort were always prepared to help them to get out of jail or at least to register strong protests on the occasion of their summary executions.[2]

On the other hand it is an encouragement to mercenaries to form when the government and popular opinion of their native land actively or tacitly supports them. Colonel Trinquier would have attempted nothing in Katanga if the French government

---

[1] There was a curious legal case in France. In 1966 a 'camp' of mercenaries was discovered in the Ardeches. The CRS raided and arrested the men and their leaders. The whole affair remained mysterious. My theory is that Thierry du Bonnay, the organizer, was raising the mercenaries 'on spec', though using Tshombe's name. In any case, the French courts decided that recruiting mercenaries on French soil for a foreign government was an offence; but Tshombe, an exile, was not a foreign *government*. Therefore, no offence had been committed.

[2] As the British government did in the summer of '67, on learning that two mercenaries of British origin had been killed in the massacre of the mercenaries at Leopoldville.

had not semi-officially supported him. The young Rhodesians and South Africans who flocked to join Five Commando knew that there was no question of their being punished and that the authorities in both countries looked with a benevolent eye upon their enlistment. Schramme was justified in feeling that he would be a hero in Belgium, particularly if he succeeded in overthrowing Mobutu. Such British mercenaries as there may have been fighting for the Federal side in the Biafran war could be sure that the British government would never threaten to withdraw their passports (besides, as a Foreign Office spokesman ingenuously explained, there was no question of this, for Nigeria is a member of the Commonwealth and any British subject is legally entitled to serve in any other Commonwealth army).

Finally, from the ordinary mercenary's point of view, the country where the war is being fought must be reasonably close, both psychologically and physically, to his homeland. It was for this reason that any scheme to use Five Commando *en masse* in the Yemen was chimerical; the South African and Rhodesian mercenaries would have fought in Africa, in the Biafra war for instance, in a situation and against opponents whom they understood, but only the most sophisticated (of whom there were not many) would seriously have considered going to Arabia.

Such are the conditions necessary from the potential mercenary's point of view. From the potential employers' point of view there is, obviously, one overriding question: are the mercenaries available better troops by far than their own soldiers? Cyrus, considering the Greeks, answered yes. The kings of France, considering the Swiss, answered yes, in their field of action. Tshombe, considering the French former paratroops, answered yes. But the reputation of the white mercenaries was badly shaken by Schamme's retreat and by the Dilolo episode. Their military superiority had been proved in the Simba revolt, but their revolt had in the end been quashed by the black army with the lowest reputation on the African continent, the ANC. The military leaders of Nigeria and Biafra, nearly all of whom had been educated at Sandhurst and had themselves seen action against the Congolese as part of the United Nations force, must surely have concluded that man for man the average Nigerian or Biafran soldier, far superior to the Congolese, was almost as good as the average white mercenary. Where the white mercenaries were obviously superior was not in their courage nor in any massed tactical formation (such as the Swiss in their pike phalanx) but in their technical mastery of more sophisticated modern weapons; therefore both sides in the Biafran war employed mercenaries as pilots and as training officers, but were reluctant to employ them as fighting groups.

It looks as if this might be the pattern for the future. The conditions for the use of mercenaries exist in Africa, and it appears likely that opportunities will increase rather than diminish. Where there are a number of small states, militarily backward, involved in any number of probable conflicts, where there is no single dominant military power and no likelihood of direct military intervention by an outside power, then as in medieval Italy the correct situation exists for the growing use of mercenaries. Independent black Africa has been spared so far, though only just, wars between rival states. It seems improbable that this situation will continue long. In the case of local wars, it is also improbable that superior military powers, such as South Africa or the old colonial states, will interfere directly. Moreover, the profession of a mercenary has become almost respectable in Europe compared with what it was in 1960. True, the employment of mercenaries by African leaders is still not respectable in African eyes, but here there is a veil of hypocrisy which can hardly last much longer. Therefore the use of European mercenaries by African leaders in the event of a war between two African states is probable.

The other situation in which mercenaries have normally sprung up occurs when a large and ramshackle empire, under weak central control is torn by civil war. This was the case in ancient Persia; it has been the case in the modern Congo. There are other countries in Africa, besides Nigeria, which resemble more an empire in their structure and loyalties than a nation or city-state. Many of them are—at the moment of writing—held together by the existence of 'the Liberator'; in others the army is still led by officers of the former colonial power or indirectly by officers of an official military mission. But neither of these two saving factors are likely to endure. Therefore, objectively, it seems probable that civil wars led by 'pretenders' will take place in several imperial-type states, and that the pretenders will try, as the exiled Tshombe did, to support their cause by the use of white mercenaries.

A possible objection is that there will not be enough white mercenaries willing to come forward. It is true that normally mercenaries swarm only after major wars and that it is over twenty years since the last major war in Europe ended. Yet there have been enough minor wars to give many whites a taste for professional soldiering, as well as the necessary training. Letters of inquiry following articles in the press or television programmes prove that many young men did at least consider the idea of becoming a 'Congo mercenary,' and reports of two or three men who have 'formed' mercenary armies on paper and offered these bands (for instance) to fight communism anywhere in the world for fifty thousand pounds a week show at least what lines wishful thinking can take.

White governments began by being highly suspicious of mercenaries from their countries. They have now seen how effective mercenaries can be and how useful as instruments of policy, for, though unreliable, they can be disowned absolutely. The South African and Portuguese governments have certainly already attempted to use mercenaries as an instrument of foreign policy; sections of the French government have also done so. The American government has both used them and tried to be rid of them, being evidently of two minds about their value. In any case it seems probable that this trend will continue and that instead of sending direct military technical assistance to the conflicting side they favour, white governments will allow, and semi-officially encourage, mercenaries to join in this or that conflict and will attempt to control mercenary leaders.

A Congo-type situation may not recur. It seems more likely that African rulers will prefer to employ a few highly trained mercenaries rather than a body of mercenaries militarily none too superior to their own native troops. In that way they will obtain the advantages without running the risks attached to the use of mercenary troops. Yet this need not necessarily be so. If a mercenary 'condottiere' of sufficient military ability, more so than any who have yet appeared, were to win a reputation and form his own permanent band of white soldiers, he would probably find an employer.

Indeed the advantages of using mercenary troops may become apparent to other than African leaders. It would no doubt seem frivolous to suggest that the government of Great Britain should enlist mercenaries in order to crush the Rhodesian rebellion by force, although seeing that the real argument for not using force is that British soldiers cannot be expected to fire on their kith and kin and cannot be permitted to be killed by them, it would seem a logical way out of an impossible situation. On the other hand, if white mercenary officers were to appear training and leading the 'terrorists' or 'freedom fighters' of the black Rhodesian and South African groups in Zambia, this would be no more than the natural development of a situation in which British national policy and international mercenary tradition temporarily coincide.

In any case, as the militaristic nationalism of the European nation states fades, to be replaced by either vague supranational loyalties or fierce but local patriotisms, it becomes more and more likely that mercenary soldiering will increase. It will be interesting, from an academic point of view, to see how often and how completely history, so repetitious in this field, will continue to repeat itself.

Appendix 1

CONTRACT OF AGENTS IN THE SERVICE OF THE DEMOCRATIC REPUBLIC OF THE CONGO

BETWEEN THE DEMOCRATIC REPUBLIC GOVERNMENT OF THE CONGO, represented by the Prime Minister in agreement with the National Security Council on the one side, and Mr: *Name, Christian name, place of birth, date of birth, nationality, left or right-handed, father's full name, mother's maiden name, profession, marital status, wife's name, wife's address, children's names and ages, last address, address of next of kin, bank account number, bank address, previous military experience, rank held in foreign army* on the other side, hereinafter referred to as the Foreign Volunteer, the following has been agreed to:

CHAPTER 1

Article 1. Conditions to be fulfilled in order to be eligible for enlistment.

To be eligible for enlistment into the Congolese national army, the Foreign Volunteer must have been in a Regular Foreign Army and be accepted by the Commander-in-Chief.

Article 2. Military pledge required by this contract.

a) A Foreign Volunteer must pledge himself to serve in the Congolese National Army in a military capacity.

b) The military pledge involves learning the rules and regulations of the Congolese army.

Article 3. Submission to the Laws of the Republic.

A Foreign Volunteer must submit to the Laws of the Republic and the judgement of their military tribunals, the same applying to infractions of common law as for infractions of military law. The Order in Council of December 18, 1964, decrees severe punishment for the waste of arms and ammunition, pillage, theft and violence towards civilians. In certain particularly odious cases of pillage and violence the death penalty or imprisonment for life could be imposed. Every infraction of common or military law will automatically involve the application of the clause, Article 9, paragraphs a) and c) of this contract. The Foreign Volunteer must acknowledge and declare that he understands Chapter 2 of the Order in Council of December 18, 1964, in relation to the rules and regulations of Congolese military discipline, and that he understands their terms in this capacity in the end, and see that he must submit to all of their provisions.

Article 4. Rank awarded to Foreign Volunteers.

Promotion a) At the time of the signing of the contract, the signee is awarded the same rank which he held in the Foreign Army, provided that he has effectively carried out the function for this rank. The contractor cannot take into account honorary ranks awarded by a Foreign Army.

b) Proof of a person's rank in a Foreign Army must be provided by original official documents or certified copies accepted by the Congolese military attache or the Chief of Service G.1 of the A.N.C. Non-certified photostat copies are not valid.

c) The awarding of rank at the time of signing this contract is made according to the following scale:

Foreign ranks	A.N.C. ranks
Private and Corporal	Volunteer
Sergeant	Sergeant
1st Sergeant to Adjutant	Adjutant
Sergeant Major	Adjutant Chief
Warrant Officer	Corresponding Rank
Officer	Corresponding Rank

d) The Foreign Volunteer enlists at the rank of Volunteer. If it is considered that he merits it, a Foreign Volunteer may be promoted to a higher rank. Only the Commander-in-Chief has the authority to promote, on the recommendation of the Corps Commander of a Foreign Volunteer, taking into account the necessity of leadership.

Article 5. Functions of the Foreign Volunteer.

The nomination of rank does not entitle a person to carry out the functions of that rank. These functions are independent of rank. The functions to be carried out are determined by the C. in C. for the better interests of the A.N.C.

Article 6. Various things are forbidden.

It is forbidden for a Foreign Volunteer to:

a) Bring their families to the Congo without previous permission of the C. in C.

b) Engage in any lucrative business activity while they are within the territory of the Republic.

c) Edit a newspaper or any other periodical of any nature whatsoever, or contribute to its administration or composition.

d) Participate in any political strife.

e) Publish any anonymous articles in newspaper or any other periodical, to write books or to give interviews.

CHAPTER 2
DURATION OF CONTRACT, RE-ENLISTMENT, CESSATION OF CONTRACT, ETC.

Article 7. Duration of contract.

The present contract is for a term of six months following the date of signature.

Article 8. Re-enlistment.

A Foreign Volunteer may ask for a renewal of his contract for a further six months. He should make his application in writing within two months of the expiration of his contract. The request should be addressed to the C. in C. and sent through the normal channels. The C. in C. has the final decision.

Article 9. Causes for the annulment of the contract.

a) The contract will be annulled in all cases in which sentences have been pronounced for infractions of military regulations, as shown in Chapter 2 of the Order in Council, December 18, 1964, and infractions of common law by a sentence of less than six months imprisonment have been pronounced.

b) Full causes for a possible annulment of the contract. Bad conduct; grave insubordination; repeated bad discipline. All infractions are conditions of Article 6 of this contract.

c) The annulment of contracts shown in paragraphs a) and b) may be pronounced by the C. in C. or his deputy without prior notice. When a contract is withdrawn, the Foreign Volunteer concerned will be expelled *ipso facto* from the territory of the Republic. The costs of repatriation will be charged to the Foreign Volunteer who is expelled.

Article 10. Cancellation of contract.

The government of the Democratic Republic of the Congo reserves the right to cancel this contract before its expiration for any obligatory cause, or any cause beyond the control of the present contractor.

Article 11. Indemnity for the cancellation of contract.

In the case of the preceding article the Foreign Volunteer is entitled to a cancellation-of-contract indemnity equal to fifteen days' salary (Article 15) and fifteen days' daily indemnities (Article 17) for each month of service up to a maximum of three months. This indemnity is transferable, in its entirety, into Belgian francs.

Article 12. Notice of termination of contract.

a) Should either party fail to comply with the terms of this contract, the wronged party may terminate the contract. Failure to comply with the terms of this contract render the state of execution, and a continuation of mutual good relations impossible. The party breaking the contract is not bound to pay any indemnity to the other.

b) Should the Foreign Volunteer be guilty of any fraudulent act, making false statements, concealing any physical disabilities or any infirmities whatsoever at the time of his enlistment, or of inflicting any injury to himself after enlistment, the contract will be terminated.

c) Notice of termination of contract by the wronged party must be given in writing in the manner prescribed hereafter. If the Foreign Volunteer takes the initiative in terminating the contract, the termination will not become effective until the sixteenth day after the notification in writing has been submitted to the first authority in the hierarchy unless this first authority is in a position to remedy the reason for the Foreign Volunteer's decision to terminate his contract. If the field C.O. or his deputy takes the initiative in terminating the contract, the termination only becomes effective the day after this termination of contract has been given in writing to the Foreign Volunteer and passed through the normal channels.

Article 13. Cessation of contract.

The Foreign Volunteer may ask to break his contract for personal reasons only when this is caused through an Act of God. The request must be sent through the normal channels to the C. in C. or his deputy, who has the final decision. If the request is accepted, the cessation of contract will not take effect until the day after the favourable decision has been communicated to the Foreign Volunteer in person through the normal channels.

CHAPTER 3
PECUNIARY ACTS

Article 14. Remuneration. (See Article 26)

a) The Foreign Volunteer is entitled to a monthly salary, various indemnities and certain advantages in kind.

b) These remunerations are susceptible to variations of the index.

Article 15. Monthly salary while in action.

The Foreign Volunteer will receive a monthly salary in advance at the beginning of each month. The salary while in action will consist of:
a basic salary, and a six-monthly augmentation for voluntarily re-enlisting.

c) The monthly basic salary is fixed according to the following scale:

Volunteer—10,053 francs × index
Up to
Lieutenant Colonel—37,916 francs × index[1]

d) From the seventh month of service, and for each six-monthly period following, the basic salary is augmented by two thousand francs multiplied by the index. A new augmentation of the same amount is awarded for each following term in favour of a Volunteer who has re-enlisted.

---

[1] Only the two extremes of the salary scales are quoted. A second lieutenant received 21,250 francs × index.

e) Each month is taken as thirty days. When the contractor has to work out the daily salary and indemnity shown in this chapter the daily salary is equal to one thirtieth of the total of the monthly total. The exact amount is calculated as shown in paragraph b) of Annex 2.

Article 16. Wife and family allowances.
a) The Foreign Volunteer is entitled to the following allowances payable in advance at the same time as he receives his salary:

Wife—monthly allowance of 2,127 francs $\times$ index	
First child	1,277 francs $\times$ index
Second child	1,360 francs $\times$ index
Third child	1,530 francs $\times$ index
Fourth child and others	1,787 francs $\times$ index

Example: A Volunteer, married, father of five children for whom he is responsible, will receive a total of 9,868 francs multiplied by the index. This family allowance is payable only for legitimate children of the Foreign Volunteer for whom he is responsible.

Article 17. Daily indemnity for board and lodging.
The Foreign Volunteer is entitled to a daily indemnity of two hundred francs multiplied by the index. This indemnity is in place of an allocation for lodging; it is payable in advance at the same time as the salary is received.

Article 18. Daily danger pay.
The Foreign Volunteer is entitled to danger pay as follows, payable in arrears:
a) While in a danger zone 500 francs $\times$ index.
b) While in an insecure zone 200 francs $\times$ index.
These zones are determined at the beginning of each month for the previous month by Q.G.(A.N.C.) G.3, who also determines the dates of the beginning and end of danger and insecure zones.

Article 19. Indemnity for billets.
a) The Foreign Volunteer on operation cannot claim an indemnity for billets.
b) While he is not on operation and is not accommodated in a hotel or state building, but is in a place where he has to pay personally for lodging, he is entitled to a daily indemnity of two hundred and fifty francs multiplied by the index.

Article 20. Advantages in kind.
a) The Foreign Volunteer is entitled, in principle, to free food.
b) When food cannot be given to a Foreign Volunteer and he is obliged to purchase his own, he is entitled to a daily indemnity for food fixed on the following scale:
  120 francs $\times$ index when he is in a sedentary post.
  175 francs $\times$ index when he is on patrol.

Article 21. The Index.
The Index mentioned in the preceding articles is actually fixed at 4.69. It is, however, liable to variation. A new index is fixed by the Prime Minister. Annex No. 2 of this contract gives the full salary with the various indemnities at the index at 4.69 included.

Article 22. Monetary deductions for punishment.
The following monetary deductions may be made by the Chief of the Corps after receiving a written report from the Platoon Commander.
 a) For infraction of those disciplinary rules which demand monetary deductions on the basis of: one thirtieth of the salary (Article 15) and daily indemnities (Article 17) for each day under house arrest. One fifteenth of the salary (Article 15) and daily indemnities (Article 17) for each day under close arrest.
 b) The total monthly monetary deductions cannot exceed two thirds of the total monthly salary plus daily indemnities.

Article 23. Travelling Expenses.
The Democratic Republic of the Congo will pay all travelling expenses of Foreign Volunteers from the place of enlistment to the place of execution of the contract.

Unless they make a contrary decision the contractors will pay travelling expenses for the repatriation of Foreign Volunteers from the place of execution of the contract to place of enlistment

The mode of transport will be, in both cases, the least onerous to the treasury.

CHAPTER 4
SOCIAL ADVANTAGES

Article 24. Lump sum compensation in the case of the death of a volunteer.
In the case of the death of a Foreign Volunteer as a direct and exclusive result of action while on service, the following is granted to his beneficiary:
 a) One million Belgian francs, approximately twenty thousand Swiss dollars, for the wife of a married Foreign Volunteer who at the time of enlistment was not legally separated or estranged—proof of this must be provided by an attestation from the Burgermaster, Mayor or other Authority; for the next of kin in the case of an unmarried, widowed, divorced or separated Foreign Volunteer who has not named any other beneficiary; for the person named in this contract by the Foreign Volunteer who is unmarried, a widower or a divorcee.
 b) One hundred thousand Belgian francs for each legitimate child. The Government of the Democratic Republic reserves the right to make all arrangements for the compensation of the children to be made to an official institution in their country who will be charged to manage the estate until the children reach their majority.

Article 25. Insurance.

The Government of the Republic will give to an injured Volunteer free insurance up to a maximum of one million Belgian francs plus one hundred thousand Belgian francs for each child he is responsible for. This insurance will be paid out according to the degree of injury laid out in the following article.

Article 26. Compensation given to those totally and permanently injured.

In cases of wounds involving a total and absolute loss of sight, the entire removal or complete loss of the function of both hands or feet, or one hand or foot, complete paralysis, incurable mental illness excluding the possibility of carrying out any form of work or occupation, the Government of the Republic will pay 100% of the total insurable amount.

Article 27. Compensation awarded to those partially and permanently injured.

In cases of partial and permanent injury compensation is fixed as follows, as a percentage of the total:

a) The total and absolute loss—that is the complete loss or complete loss of the function of—the right arm 75%, left 60%, the right forearm 65%, left 55%, the right hand 60%, left 50%, a thigh 60%, one leg 50%, one foot 40%, one eye 30%, the right thumb 20%, left 13%, the right index finger 16%, left 14%, the right middle finger 10%, left 8%, the right small finger 8%, left 6%, the big toe 5%, all other toes 3%, the hearing of one ear 15%, the hearing of both ears 40%. For a left-handed person, on condition that this has been declared before receiving the wound, the scale fixed for the right members will apply to the left members.

b) The partial loss of one of the members or organs mentioned in a). Compensation will be paid in proportion to the loss of usage as a percentage, but not exceeding 60% of the whole amount. All wounds causing permanent or partial injury to the organs not mentioned above will be compensated for after the degree of incapability has been assessed by examination before a medical board, taking into account the preceding scale.

c) The total amount of compensation for permanent partial injury cannot be more than three quarters of the total insurable amount, whatever the case of the number of organs or members lost, whether total or partial.

Article 28. Compensation in cases of temporary injury.

a) In cases of temporary injury the Foreign Volunteer is entitled to his salary, compensation and other allocations as laid out in Articles 15, 16 and 17.

b) A temporary injury. As shown in this Article, it must be recognized that it is impossible for the volunteer to carry out any activity whatsoever. This should be duly ascertained by a medical certificate.

Article 29. Accumulation of compensation.
Compensation for the deceased, totally and permanently injured, and partially injured, can in no case be accumulated. Payment of compensation as shown in Article 28 ceases on payments of compensation detailed in Articles 23, 26 and 27.

Article 30. Treatment of illnesses.
Medical treatment, surgery and hospitalisation of a person under contract is paid for by the Government for the duration of the contract and during the leave period. Any treatment paid for in a foreign country will be reimbursed upon presentation of the medical bill.

Article 31. Leave.
   a) At the normal expiration of his contract of 6 months, the Foreign Volunteer is entitled to 20 days paid leave. He may spend his leave in the country where he was enlisted.
   b) While on leave he is entitled to his salary and to indemnities as shown in Articles 15, 16 and 17.
   c) Travelling expenses are paid for by the State, this journey being considered as the termination of the contract.

CHAPTER 5
TRANSFERS, TAX IMMUNITY, SETTLEMENT OF COMPENSATION FOR THOSE KILLED AND WOUNDED

Article 32. Guarantee of Transfers.
   a) Each month the foreign volunteer may have the following remuneration transferred into a foreign currency: 50% of the monthly salary, 100% of the wife and family allowances, 50% of the daily indemnity due for one month, 50% of danger pay due for one month.
   b) In case of temporary incapacity the Foreign Volunteer will be hospitalised, treated or convalesce in the Congo. He may have the following remuneration transferred into a foreign currency: 50% of the monthly salary, 100% of the wife and family allowance, 50% of the daily indemnity due for one month. However, the monthly salary and indemnities due in virtue of Article 28 for the Foreign Volunteer who is hospitalised, under treatment or is convalescing in a foreign country, will be transferred in total into a foreign currency for the duration of his term of convalescence.
   c) After six months of service, in the same way as for the expiration of his contract, the foreign volunteer may transfer into a foreign currency the money saved during the six months period. However, the amounts transferable may not exceed: 25% of the amount received as laid out in Articles 16, 17 and 18: 100% of the leave pay and indemnity as laid out in Article 31.
   d) In cases where a contract is broken or terminated, the Foreign Volunteer may transfer the money saved during his term of contract. However, the

amount transferable may not exceed 25% of the money received, as laid out in Articles 16, 17 and 18.

e) In cases where the contract is cancelled, the Foreign Volunteer may further to the amount laid out in paragraph c) transfer 75% of the indemnity mentioned in Article 11.

f) Transfers laid out in paragraphs a), b), c), d) and e) above are subject to the approval of $G_{.1}$.

Article 33. Settlement of compensation for those killed and wounded.

The settlement of compensation as laid out in Articles 24, 26 and 27 is effective, subject to the approval of $G_{.1}$: within a maximum of three months from the date on which compensation as laid out in Articles 24, 26 and 27, is granted: within a maximum of three months from the date on which the amount of compensation has been set out by the Medical Board (compensation as laid out in Articles 26 and 27).

Article 34. Transfer Expenses.

Transfer expenses resulting from the application of Articles 32 and 33 are paid for by the State.

Article 35. Tax Immunity.

Salaries, allowances and compensation of any nature as laid down in this contract are free of all tax.

CHAPTER 6
FINAL REMARKS

Article 36. Litigation.

In cases where the subject, interpretation or execution of any clauses in this contract are contested, the dispute will be heard before a tribunal.

Signed at   Date

For the Democratic Republic of the Congo in . . . original copies.

The Prime Minister—

The Foreign Volunteer—

Note 1. The Foreign Volunteer must append in his own hand the words 'read and approved', *lu et approuvé*.

MINOR POINTS FROM ANNEXES TO THE CONTRACT

Article: Extension of Contract.

Volunteers may for personal reasons prolong the duration of their contract indefinitely. The Battalion commander has the right with the agreement of the C. in C. to prolong for administrative or security reasons a Volunteer's contract. However, these Volunteers are entitled to all advantages laid out in this contract.

Signed: Bobozo L. Major General. Commander in Chief.

Article: Promotion.
The scale of promotion for Volunteers joining the A.N.C.s is as follows: Volunteer, Sergeant, Adjutant, Adjutant-Chief, Second Lieutenant, Lieutenant, Captain, Commandant, Major, Lieutenant-Colonel. It is obligatory to abide by this scale, no person may jump two ranks in a single nomination.

Article: Requirements for indemnities.
Official Congolese death certificate, doctor's certificate of death, witnesses' report, report of commanding officer [and many more for South Africa and Rhodesia: affidavits, etc. etc. This article is headed: *from Albertville*].

Appendix II

TRANSLATION OF A TREATY between his Majesty and the Landgrave of Hesse-Cassel. Signed at Cassel, January 15, 1776.

His Britannic Majesty, being desirous of employing in his service a body of 12,000 men, of the troops of his most serene highness the reigning landgrave of Hesse Cassel; and that prince, full of attachment for his Majesty, desiring nothing more than to give him proofs of it, his Majesty, in order to settle the objects relative to this alliance, has thought proper to send to Cassel the sieur William Faucitt, his minister plenipotentiary and colonel in his service, and his most serene highness has named, on his part, for the same purpose, the baron Martin Erneste de Schlieffen, his minister of state, lieutenant general and knight of his orders, who being furnished with requisite full powers, have agreed, that the Treaties formerly concluded between Great Britain and Hesse shall be made the basis of the present Treaty, and to adopt as much of them as shall be applicable to the present circumstances, or to determine by new articles such points as must be settled otherwise; every thing that shall not be differently regulated, shall be deemed to subsist in full force, as it shall appear to be declared in the above-mentioned Treaties; and as it is not possible to specify each particular case, every thing that shall not be found regulated in a precise manner, neither in the present Treaty, nor in the former Treaties, ought to be settled with equity and good faith, conformably to the same principles which were agreed on each part to be pursued for regulating all such cases, whether during or after the last war.

I. There shall be therefore, by virtue of this Treaty, between his Majesty the king of Great Britain and his most serene highness the landgrave of Hesse Cassel, their successors, and heirs, a strict friendship, and a sincere firm and constant union, insomuch that the one shall consider the interests of the other as his own, and shall apply himself with good faith to advance them to the utmost, and to prevent and avert mutually all trouble and loss.

II. To this end it is agreed, that all former Treaties, principally of guaranty, be deemed to be renewed and confirmed by the present Treaty, in all their points, articles and clauses, and shall be of the same force as if they were herein inserted word for word, so far as is not derogated from them by the present Treaty.

III. This body of 12,000 men of the troops of Hesse, which is to be employed in his Britannic Majesty's service, shall consist of four battalions of grenadiers, of four companies each, fifteen battalions of infantry, of five companies each, and two companies of chasseurs, the whole provided with general and other necessary officers. This corps shall be completely equipped and provided with tents and all accoutrements, of which it may stand in need; in a word, shall be put on the best footing possible, and none shall be admitted into it but men fit for service, and acknowledged for such by his Britannic Majesty's commissary. Formerly the signature of the Treaties has usually preceded, by some time, the requisition for the march of the troops, but, as in the present circumstances, there is no time to be lost, the day of the signature of the present Treaty is deemed also to be the term of the requisition, and three battalions of grenadiers, six battalions of infantry, with one company of chasseurs, shall be in a condition to pass in review before his Britannic Majesty's commissary on the 14th of February, and shall begin to march on the day following, the 15th of February, for the place of embarkation. The rest shall be ready in four weeks after, if possible, and march in like manner. This body of troops shall not be separated, unless reasons of war require it, but shall remain under the orders of the general, to whom his most serene highness has entrusted the command; and the second division shall be conducted to the same places only, where the first shall actually be, if not contrary to the plan of operations.

IV. Each battalion of this body of troops shall be provided with two pieces of field artillery, with the officers, gunners, and other persons, and the train thereunto belonging, if his Majesty is desirous of it.

V. Towards defraying the expenses, in which the most serene landgrave shall be engaged, for the arming and putting in condition the said corps of 12,000 men, his Majesty, the king of Great Britain, promises to pay to his serene highness for each foot soldier 30 crowns Banco, levy money, as well for the infantry as for the chasseurs, or artillery, if there should be any, the sum total of which shall be ascertained, according to the number of men composing this corps, and as they have been reckoned in former alliances. The sum of 180,000 crowns Banco, valued as in the following Article, shall be paid on account of this levy money, on the 10th of February, and the residue shall be paid when the second division of this corps shall begin their march.

VI. In all the former Treaties a certain number of years is stipulated for their duration; but, in the present, his Britannic Majesty, choosing rather not to engage himself for any longer time than he shall have occasion for these troops, consents, instead thereof, that the subsidy shall be double, from the day of the signature of this Treaty to its expiration; that is to say, that it shall amount for this body of 12,000 men to the sum of 450,000 crowns Banco per annum, the crown reckoned at 53 sols of Holland, or at 4s 9¾d. English money, and that the subsidy shall continue upon this foot during all the time that this body of troops shall remain in British pay. His Britannic Majesty engages also to give notice to the most serene landgrave of its determination, 12 months, or a whole year, before it shall take place, which notice shall not even be given before this body of troops is returned, and actually arrived in the dominions of the said prince, namely, in Hesse, properly so called: his Majesty shall continue equally to this corps the pay and other emoluments for the remainder of the month in which it shall repass the frontiers of Hesse, and his most serene highness reserves to himself, on his side, the liberty of recalling his troops at the end of four years, if they are not sent back before, or to agree with his Britannic Majesty at the end of that time for another term.

VII. With regard to the pay and treatment, as well ordinary as extraordinary, of the said troops, they shall be put on the same foot in all respects with the national British troops, and his Majesty's department of war shall deliver, without delay, to that of his most serene highness, an exact and faithful state of the pay and treatment enjoyed by those troops; which pay and treatment, in consideration that his most serene highness could not put this corps in a condition to march in so short a time, without extraordinary expenses, shall commence for the first division on the 1st day of February, and for the second seven days before it shall begin to march, and shall be paid into the military chest of Hesse, without any abatement or deduction, to be distributed according to the arrangements which shall be made for that purpose; and the sum of 20,000l. sterling shall be advanced immediately on account of the said pay.

VIII. If it should happen, unfortunately, that any regiment or company of the said corps, should be ruined or destroyed, either by accidents on the sea, or otherwise, in the whole, or in part, or that the pieces of artillery, or other effects, with which they shall be provided, should be taken by the enemy, or lost on the sea, his Majesty, the king of Great Britain, shall cause to be paid the expenses of the necessary recruits, as well as the price of the said field pieces and effects, in order forthwith to reinstate the artillery, and the said regiments or companies; and the said recruits shall be settled likewise on the foot of those which were furnished to the Hessian officers, by virtue of the Treaty of 1702, Article 5th, to the end that the corps may be always preserved and sent back in as good a state as it was delivered in.[1] The recruits annually necessary shall be

---

[1] Article XI of the Brunswick Treaty reads: According to custom, three wounded men shall be reckoned as one killed. A man killed shall be paid for at the rate of levy money. If it shall happen that any of the regiments, battalions, or companies of this corps should suffer a loss altogether extraordinary, either in a battle, a siege, or by an uncommon contagious malady, or by the loss of any transport vessel in the voyage to America, his Britannic Majesty will make good, in the most equitable manner, the loss of the officer, or soldier, and will be at the expense of the necessary recruits to re-establish the corps that shall have suffered this extraordinary loss.

sent to the English commissary, disciplined and completely equipped, at the place of embarkation, at such time as his Britannic Majesty shall appoint.

IX. In Europe his Majesty shall make use of this body of troops by land, wherever he shall judge proper; but North America is the only country of the other parts of the globe where this body of troops shall be employed. They shall not serve on the sea; and they shall enjoy in all things, without any restriction whatsoever, the same pay and emoluments as are enjoyed by the English troops.

X. In case the most serene landgrave should be attacked or disturbed in the possession of his dominions, his Britannic Majesty promises and engages to give him all the succour that it shall be in his power to afford, which succour shall be continued to him until he shall have obtained an entire security and just indemnification: as the most serene landgrave promises likewise, on his part, that in case his Majesty, the king of Great Britain, is attacked or disturbed in his kingdoms, dominions, lands, provinces, or towns, he will give him in like manner all the succour that it shall be in his power to afford, which succour shall likewise be continued to him until he shall have obtained a good and advantageous peace.

XI. In order to render this alliance and union the more perfect, and to leave no doubt with the parties about the certainty of the succour, which they have to expect by virtue of this Treaty, it is expressly agreed, that to judge for the future whether the case of this alliance, and the stipulated succour, exists or not, it shall suffice that either of the parties is actually attacked by force of arms, without his having first used open force against him who attacks him.

XII. The sick of the Hessian corps shall remain under the care of their physicians, surgeons, and other persons, appointed for that purpose, under the orders of the general commanding the corps of that nation, and everything shall be allowed them that his Majesty allows to his own troops.

XIII. All the Hessian deserters shall be faithfully given up, wherever they shall be discovered, in the places dependent on his Britannic Majesty, and above all, as far as it is possible, no person whatever of that nation shall be permitted to establish himself in America without the consent of his sovereign.

XIV. All the transports for the troops, as well for the men as for the effects, shall be at the expense of his Britannic Majesty; and none belonging to the said corps shall pay any postage of letters in consideration of the distance of the places.

XV. The Treaty shall be ratified by the high contracting parties, and the ratifications thereof shall be exchanged as soon as possible.

In witness whereof, We, the undersigned, furnished with the full powers of his Majesty, the king of Great Britain on one part, and of his most serene highness the reigning landgrave of Hesse Cassel on the other part, have signed the present Treaty, and have caused the seals of our arms to be put thereon. Done at Cassel, the 15th of January, in the year 1776.

WILLIAM FAUCITT. (L.S.)
M. DE SCHLIEFFEN. (L.S.)

Index

Abbas, Dr Mekki, 162–4, 166
Accaiouli, Nerio, 54
Adekunle, Col., 261
Africa Addio, 152, 153
Aimery, Sir John, 30
Alberigo di Barbiano, 60, 61, 66, 70, 72, 73
Albret, Perduccas d', 32
Alexander, Gen., 147n
Alfonso II, of Naples, 88, 89, 92
Almogavares, the, 53
Alviano, Bartolomeo, 48
Amilakvari, Col. Prince, 138
Andronicus II (Palaeologus), Emperor, 53
Ancona, March of, 45
Angola, 170–71
Anhalt-Zerbst, Prince of, 128
Anspach-Bayreuth, Margrave of, 127–8
Appenzell, 78, 86, 100
Aquinas, Thomas, Saint, 32
Arab Legion, Jordanian, 17, 143
Armagnac, Count of, 34, 36
Armagnac, Duke of, 60, 68
Armagnacs, the, 68–9, 78
Armand, Capt., 268
Arras, Treaty of, 68
Athens, 54
Auberchicourt, Eustace d', 30
Augusta, sister of George III, 116
Auray, Battle of, 30

Badefol, Geguin de, 31
Baglione, Gianpaolo, 48, 49
Baluba war, 149, 157, 158, 199–200
Barbastro, Battle of, 135, 136
Barbute, German and Hungarian, 55–6
Barré, Col., 125
Barvaux, Major, 169

Bartholomew of Saliceto, 32
Basel, 100
Bathurst, Lord Chancellor, 113
Bavaria, Elector of, 120
Belgians, the, 157, 174, 176
Bentivoglio, Giovanni, 45
Bergerac, Cyrano de, 141
Bernard, Saint, of Siena, 49–50
Berne, 76, 80, 83, 84, 85, 86, 95
Bernelle, Col., 135, 136
Biafra, 259–75
Bismarck, Count von, 15
Blasey, Jean de, 35
Blois, Comte de, 30
Bobozo, Gen., 182, 236
Bodenan, François, 209
Bohun, Humphrey de, Earl of Essex, 26
Boldrino da Panigale, 49
Bologna, 65
Bongard, Hans von, 58
Bongo, President of Gabon, 266n
Borgia, Cesare, 47, 48, 49, 63
Bosquet, Major, 169
Bourc Anglais, the, 30
Bournonville, Enguerrand de, 35
Boyne, Battle of the, 22
Boynton, Sir Henry, 35
Bracco, mercenary, 216
Bretigny, Treaty of, 28, 33, 34, 36, 40, 68
Breton Company, 59, 60
Brienne, Walter de, Duke of Athens, 54
Brignais, Battle of, 30, 31, 33, 38, 39
Brincourt, Christian, 264
British Auxiliary Legion, 135
Brown, 'Kamikaze', 271
Browne, Capt. Richard, 162–4, 166
Brunswick, 116, 295n

298 | INDEX

Brunswickers, 116–17, 127
Bude, Sir Silvester, 59, 60
Buissey, Antoine de, 90, 95, 98
Bukavu, Congo, 137, 173, 187–91, 201–2, 214–17
Bull, Alderman, 120, 121
Bunker Hill, Battle of, 107, 108
Burckhardt, Jakob, 66, 88
Burger, RSM, 225
Burgoyne, Gen., 128
Burgundy, 79–80, 81, 83
Burke, Edmund, 119

Calveley, Sir Hugh, 30, 71
Camden, Lord, 124, 126
Campobasso, Conte di, 71, 82
Cane, Facino, 61, 71
Cao Bang, 141n
Capenne, Bourc de, 30, 31
Captal de Buch, the, 30, 34
Cargill, Russell, 163
Carleton, Gen., 108
Carlos, Don, of Spain, 16, 135
Carmagnola, Count of, 48, 70, 72, 78
Caroline of Brunswick, 116
Carthage, 16, 218
Castiglione, Baldassare, 43, 71
Catherine the Great, of Russia, 108, 109–10
Catherine, Saint, of Siena, 58, 60
Cavendish, Lord John, 119
Central Intelligence Agency, 209
Chandos, Sir John, 38
Charles, of Anjou, 18, 53
Charles, Duke of Brunswick, 116–18, 128
Charles, Duke of Burgundy, 71, 79–82
Charles VI, of France, 34, 35
Charles VII, of France, 68, 69
Charles VIII, of France, 88–95
Charles IV, Emperor of Germany, 58
Charles V, Emperor of Germany, 17
Charles XII, of Sweden, 270
Charles Augustus, of Saxe-Weimar, 127
China, 172
Church, the, 39
Clary, Michel de, 168, 265
Clemens, René, 178
Clement VI, Pope, 54
Clement VII, Pope, 59, 60
Clive, Robert, 106
Clos, Max, 194
Cocherel, Battle of, 30, 34
Colleoni, Bartolommeo, 42, 43, 61, 72

Colonna, Prospero, 92
Comines, Philippe de, 80
Compagnia: del Capellotto, 58; del Fiore, 58; della Stella, 58; di San Giorgio, 58, 73
Compagnie: de la Margot, 35; des Bâtards, 35; des Tards-Venus, 25; Internationale, 163–4, 166
Compagnons de la Folle Vie, 83–4
Company of St Denis, 36
condottieri, the, 42–73
Congo, the, 143–51, 155–219 passim, 236–52, 283–92
Conquistadors, the, 18
Conrad, Col., 136
Constantinople, fall of, 71
Coucy, Enguerrand de, 68
Couve de Murville, M., 160
Crécy, Battle of, 28
Cristina, Queen of Spain, 135
Cumberland, Duke of, 121

Daily Telegraph, 145
Danjou, Capt., 137
Dayan, Gen. Moshe, 217
Delamichel, 'Frenchie', 179, 180, 198
Delperdange, Gen., 177, 179
Denard, Bob, 148, 151, 162, 165–6, 170, 173, 178–90 passim, 195–9, 204–18 passim, 253, 255, 257, 260, 275
Dernier Train du Katanga, Le, 149
Diaz, Bernal, 18
Dien Bien Phu, 137, 140, 141
Dionysius of Syracuse, 22
Dijon, Antoine de Buissey, Bailli of, 90, 95, 98
Dresnay, Renaud, 61
Dufour, Col. Henri, 141
du Guesclin, Sir Bertrand, 30

Écorcheurs (Scorchers), 69
Edward, Black Prince, 28, 32, 34
Edward I, of England, 26
Edward III, of England, 27–8, 33, 34, 37, 40
Elizabeth I, of England, 114
Elizabethville, 155
England, 17, 19, 26, 106–10, 114, 293–6
Espresso, L', 152
Este, Isabella d', 89
Ethiopian troops, 162, 169, 204
Evans, Sir de Lacy, 135

INDEX | 299

Faucitt, Col. William, 116–18, 127, 296
Faulques, Robert, 148, 159, 161–2, 166, 169, 173, 203, 204, 255, 257, 260–62, 275
Feisal, of Saudi Arabia, 255
Ferdinand, of Aragon, 93
Ferdinand, of Brunswick, 116
Fermo, Oliverotto da, 49
Feronie, first minister of Brunswick, 116
Ferrante, King of Naples, 48–9, 88
feudalism, 19, 25–8, 39
Figaro, 143, 145, 194, 214
Five Commando, 174–8, 180–82, 185, 201, 205, 221–32, 244–5
Florence, 51, 52, 59, 65, 79
Foccart, Jacques, 209n, 266n
Foix, Gaston Phoebus, Count of, 34
Foreign Legion, French, 17, 18, 130–42
Fornovo, Battle of, 93
Fortebraccio, Braccio, 42, 44, 45, 49, 51, 61, 66, 67, 70
France, 14–16, 69, 101–3, 132, 141
Francis I, of France, 102–3
Franco, Gen., 16, 22
Franco-German War, 15
Frederick, Duke of Austria, 78
Frederick III, Emperor, 68, 78, 84
Frederick, Landgrave of Hesse-Cassel, 117–18, 127–8
Frederick of Prussia (the Great), 14, 106, 107, 115, 120, 127
Frederick William I, of Prussia, 14
Free Companies, 28, 30–41, 56–60
Fribourg, canton, 86
Froissart, Sir John, 30, 31, 38, 39, 40, 59, 113

Gage, Gen., 107, 108
Gaulle, Gen. Charles de, 138, 209n
Gbenye, Christophe, 172, 176
Geneva, 84
Geoffrey Têt-Noire, 30, 31, 36
George III, of England, 19, 110, 113, 115
George IV, of England, 116
Germaine, Lord George, 119, 126
German Legion, King's, 131, 140
Germani, Dr Hans, 150
Gessler, Governor, 75
Gibbon, Edward, 109
Giustiani, Giuliano, 71
Gizenga, 158
Glarus, 76, 86
Glubb Pasha, 143

Godard, Col., 159
Goering, Hermann, 270
Goethe, 127
Goosens, Marc, 255, 267
Goualt (or Gouhaux), mercenary, 179
Gouhaux, Lt, 143
Grafton, Duke of, 111, 123
Grand Catalan Company, 53–4
Grandson, Battle of, 81
Great Company, Fra Moriale's, 56–7
Great Company, Knollys', 32, 33
Great Schism, 58, 60
Gregoretti, Piero, 152
Gregory XI, Pope, 58
Guardian, The, 146, 258n
guards, mercenaries as, 22–3
Gunning, British Ambassador to Russia, 108, 109
Guntram the Rich, 74
Gurkhas, 16, 17, 18, 20, 140, 169

Hammerskjöld, Dag, 160n, 167, 168
Hanau, Count of, 118, 119
Hapsburgs, the, 74, 75, 116
Harmel, M., 212
Hartingdon, Prof. Samuel, 217n
Hartley, Mr, 120
Hawkwood, Lady, 62n, 67
Hawkwood, Sir John, 30, 33n, 39, 42, 43, 49, 50, 57–63 *passim*, 67, 71
Hazelius, Per, 273n
Heath, Edward, 278
Henry II, of England, 26
Henry IV, of England, 35
Henry V, of England, 38
Henry the Bastard, of Trastamare, 30
Hesse-Cassel, 116, 293–6
Hessians, 112, 117–18, 126–7, 134
Hita, Archpriest of, 31n
Hoare, Col. T. M. B., 18, 23, 144, 148, 150, 165, 173–9, 200, 202n, 208, 223, 224, 233n, 237, 249, 250, 252, 255n, 257, 275
Housman, A. E., 13
Hundred Years' War, 27, 28, 68
Huyghe, Carlos, 163

Ianarelli, Armand, 264, 268
Indian troops in Katanga, 204
Innocent VI, Pope, 31, 39, 40, 41
International Brigade, 16, 17, 18, 20
Irham, Lord, 119

Irish mercenaries, 22
Irish troops, in Katanga, 204
Italy, 51–3, 60, 88–90

Jacques, Major, 169
James, King of Majorca, 59
Jiacopetti, 151, 152, 153
Joanna I, Queen of Naples, 54, 55
Joanna II, Queen of Naples, 49, 67
John the Good, of France, 28, 32
Johnson, President Lyndon B., 186, 217n
Johnstone, Governor, 112
Jourdan, Gen., 15
Juglers, 68
Julian, Col. H. F., 190
Julius II, Pope, 101

Kant, Immanuel, 127
Kasavubu, President, 157, 171, 177
Katanga, 144, 156–71, 180–81, 192, 205, 208, 209, 253
Kaunda, President of Zambia, 189
Khiary, UN delegate, 161
Kimba, Prime Minister of Congo, 185
Knollys, Sir Robert, 30, 32–4, 39
Kyrellis Plan, 208, 209, 212

Laboudigue, mercenary, 219, 255
Ladislas, King of Naples, 66
Lamouline, Col., 176, 177
lance, the: English, 58; French 69n
Landau, Count, 55, 56, 57
Lansquenets, 99–100, 101–2, 134
Larteguy, Jean, 140, 149
La Salle, Bertrand de, 30, 59, 60
Leleup, Guy, 218
Leo X, Pope, 48
Leopold, Duke of Austria, 75
Leopold III (the Valiant), Duke of Austria, 75
Leopoldville, 155
Lessing, Gotthold Ephraim, 127
Le Tremouille, Gen., 96, 97, 102
Lexington, Battle of, 107
Liegois, Col., 176
Lodi, Peace of, 51, 71
London, in Middle Ages, 52
Lorenzo the Magnificent, 88
Lorraine, René, Duke of, 82
Louis XI, of France, 79, 84, 85
Louis XII, of France, 93–6
Louis, King of Hungary, 44, 54–6

Louis-Philippe, King of France, 134, 135
Lowenbrügger, Nicholas, 87
Lucerne, 75, 84, 94
Lucien-Brun, Maurice, 266
Lumumba, Patrice, 160n, 171
Lyautey, Marshal, 135
Lyttleton, Lord, 111, 124

Machiavelli, Nicolò, 43n, 47–51, 63, 74
McKeown, Gen. Sean, 166, 168
Mader, Adjutant-Chef, 132
Malatesta, Sigismondo, 56, 72
Malestroit, Jean, 59, 60
Manchester, Duke of, 110, 111, 122, 123
Mantua, Francesco Gonzaga, Duke of, 93
Marcel, Ambrogiot, 31
Marcel, Aymerigot, 30
Marche, Jacques, Compte de la, 31
Marignano, Battle of, 102–3
Marino, Battle of, 60, 66
Marlborough, Duke of, 106
Marlière, Col., 179
Martin, V, Pope, 45, 66
Martinez, mercenary, 219
Mary of Burgundy, 84, 93
Massu, Gen., 159
Masters, John, 140
Mauleon, Savari de, 30, 31, 38, 40
Maximilian, Emperor, of Austria, 84, 85, 93, 96, 99–100
Melchingen, Hugo von, 58
Mendès-France, Pierre, 166
Mercenaries: categories of, 22–3; definition of, 14, 17, 18–21, 123
Merigot Marches, trial of, 35–6
Messmer, M., 141n, 160
Michel, mercenary, 210, 213
Micombero, Col., 188
Milan, 52, 64, 65, 96
Mirabeau, Honoré Gabriel, 129
Mobutu, Gen., 155, 156, 172, 177–92, 205–7, 211
Monde, Le, 146, 159, 186
Mondo Cane, 151
Monga, Col., 187, 191, 192, 217, 218
Montefeltro, Federigo da, Duke of Urbino, 43, 71, 72
Montefeltro, Guid'Antonio da, 45
Morat, Battle of, 82
Morgarten, Battle of, 75
Moriale, Fra, 48, 55, 56–7, 62, 63
Moroccan troops, 16

INDEX | 301

Mueller, Siegfried, 148, 149, 150, 177, 252
Muke, Norbert, 157-8, 171
Mulamba, Col., 173, 180
Mulele, Pierre, 171, 172n
Munongo, Godefroid, 160, 189, 218

Nancy, Battle of, 82, 83
Naples, 52; Kingdom of, 42n, 52, 53, 92
Napoleon I, 17
Napoleon III, 137
Nasser, President, 255
Navarre, King of, 30, 34
Nawej, Col., 192, 216
Neal, Major David, 255n
Niebuhr, K., 127
Nigeria, 259, 261, 265, 271, 279
Nodyn, mercenary, 214
Noel, mercenary, 210, 213, 214
Norbiatto, Giorgio, 262
North, Lord, 107, 108, 114, 119
Novara, Battle of, 101

O'Brien, Conor Cruise, 160n, 167, 168
Ojukwu, Col., 261, 262, 267, 268, 273
Olenga, Gen., 200, 222
Opke, Augustus, 271, 274
Organization of African Unity (OAU), 181, 189, 192
Orsini, Paolo, 49

Panin, Russian PM, 108, 109
Papacy, 44n, 71n
Papal States, 52
Paris, 52, 153-4, 236
Parliament, British, 110-13, 119-26
Pedro, of Aragon, the Ceremonious, 59
Pedro the Cruel, 30
Perrot le Bearnais, 30, 31, 34, 38, 40
Peter III, of Aragon, 53
Peters, John, 148, 175, 178, 179, 181, 208, 232-6, 239, 245, 250, 258, 265, 275
Philip, Duke of Burgundy, 80
Philip VI, of France, 28
Piaf, Edith, 131
Piccinino, Iacopo, 43, 48, 67, 70, 72
Piccinino, Niccolo, 67
Picot, mercenary, 261
Piper, Sir James, 30
Piret, Major, 180, 195, 198
Piscopo, Pandolfello, 67
Pitt, William, the Elder, 106, 108, 111, 129
Pius II, Pope, 69, 72
Poitiers, Battle of, 28

Pompidou, President, 141, 259
Praetorian Guard, 23
Protin, Commandant, 169, 176, 177, 251
Puren, Jeremiah, 165, 173, 174, 192, 212, 216, 233n, 250

Quintin, Maurice, 193, 210

Raja, Brig., 168, 170
Ravenna, Battle of, 101
Regnault de Cervolles, Archpriest, 30, 31, 33-4
Rhenish League, 82
Richard II, of England, 30, 39, 62
Richmond, Duke of, 112, 121, 122
Riedesel, Col., 117
Rienzi, Cola di, 48, 62
Rikhye, Gen., 170
Roger di Flor (von Blum), 53-4, 62
Rome, 90-92
Romont, Count of, 80
Rosen, Count Carl Gustaf von, 190n, 269-76
Rosen, Count Eric von, 270
Roux, Alleyne and Peter, 36n
Rudolph I of Hapsburg, 74

Saint Albans, Abbot of, 27n
Saint-Marc, Elie de, 141n
Saint Paul, Tony de, 256
Saint Pol, Count of, 37
Saquanville, Pierre de, 35
Saqr Bin Mohammed al-Quassini, Shaikh, 255n
Saratoga Springs, 128
Savile, Sir George, 119
Saxe-Weimer, 127
Schaffhausen, 100
Schiller, J. C. F. von, 127
Schlieffen, Gen. M. de, 117, 296
Schramme, Jean, 23, 137, 148, 151, 165-7, 170, 173, 177, 179, 181, 188-9, 192-3, 201-19 *passim*, 249, 251, 275, 279
Schroeder, George, 178, 181-5, 249, 255, 258
Schrot, mercenary, 265
Schwarz, Walter, 258n
Schwyz, canton of, 74, 78, 83, 86, 94
Scottish mercenaries, 22
Sempach: Battle of, 75; Covenant of, 76
Seven Years' War, 106
Sforza, Cardinal Ascanio, 88, 96

302 | INDEX

Sforza, Bianca, 92
Sforza, Drusiana, 48
Sforza, Francesco, 47, 48, 51, 63, 67, 70, 71, 88
Sforza, Galeazzo Maria, 88
Sforza, Gian Galeazzo, 89
Sforza, Isabella, 89
Sforza, Ludovico (il Moro), 88–9, 92–100 *passim*
Sforza, Massimiliano, 101
Sforza, Muzio Attendolo, 48, 49, 61, 63, 67
Shelburne, Earl of, 123
Sidi-bel-Abbès, 134, 137, 142
Sigismond, Emperor, 78
Simba war, 147, 156, 171–8, 200–201
Six Commando, 176, 178, 180, 185, 208, 214
Smith, Wilbur, 149
Solothurn, canton of, 86
Soult, Marshal, 130
Spandre, Mario, 178
Spanish Civil War, 16, 18
Spanish Foreign Legion, 140, 141
Spanish Succession, War of, 106, 115
Spencer, Lt Jeremy, 221, 224
Sprecch, 55
Stanleyville, 155, 172, 176
Stefan III, Duke of Bavaria, 61
Steiner, Rolf, 262, 264–7
Sterz, Albert, 48, 57
Stoffel, Col., 134
Suffolk, Earl of, 108, 109, 116, 118, 121–3
Swabian War, 86–7, 100
Swedish troops, in Katanga, 169, 203
Swiss, mercenaries, 15, 22, 23, 74–104

Tell, William, 75
Telli, Diallo, 192
Ten Commando, 205, 206
Ten Thousand, the, 24, 194, 215, 219, 248
Terzo, Ottobuono, 48
Thierry du Bonnay, 278n
Tilly, Count Johann von, 17
Times, The, 144, 150, 257
Townshend, Viscount, 114
Trèves, Prince-Bishop of, 127
Trinquier, Col., 149, 159–61, 209n, 278
Tshatshi, Col., 179, 180
Tshipola, Col., 179
Tshombe, President, 155–60 *passim*, 168–73 *passim*, 177–8, 186, 190, 208, 209, 212, 213, 218

Turmann, Swiss mercenary, 98
Tyler, Wat, 39
Tyrel, Jean, 37

Union Minière, 144, 208, 209, 253
United Nations, 20, 144, 147, 158, 162, 166–71, 203, 252
United Provinces, 14
United States, 107, 126, 128–9, 172, 245–7, 278
Unterwalden, canton, 74, 78, 83, 87
Urban V, Pope, 58
Urban VI, Pope, 60
Uri, canton, 74, 75, 78, 83, 86, 94, 101
U Thant, 168

Vanderveuken, mercenary, 218
Vanderwalle, Col., 174–9
Varangian Guard, 22
Venice and Venetians, 16–17, 48, 52, 64
Vergennes, Comte de, 109, 114
Vergerio, Pier Paolo, 60
Verme, Iacopo del, 60, 61
Verwoerd, Dr, 234, 235, 236
Vettoni, the Florentine, 102
Visconti, the, 61, 62
Visconti, Bernabò, 67
Visconti, Bianca, 88
Visconti, Filippo Maria, 63, 71, 78, 88, 95
Visconti, Gian Galeazzo, 78
Visconti, Valentina, 95
Vitelli, Vitelozzo, 49
Vivre pour Vivre, 149
Voltaire, 105, 117, 120
Vorster, B. J., 235, 236

Waldech, Prince of, 115, 127, 128
Waldstätte, 75, 86, 94, 101, 134
Wallenstein, Albrecht von, 17
Walton, Robin, 37
Wartenstein, Hartmann von, 58
Washington, George, 126
Wauthier, Commandant, 179, 180
Weber, Col. Guy, 158, 160, 161
Welensky, Sir Roy, 158
Werner of Urslingen, 42–5, 55, 56, 66
Wharton, Hank, 259, 266, 271
White Company, 35, 39, 48, 51, 57, 59, 60
Wicks, Alastair, 146, 148, 164–5, 167, 174, 177–9, 224n, 252, 258, 260, 275
'Wild Geese', 22

Wilhelm II, of Germany, 13, 14
Wilhelm, mercenary, 179, 180
William III, of England, 22, 112, 114
William of Diesbach, 86
Williams, 'Taffy', 262, 264, 267, 268, 275
Wilson, Lt Gary, 175
Wolf, Conrad, 55, 56, 62
Wren, P. C., 138, 139, 140
Wurtemberg, Duke of, 127

Xenophon, 21, 23, 248, 249

Yemen, the, 255-6
Yorke, Sir Joseph, 114, 128
Yorktown, 128
Young, Brig. Peter, 147

Zug, 76, 83, 86
Zurich, 76, 78, 84, 86, 96

A Sh[...]

The Almogavares (Aragon, c. 1200 – 1300)   Semi-Feudal

The Grand Catalan Company (Byzantine Empire, 1306 –1374)   Th[...]

The 'Compagnie di Ventura' (Italy, c. 1350 – 1400)

The 'Compagnia di San Giorgio' (Italy, 1379)

The 'Braccheschi' and 'Sforzeschi' (Italy, c. 1400)

(Burgun[...]

The Condottieri (Italy, c. 1400 – 1530)

Swiss Guards   Offic[...]
(Europe, c. 1500 – 1848)   (France – Ar[...]

The Swiss Guard   The Spanish Foreign Legion — - — The F[...]
(The Vatican)

Five Commando — — — — — — Leopard Group — — — — —

STRAIGHT LINE ——— = direct descent

——— — ——— — ——— = bastard descent/relation